The Labor of Hope

THE LABOR OF HOPE

*Meritocracy and
Precarity in Egypt*

Harry Pettit

Stanford University Press
Stanford, California

Stanford University Press
Stanford, California

Printed in the United States of America on acid-free, archival-quality paper

Cataloging-in-Publication Data available upon request.
Library of Congress Control Number: 2023007574
ISBN: 9781503636538 (cloth), 9781503637443 (paper) 9781503637450 (ebook)

Cover design: Daniel Benneworth-Gray
Cover photographs: Unsplash/ Nassim Wahba and Yassin Mohamed

CONTENTS

Acknowledgments		vii
	Introduction	1
1	Selling Hope	23
2	The Drugs of Life	55
3	Without Hope There Is No Life	84
4	The Labor of Love	113
5	The Migration of Hope	146
	Conclusion	175
	Notes	189
	Bibliography	209
	Index	223

ACKNOWLEDGMENTS

THIS BOOK IS A PRODUCT of so many people and so much labor beyond myself. I cannot begin to thank them for all the support they have given me. Here is an insufficient attempt.

First and foremost, the book would not have been possible without the people whose story it tells. This is your story, and I hope I did some justice to it. I wanted to depict the pain that you, as well as countless others, go through daily as a result of a broken system that promises so much but offers little to so many. I only hope that writing this book can put the spotlight on it.

I want to thank Sharad Chari, Murray Low, and Claire Mercer for setting me on the path toward a research career by planting the initial seed. Without their encouragement I would not be where I am today. Sharad Chari, John Chalcraft, and Gareth Jones, thank you for showing me that geography and the social sciences can be outward-facing and fluid. It was through exposure to their interdisciplinary academic approach and intellectual interests that the conceptual and empirical approach behind this book was first developed. They enabled me to read and engage with books—such as Paul Willis's *Learning to Labour*, Michael Burawoy's *Manufacturing Consent*, or Saba Mahmood's *Politics of Piety*—that used an ethnographic methodology to understand the complex and ambivalent ways through which people invest in and reproduce hegemonic regimes. This interest has stayed with me and now permeates my academic project.

I have to make special mention of Claire Mercer and Gareth Jones, who—after agreeing to "share" me—have provided generous care, sharp insights and critique, a push now and again, and a confidence boost in difficult times. In particular, I will always be grateful for the nudge to write in a way that told a story and put temporality rather than themes front and center. I have also come to appreciate the influence of the cluster of human geographers at the London School of Economics—Sylvia Chant, Murray Low, Ryan Centner, Austin Zeiderman, and Megan Ryburn. They have shaped my own approach to research through their inspiring combination of foregrounding empirical accounts with critical theoretical engagement and an unequivocal focus on power and inequality. In particular I want to thank Megan and Austin for paving the way and providing inspiration and advice on beginning the process of writing this book. A special mention must also be made to Asher Ghertner and his PhD students at Rutgers University who stimulated different ways of thinking about my data during my visit there. During this trip I was also introduced to the work—and very briefly the person—of Lauren Berlant. This was transformative for me, as *Cruel Optimism* provided a beautiful framework to begin understanding the practices of the young men in this book, while also encouraging me to push forward the project of taking emotion seriously in the analysis of economic relations. Finally, a special thank you to Farha Ghannam and Tatiana Thieme, for engaging so meaningfully with this material and suggesting stimulating new directions.

I have been on quite a journey in academia—both unstable but also fulfilling. This has included numerous institutions: the University of the West of England, the University of Oxford, Newcastle University, the University of Reading, Northumbria University, and the University of Amsterdam. Along the way I have been extremely fortunate to have mentors—Alex Vasudevan, Sally Lloyd-Evans, Kate MacLean, and Rivke Jaffe—who have provided invaluable critical engagement with the book's material alongside so much emotional support that has enabled me to keep making steps forward. The writing of the book has been generously supported by grants from the Economic and Social Research Council, university research funding, and the Leverhulme Trust along the way. I feel extremely lucky to have enjoyed the freedom this funding has afforded me to develop ideas and ride the ups and downs of the writing process. I hope that many more are able to do the same. During the last two years of the publishing and writing process with Stanford, I have been very thankful to Kate Wahl and the three anonymous reviewers for pushing the manuscript and its arguments toward more clarity and authority.

This book, from the beginning of fieldwork to publishing, has been years in the making. During this time, I have picked up and held on to so many wonderful friends who have all contributed to infusing life with the joy, comfort, and meaning that has been fundamental in enabling me to complete this book. This journey would have really been impossible without Wiebe Ruijtenberg. Wiebe began as a wonderful companion during fieldwork in Egypt but has since become a best friend who provides incredible academic engagement and support on a daily basis, alongside care and empathy in difficult times and joy and laughter in good times. Mara Nogueira and Ganga Shreedhar were with me every step of the journey, through all its highs and lows, and continue to provide the necessary mix of stability and chaos in life. Thanks also to Ahmed, Josh, James, Daniel J., Daniel O., Kat, Becka, Charlotte, and Ellie, who provide continual grounding through years-long friendships. Cristina Inceu, thank you for sharing so much of the journey with me—and for your sharp intellect and enduring care.

Beyond London, during fieldwork in Cairo I found a second family with Pam, Stef, Eduard, and Lucia. This family was crucial in maintaining my psychological state during an emotionally taxing process. During my academic journey, I have enjoyed engaging academic conversations and letting off steam with Alessandra Radicatti, Tom Cowan, and Olivia Mason. Finally, in more recent times I have developed an amazing network of friends in Amsterdam through the UvA, church, and random occurrences. To Riet, Mari, Dolly, Solene, Signe, Shoushan, Max, Jiska, Bram, Kris, Ysanne, Amelia, and Afra. You have all made the transition to Dutch life so much easier and I hope that you will be in my life for a long time to come.

I would like to end by thanking and expressing my love for my family: Omi and Grandad, my parents Sylvia Finch and Peter Pettit, and siblings Michaella, Tom, and Will. Thank you for providing meaning and grounding, and for being there, all the way from Retford to London and across the continent.

Finally, I must say thank you to God for providing eternal acceptance and love.

The Labor of Hope

INTRODUCTION

ON A HOT JULY EVENING, Gamal and I were walking along Qasr al-Nil Bridge toward Tahrir Square in the center of Cairo. Gamal had graduated from Cairo University's Faculty of Law five years earlier. Once a prestigious department producing Egypt's highest-ranking judges, in recent years it has become colloquially known as one of the "faculties of the people" (kulyat al sha'b), due to its ever-increasing volume of students and low-quality education.[1] Many graduates can now be found not in the law courts but working as taxi drivers or serving shawarma sandwiches in the city. Gamal, like many of his friends, did not want that life. He dreamed of escaping what he described as a crowded, decrepit lower-class to lower-middle-class neighborhood in northeast Cairo and inhabiting another kind of life and city. He imagined working as an international trade lawyer in the glamorous Nile City towers, a modern office block on the banks of the Nile, living in one of the newly built gated communities on the city's outskirts, marrying a European woman, and eventually moving abroad to work in London.

For the last few years Gamal had worked hard to realize this dream. While intermittently taking freelance family law cases and working in a clothing shop to earn money, he optimistically and intensively developed his English, studied international trade law on the internet, earned a master's degree at Cairo University alongside courses in CV writing and interview techniques, and obtained unpaid work experience. Gamal was repeatedly told by course trainers and people working in law firms that he would make it eventually if he worked hard enough. I had been following Gamal and other young male graduates like him over the last year as they chased this dream. They took low-end jobs in the hope of securing promotion, attended training courses and job fairs, submitted CVs to prestigious companies, relentlessly planned their dream start-up, read self-help literature, prayed to God for guidance, sat in cafés talking about their ideal future, hung out in shopping malls imagining what they wanted to buy, and attempted to sustain intimate relations with women. These activities all stimulated intense hope, the sense that their ambitious globalized dreams were drawing nearer.

But for Gamal, this all remained a long way off. Over the years he had experienced many false starts, holding three unpaid positions in small law firms before leaving each due to broken promises of a forthcoming salary, struggling to even receive answers from countless scholarships and jobs to which he had applied, and experiencing heartache every time a European woman he had started dating left Egypt and ended things. Each moment Gamal thought he was on the cusp of mobility, it proved an illusion. These disappointments induced much anguish, angry rails against corruption in the labor market and the decrepit state of Egypt's economy, and even a questioning of God's presence. Gamal faced incessant calls from his parents to give up, take work, and begin preparations for marriage with a woman in his neighborhood. However, he would not give up. Doing so, he described, would result in "death," an empty life in which he would have nothing to look forward to. Instead, after each disappointment Gamal distracted himself for a few days with friends, hashish, and television, before moving on to his next attempt, reintroducing hope by focusing on what he had done wrong and what he might do differently now in order to secure God's reward for his efforts.

On this July day, Gamal was continuing his attempts to partake in Cairo's global city. We had been hanging out at an open event at the Cairo Opera House for the end of Ramadan. As we walked along the bridge in good spirits, Gamal excitedly told me about an internet search earlier that day identifying an international law course in the UK. But our conversation was interrupted when we came across a group of men staring anxiously into the water below. A man had just jumped. As we looked out over the edge trying to spot him, we were told that the body had disappeared. After waiting a few minutes for the police to arrive, we walked on. I said it was sad to think of someone being driven to kill themself. "Of course, it is sad," he replied, "but it is weak, to do something like that is giving up, you have to withstand the tough circumstances like I am doing." Gamal assumed the man had jumped because he could not tolerate Egypt's labor market. I replied that I knew of young men in similar situations to Gamal who had talked of suicide. "But they can find a job!" he responded in shock, "then move out and rent a flat, they just need independence, like me. They will make it . . . you know there is a phrase in Egypt, 'the journey of a thousand miles starts with a single step,' you just have to take the step and keep going. You need to be positive; you need to keep hope."

In this same spot back in 2011, nearly one thousand Egyptians, mostly men, died at the hands of Egypt's security forces as millions marched to demand an end to the thirty-year rule of Hosni Mubarak. Egyptians generally recall with great nostalgia the feeling they experienced during those days. It was hope, a feeling that their country and thereby their own lives were once again moving toward a fulfilling future. This hope demanded "bread, freedom, and social justice" (aish, huriyya, w 'adala igtima'iyya), the overhaul of a system that was denying access to a dignified life for so many. Those who died were held up as martyrs who had sacrificed themselves for the security of that hope. But now several years on, Gamal's interpretation of another who died in the same place was quite different. His was not a heroic act of defiance against an unjust system but an act of weakness. He was blamed for refusing to hope, to persevere with the belief that his efforts would be compensated within Egypt's current economic landscape. Instead, it was Gamal's individualized stoicism and refusal to give up that secured respect.

This book examines how Gamal and other young men like him struggle to keep on going within conditions that strip them of the ability to lead a livable life. They belong to a middle-class group in contemporary Egypt that lives with a disconnect between their globalized aspirations and their inability to obtain secure work, get married, and afford a dignified lifestyle. This disconnect emerged on the back of late-twentieth-century neoliberal reforms that enabled a select few to accrue vast wealth—as symbolized by the exclusive gated communities, glitzy shopping malls, securitized office blocks, and expensive private educational institutions that sprang up around Cairo. At the same time, many in the middle class whose status had been built on the country's state-socialist project have been pushed into low-quality state education and un- or underemployment, forced to watch Cairo's glamorous construction from afar.

Once I began following the lives of young men like Gamal, I became interested in the fluctuation of their emotional states. This emerged as key to explaining how they kept going within an economic system that denied them access to what they desired. They frequently descended into anxiety, boredom, and despair as the labor market stalled their pursuit of a desirable career and durable intimacy. But they also constantly managed to overcome these emotions by engaging in certain activities that provided brief distraction and relief, as well as a vital sense of hope for the future.

Maintaining hope is key to forging a livable life. Egypt's uprising and the period that followed briefly provided renewed hope for the future. This rested on the promise of tackling the structural conditions that produce inequality, poverty, and precarity. However, as I spent time with young men like Gamal years later, this hope felt remote. They were investing in the hopes generated by a neoliberal economic regime that entrenched itself over the turn of the millennium. They craved a private-sector career, modern consumption, and international mobility, and their hope rested on objects, narratives, and practices that, in Gamal's words, turned revolutionary martyrs into cowards, establishing the individual as the determinant of success.

In tracing how young middle-class men sustain a livable life, this book reconsiders key approaches to understanding the everyday emotional politics of contemporary capitalism. The condition of Egypt's middle class is not unique. Globally populations are grappling with a simultaneous diminution of employment pathways as a result of neoliberal economics and work precarity, alongside a structural raising of aspirations in the context of globalization, expanding education, and technological advancement. This is producing widespread feelings of anxiety, frustration, and despair. In recent years scholarship has responded by tracing how marginalized communities enact alternative hopes, through either overt resistance or sustaining life seemingly outside capitalist regimes of value. But this focus sidelines the empirical reality that, despite the production of disconnection and precarity, most people continue to invest in the hopes and dreams offered by capitalist systems.

Understanding why this is happening requires examining the politics and political economy of emotion and hope. It requires tracing how harmful capitalist systems continue to produce the means for disenfranchised populations to keep going. This book does this by considering the everyday practices through which young educated underemployed men in Egypt keep going not as resistance or agentive survival but as a form of emotional labor that enables the labor market to keep functioning despite producing inequality and precarity. This labor is made up of gendered practices that produce temporary distraction from difficult emotions and sustain a vital sense of hope for future mobility. By retaining a meritocratic focus on the individual and away from structural issues, this emotional labor, or labor of hope, keeps men invested in Egypt's capitalist economy. In intricately tracing this labor, the book argues that the emotional labor required to survive precarity and disconnection represents a much broader reality in contemporary labor markets and a vital terrain of political struggle.

THE RISE AND FALL OF EGYPT'S MIDDLE CLASS

In the 1990s and early 2000s, Egypt was projected as a space of hope. Not only was economic growth strong, but the country was an important signifier for what had been advertised by development organizations, global consultancy firms, the media, and parts of academia as the surge of a new middle class across the Global South.[2] In a 2014 report, the German Development Institute concluded that Egypt's middle class increased by a factor of four from 1990 to 2010.[3] The rise of the middle was held up as a sign that countries like Egypt were leaving the "waiting room of history," finally enjoying everything that globalization, development, and economic liberalization promised to bring.[4] It was proof that wealth was "trickling down" and economic growth "sustainable" and "inclusive."

The events of 2011 abruptly punctured this hope. Development institutions, the media, and researchers claimed that "middle-class frustration fueled the Arab Spring."[5] New economic measurements revealed an alternative story, with a 2015 World Bank report that measured income concluding that Egypt's middle class shrank in the years preceding 2011.[6] A similar story emerged when wealth was measured, which is important as it provides

6 INTRODUCTION

a window into the ability of populations to afford middle-class markers such as education and property. Credit Suisse's 2015 Global Wealth Report found that Egypt's middle class—registered as only 5 percent of the population of ninety million—was halved between 2000 and 2015. What was left lost US$7 billion during that period, while those above (0.4 percent of the population) gained US$72 billion.[7]

Alternative quantitative studies also started puncturing the narrative of a rising middle class elsewhere.[8] Credit Suisse's report revealed declines in middle-class wealth in every region except China after 2000, with the distribution shifting almost universally in favor of those at higher wealth levels.[9] As a result of from these statistics, Egyptian commentators, researchers, and international organizations suddenly announced the death of Egypt's middle class in the early twenty-first century. But to understand exactly how the condition of the middle class changed, it is necessary to go beyond quantitative analysis. The middle class must be understood as an everyday practice and aspirational category for which membership requires certain kinds of jobs, education, taste, family construction, and conduct.[10]

The label "middle class," or "middle level" (al-tabaqa al-mutawasita), originates in a late-nineteenth-century Egyptian state-building project initiated by Muhammad Ali to create a bureaucratic workforce out of a secular education system.[11] But it was under the presidency of military general Gamal Abdel Nasser (1956–1970) when a huge expansion occurred.[12] Nasser increased access to public school and university while guaranteeing every secondary school graduate a government job on the back of a program of industrialization geared toward import substitution and nationalization.[13] People who had been working as petty traders, agricultural laborers, and factory workers were lifted into a middle class based on lifetime nonmanual state jobs, state education, material security aided by subsidies and rent-capped housing, and belonging to a national, modernist, and reformist Islamic culture.[14] At the same time, Nasser limited the wealth of the pre-1950s elite by sequestering land and restraining their ability to accumulate property and earn high incomes. Although inequalities persisted, Egyptian society underwent a process of socioeconomic convergence during this period.

However, in the 1980s and 1990s Egypt's socialist developmental project unraveled. President Anwar Sadat (1970–1981), while continuing to expand education and public employment, set in motion discontinuous economic liberalization. In response to a stagnating economy and rising government debt, a series of policies were introduced under the label *infitah* (opening) to make Egypt attractive to international capital and give the local private sector more freedom.[15] Liberalization continued into the twenty-first century as Hosni Mubarak—who became president after Sadat's assassination—imposed International Monetary Fund (IMF)-led reforms and structural adjustment policies in response to further revenue shortfalls.[16] This involved deep austerity measures, reductions in price controls, exchange rate depreciation, further privatization, and a reallocation of expenditure away from welfare and toward the private sector.[17]

IMF accounts paint a story of low inflation and reasonable growth figures during the 1990s. But Timothy Mitchell argued that this was enabled by speculative financial injections in real estate and importing expensive consumables instead of revived production.[18] While economic liberalization promised social mobility, it led to dramatic fissures among the middle classes.[19] The bourgeoisie of the pre-Nasser years, the bureaucratic and military strata of Nasser's reign, and the commercial nouveaux riches rapidly accumulated capital by expanding public-sector incomes, commercial private-sector activities, Gulf migration, and real estate. This accumulation centered on Egypt's capital and produced new standards of middle-classness based on modern consumer lifestyles, internationalized private sector work, foreign-language education, and global mobility.[20] These were imprinted on Cairo's urban landscape in the shape of international educational institutions, glamorous gated communities, office developments, and shopping malls as part of the government's ambition to construct a "global city."[21]

As the upper-middle classes rapidly accumulated capital, many in the Nasserist middle class faced hardship in the aftermath of the neoliberal transition. In the late twentieth and early twenty-first century the ability of many to maintain a middle-class lifestyle, which was increasingly oriented toward modern consumption, diminished because of a steady devaluation of the Egyptian pound, a stagnation of government wages, and a decline in reliable state services and subsidies.[22] But it is those coming of age since the early 2000s who have faced the most dramatic rupture in their pathway toward a middle-class life in contemporary Egypt.

INTRODUCING EGYPT'S DISCONNECTED MIDDLE CLASS
The young men who provide the focus of this book constitute part of what
I call a disconnected middle class in Egypt. Their grandfathers, growing up
in the 1950s and 1960s, worked as ceramics traders, farmers, fishermen, bar-
bers, curtain makers, factory workers, coffee shop owners, and tailors. They
did not own land and rarely had an education beyond school, signifying
membership of the popular classes. But their parents benefited from Nasser's
reforms. Their fathers and sometimes mothers graduated from postsecond-
ary technical education to obtain government jobs such as teachers or train
station officials or in the distribution of food subsidies and local tax offices.
After obtaining employment, most quickly married and secured a subsidized
rental property or built an apartment with parental help.

Some of my interlocutors grew up in Cairo's "informal" neighborhoods
that emerged in the 1950s and 1960s outside government planning as Egyptians migrated from the provinces. While not constituting part of the city's
'ashwa'yat (slums), many complained how these neighborhoods had become
overcrowded—especially with lower-class people—and dilapidated over the
years because of rural-urban migration and chronic underinvestment. These
areas are far removed—aesthetically and spatially—from historically elite
areas and gated community settlements catering to the new middle classes.
Other interlocutors grew up in towns and villages in the Nile delta and
beyond that have faced economic decline as industrial bases moved abroad
and Cairo swept up new economic activity. Again, these places are compared
unfavorably to the capital as they lack employment opportunities as well as
consumptive symbols of wealth.

My interlocutors all attended government schools and universities in the
early 2000s that have become infamous for overcrowding and poor quality.[23] While pupil numbers continued to rise into the twenty-first century,
state expenditure on education has decreased.[24] At the same time the government facilitated private investment in response to demand for alternative
options from the upper classes and the international commercial economy.[25]
Even public universities have opened fee-paying foreign-language sections.
The most notorious faculties are the Arabic sections of commerce, law, and
humanities, which make up two thirds of enrollment. They are known as
the "faculties of the people," where people end up if they underperform in

the fiercely competitive high school exam and go "just to get a certificate." My interlocutors graduated from these faculties between 2009 and 2013. Looking back, they complained of being unable to enter lectures because of overcrowding, corruption in grading, and a system where memorization is rewarded and independent thought disabled.

As low-status graduates, the men in this book were especially vulnerable to the employment struggles plaguing educated youth in a liberalizing Egypt. University graduates make up almost half of unemployed youth.[26] On average it takes the several hundred thousand graduates who enter the labor market each year seven years to find "gainful employment."[27] The government employment many of their parents enjoyed is no longer available after the state slashed recruitment as part of IMF reforms.[28] For these reasons, coupled with growth in capital-intensive sectors like construction and commerce, graduates have been pushed into un- and underemployment, with many men pushed into "informal" jobs and women out of the labor market altogether.[29]

The employment avenues that remain open make the achievement of middle-class respectability difficult. It is common to find male graduates of the faculties of the people working as outdoor salespeople or taxi/delivery drivers. With the right connections, other options are freelance family law or accounting in small firms, but these jobs often pay less than lower-skilled alternatives. An avenue in Cairo—and key focus in the book—has become sales and customer service roles in a call center or business process outsourcing (BPO) industry that employs 170,000 workers in services for approximately a hundred countries in twenty languages.[30] Although it can be highly paid, the BPO industry in Egypt is segmented with international call centers offering salaries three times those of local accounts.[31] But most public university graduates can access only local accounts because of language issues. My interlocutors complained that all of these job options do not match the years they spent chasing an education in a particular field. Additionally, they involve working among "uneducated people," and their small salaries and temporary contracts induce challenges for men in particular to secure marriage, build a home, and look after a family when all three have become more expensive.[32]

A loss of status through education and jobs means many middle-class youth, including the men in this book, are struggling to distinguish themselves from sha'by (lower-class) living.[33] At the same time, the standards against which they measure themselves have shifted through exposure to the raqy (classy) cosmopolitan lifestyles enjoyed by the upper classes. For my interlocutors, this exposure came through professional skills training inside universities and a thriving training economy, billboards and commercials advertising upper-class lifestyles, online information, success stories of friends or relatives, and fleeting interactions with the upper classes in restaurants or shopping malls. Expectations are no longer funneled through modernist aspirations for guaranteed public sector work. The young men in this book dream of working in multinational or large Egyptian companies, in law, commerce, human resources (HR), public relations, and banking; of becoming successful entrepreneurs; and of migrating abroad. They also want to be able to own cars, send their children to foreign-language private schools, live in exclusive gated communities, and shop in glitzy shopping malls.

Many in Egypt's middle class are growing up with a widening disconnect between their aspirations for certain jobs, lifestyles, and marriage and the precarious employment and lifestyle trajectories that lie before them.[34] This book delves into the lived experience of this disconnect among young men. It builds on ethnographic literature exploring the modern experience of masculinity in Egypt and the wider Middle East. Seeking to undermine damaging stereotypes of the dangerous, oppressive Arab man, this work has given primacy to the ordinary pursuit of manhood—revealing emergent spaces and practices through which men are asserting, struggling to live up to, and reshaping norms of masculinity.[35] Young Egyptian women also experience disconnection, in ways that partly overlap but also differ from men. Women are graduating from Egypt's universities in record numbers and developing desires for international employment and lifestyles. But they face high unemployment amid declines in public-sector work, while their pursuit of jobs is often more circumscribed, with mobility restricted and journeys dependent on locating a husband who can provide a decent lifestyle.[36] Although the book focuses on men, at various points I explicate the experience of young women and examine the way their practices impinge on one another.

THE EMOTIONAL POLITICS OF DISCONNECTION

I understand disconnection as a subjective condition.[37] It defines the existence of a gap between one's aspirations and one's ability to reach them.[38] This condition speaks to a capitalist economy which, as Rachel Heiman described, is producing a dramatic upscaling of aspirations alongside the diminishment of the possibility of achieving them.[39] Processes of globalization, urbanization, technological advances, and expanding access to education are exposing people to the lives of the wealthy that were previously not on show. Yet austerity regimes, neoliberal economics, and political instability are producing heightened uncertainty and precarity, making it harder for many to secure a stable livelihood.[40]

Disconnection is a condition experienced on and through emotion.[41] Once I began following the lives of young Egyptian men, I observed the intense fluctuation of their emotional states, between anxiety, boredom, and despair as they became stuck in situations that did not reflect their dreams, and distraction, relief, and especially hope as they engaged in activities that enabled them to overcome these emotions. Control of their emotional states emerged as vital to explaining how they kept going within conditions that diminished their ability to lead livable lives. Maintaining a sense of hope for the future was key to that.[42]

Hope is defined as a sense that "one may become other or more than one presently is or was fated to be."[43] It rests on motion, what Hirokazu Miyazaki terms prospective momentum toward a desired future.[44] It is distinguishable from other terms, in Egypt and beyond, that describe future orientation— such as confidence (thiqa), optimism (tafaʾwl), or expectation (tuwaqa). It defines a more basic sense of having something to live for and work toward. It is also distinct from acts of aspiring or desiring. A desire or aspiration can be an object of hope. Hope therefore can be defined as a sense that a desired future can become yours.

The human need for hope has been the subject of much debate. While philosophical and psychoanalytical approaches have contributed great understanding, it must be contextualized within the systems of value within which people orient their lives.[45] Capitalism and modern notions of progress require perpetual investment and growth accompanied by dissatisfaction with what one already has. Even beyond the life stage of youth there is pressure to strive for better jobs, lifestyles, and commodities. This produces, as Samuli Schielke argued, an "aspirational sense of existence, where one must always reach for more than what one has, a sensibility that essentially depends on its being dynamic and growing."[46]

The production of disconnection within capitalist systems places this hopeful sensibility under threat.[47] It replaces a sense of hope with a sense of feeling stuck in life. The question becomes how do people experiencing disconnection reclaim hope? Existing scholarship has predominantly focused on the emergence of anti- or postcapitalist forms of hope. This has involved philosophical work attempting to imagine more collective, equitable versions of the future, but also a large body of ethnographic work tracing how marginalized communities construct hopes that rest on the possibility of either breaking down capitalist arrangements or forging livelihoods and new social relations outside capitalist regimes of value and accumulation.[48]

This has been a valuable pursuit, especially as it has taken ethnographic work beyond accounts of stagnation and suffering to demonstrate how disenfranchised groups manage to forge livable lives.[49] However, it did not speak to the pursuit of hope I observed in Egypt. Despite experiencing intense rupture, the young men in this book did not turn to anti- or postcapitalist ideologies. They continued to invest in the individualized hopes generated by a capitalist system. They were consumed by the tasks of educating themselves, obtaining fulfilling private-sector careers, maintaining durable intimacy, and building homes. As much as the labor market produced anxiety and anger in achieving these aims, it also constantly offered tools to enjoy brief distraction and to relocate hope through objects, places, and narratives that offered the meritocratic promise of success through individual perseverance.

A careful consideration of these men's lives highlights two related limitations of the anti-/postcapitalist hope literature. First, it contains the implicit, and often explicit, assumption that dominant political and economic regimes have vacated the material and emotional worlds of marginalized peoples.[50] This overlooks the empirical reality that they continue to churn out powerful promises of happiness, and people around the world continue to invest in the imaginations and hopes caught up in these promises. This is not only in relation to nationalist movements that brought about Brexit, the success of leaders such as Egypt's Abdel Fattah el-Sisi, and the election of Trump in the

United States, Modi in India, and Bolsonaro in Brazil, but also to the stub-
bornness of the pursuit of good-life fantasies extended by labor and commodity markets. As Lauren Berlant articulated in the U.S. context, people retain
a cruel attachment to these fantasies, despite their continual breakdown, because the "continuity of its form provides something of the continuity of the
subject's sense of what it means to keep on living on and to look forward to
being in the world."[51]

Second, scholarship pins the capacity of marginalized peoples to sustain
hope, trick time, hustle, or resist on their agency. This stems from a Michel
de Certeau–inspired conceptual approach that differentiates between "confining structures" and "agentive movement."[52] This approach understates how
"agentive movement," or in this case the capacity to hope, might be enabled
by dominant material and ideological structures.[53] A similar trend is found in
scholarship on emotion and affect more generally.[54] Theorizations of affect—
which have helped recognize how emotions emerge as people interact with the
world—largely understands affect to be "non-representational," and therefore
beyond the reach of discourse and ideology. The affective realm is positioned
as a realm that represents the contingency of power, within which alternative
ways of living emerge.[55] Literature does not analyze sufficiently how affects—
and emotions as their personal manifestation—emerge and shift in response
to dominant ideologies and material arrangements.

To understand the emotional lives of young Egyptian men, I depart from
approaches that focus on the emergence of alternative sociopolitical formations amid the ruinations of capitalist systems. Instead, I interrogate a politics
and political economy of hope that may work in the service of labor markets. This requires returning to feminist literature on emotion. This literature
has revealed how particular "emotional cultures" or "structures of feeling"
are produced by dominant economic, political, and sociocultural configura-
tions.[56] It also investigates how these emotional cultures can become a critical
mechanism through which capitalist relations—and their associated structures of inequality and exploitation—are reproduced and challenged.[57]

Investigating the politics and political economy of hope therefore requires
tracing how dominant ideologies and techniques of governing constrain and
enable the possibilities for hope as it emerges and shifts within marginalized
communities.[58] This does not assume linear subjectification or governance

from above. It traces how affects produced by corporate and governmental knowledges and techniques are taken up and reworked in lived experience. It also requires tracing how hope then feeds into the reproduction, legitimation, and potential disruption of modes of capital accumulation and exploitation, and the structures of gendered, sexualized, classed, racialized, and colonial inequality they produce.[59]

THE LABOR OF HOPE

I want to foreground the politics of hope among disconnected populations by applying the analytic of labor, which centers the relationship between the activities, knowledges, and techniques that go into keeping hope alive and their political economic origins and effects. I propose conceptualizing practices of hope-making and distraction among young men in Egypt as a form of emotional labor. Coined by Arlie Russell Hochschild, this concept has been used to describe the management of emotions within forms of paid labor.[60] This management is crucial to the extraction of economic value from workers. But I want to switch attention to the practices required to manage emotions that take place outside work hours but are vital to workers being able to continue providing their bodies to the labor market.[61]

Shifting the concept of emotional labor to the realm of social reproduction owes great debt to two generations of feminist scholars pointing to the importance of the unpaid labor of care in producing labor power.[62] Diversifying understandings of the labor practices supporting life and capitalist value creation has been reinvigorated in recent years amid recognition that waged employment is and never was the global norm.[63] This literature has revealed the multitude of hidden gendered, racialized, even nonhuman labor producing value, but there remains much to do. Penny Harvey and Christian Krohn-Hansen emphasize the need to analyze not only how people "make a living," but how people "make life worth living."[64] Key to "making life worth living" is maintaining an emotional state that enables one to keep engaging with the world—and providing one's body to the labor market.

In this vein, I propose a broader understanding of the emotional labor that goes into upholding oneself, family, community, and therefore labor power. I define emotional labor as the material practices, social relations, and moral terrains that go into making life livable, emotionally and psychologically sustaining the bodies and minds of those engaged in the toil of preserving life and capitalist value creation. Much of this labor takes place beyond the workplace in homes, in cafés, and online, but it is crucial to producing emotionally stable workers from which value can be extracted. It involves dissipating negative emotions—anxiety, frustration, shame, and boredom—that build up during the navigation of difficult jobs and labor markets. Crucial is the maintenance of a sense of hope that one's future will live up to one's desires.[65]

The practices that go into emotional labor differ according to historical and geographical context. Emotional labor is exercised in gender-specific ways and therefore always has a gender politics.[66] It is both an individual and collective endeavor reliant on networks of friends and family, while also being open to the same commodification forces as care work more widely. Like any form, this labor has a politics that must be traced: both how it feeds into the extraction of value through the production of consenting laboring bodies and how it might enable the emergence of new social relations and forms of living. It therefore represents a vital terrain of political struggle within contemporary labor markets.

In the pages that follow I trace the emotional labor of young Egyptian men as they navigated a precarious, segmented labor market. This labor includes a variety of practices: engaging in masculinized humor, taking training courses, applying for jobs, planning fantasy start-ups, reading self-help literature, imagining the purchase of desirable commodities, praying to God, and searching for intimate connection with women. These practices become key in enabling men to forge livable lives and continue offering themselves to the labor market—by providing both temporary distraction and a vital sense of hope. Throughout, the book maintains focus on the politics of this labor: both how it emerges at the intersection of dominant ideologies, regimes of accumulation, and lived experience and how it enables the reproduction of forms of accumulation and inequality. I argue that, while crucially enabling Egyptians to forge meaningful lives, this labor becomes crucial in legitimizing an unequal capitalist regime by retaining focus on the individual as the determinant success and displacing attention on the need for structural transformations.

AN ETHNOGRAPHY OF HOPE IN EGYPT

Interrogating the everyday emotional life of young Egyptian men requires an immersive methodology. I sought to gain rare ethnographic insight onto undulations of emotion during thirteen months of ethnography stretched over five years. I arrived in Cairo in June 2014 intending to examine how educated underemployed youth were negotiating a disconnection between their aspirations for a successful career and ability to reach them. I contacted nongovernmental organizations (NGOs) working in youth unemployment and secured permission to attend a two-month training course designed to teach unemployed university graduates the "soft skills" they were supposedly lacking to succeed in the private sector. Between sessions I introduced myself as an independent researcher interested in the difficulties faced by graduates in the labor market, to which the response came: "Well, you are in the right place in Egypt!" This led to conversations, mostly with men as women were reticent to interact with a foreign man in public, about the course and their backgrounds, before I asked those with whom I developed closer relationships if they were comfortable being part of the research.

Thereafter I asked to meet friends and colleagues in order to reach beyond course participants but maintain focus on this social group. In total I spoke to forty-nine men and eighteen women, but thirteen men became the focus of the ethnography.[67] They were aged between twenty-two and twenty-seven in 2014, recent graduates from the "faculties of the people," self-defined Muslims, and raised in a mixture of lower-class to lower-middle-class areas in Cairo and towns and villages around Egypt. The gendering of interlocutors occurred because, as other researchers have found, I developed the possibility for deeper interactions with men as we could meet alone, whereas interaction with women was restricted to brief conversations during group outings. Ethnographic fieldwork began with six months in the second half of 2014. I then left for a period of five months, returning to Cairo in May 2015 for three months, again in November 2015 for one month, in September 2016 for a further month, in June 2018 for three weeks, and finally in October 2019 for three weeks. These breaks enabled me to introduce a longitudinal perspective that proved vital in understanding shifting trajectories and emotional labors as these young men navigated their twenties.

I met each interlocutor at least once a week, and some almost daily. I went to their homes to eat, chat, or watch films; we hung out in cafés or shopping malls; and we went for walks. We also looked for jobs, training opportunities, educational scholarships, or entrepreneurship funding in job fairs, online, or around the city, and learned skills like English, entrepreneurship, accountancy, law, or HR in events and lectures, in courses, or in their homes. I spent four months living in a flat with three men who had migrated to Cairo in search of work. This experience was vital in enabling me to observe the day-to-day emotional world of young men and become a more everyday presence. I did not spend much time in either family homes or workplaces. Both places were difficult to access as a single foreign man in Egypt. While I received invitations to family homes for special occasions, young men did not wish to spend much time with me there.

Topics of conversation varied. They included personal and family histories; future dreams and plans for reaching them; frustrating experiences such as job rejections or low-status employment; problems with Egypt's economy and government; women and relationships; desirable commodities; TV programs and films; opinions on world politics; Egyptian or European football; and funny situations they had encountered. The research was conducted mostly in Arabic. My Egyptian Arabic became fluent during the fieldwork, but some interlocutors preferred to communicate in English in order to practice a skill considered essential for career advancement.

Over time I became interested in the emotional dynamics of the pursuit of employment and marriage. This invites questions about how one accurately observes emotion, particularly cross-culturally. Initially I noted visible fluctuations between feelings of hope, enthusiasm, happiness, frustration, fear, confusion, anger, and sadness in response to specific events, practices, and conversations—for example, talking about the possibility of a new job or recent rejection. The ethnographic method is vital to observing emotions as they are expressed in situ, seeing not what people say they feel but what they actually feel. But to avoid misinterpretation, I asked interlocutors to describe their emotions at various moments. These conversations revealed important particularities to emotional experience in Egypt. For example, *ikti'ab* is often translated by Egyptians as "depression," but it differs from the medically determined Anglo-American term, rather connoting an elongated, paralyzing sadness. Furthermore, Egyptian men tend to conceal negative emotion around friends. Although presenting difficulties understanding emotional trajectories, the practice of distracting oneself from negativity is an important part of the story. As a foreign researcher I was sometimes able to circumvent this concealment because of my positioning outside the moral community of these men. We were not in competition, nor would I react to complaints with judgment.

During fieldwork I shifted attention to how places, objects, and discourses induced certain emotions. This required analysis of the atmospheres created within employment fairs or training courses, or by a business card or a laptop, and a self-help metaphor or religious proverb. These atmospheres are rendered visible through their materialization in bodies as feeling and emotion. Methodologically, therefore, this requires a focus on interlocutors as they interact with places, objects, and discourses. This approach is most prominent in Chapter 1, which explores how training courses, employment fairs, and entrepreneurship events incite hope as aspirational youth interact with them. These were predominantly one-day events, but I attended a soft-skills training course daily for three months in 2014. This involved sitting in lessons observing classroom activities, information they were learning, and student reactions, and speaking with students in breaks and after classes. In order to trace the logics and political economy that lay behind the production of these places, I conducted twelve interviews with employees of training organizations, recruitment agencies, and entrepreneurship platforms.

Tracing the labor of hope among Egyptian men, as a white British man, incites issues around the ethics of ethnographic knowledge production.[68] To explicate these ethics, I found it useful to place attention on what Nicole Laliberté and Carolin Schurr call the "emotional entanglements" of fieldwork.[69] I recollected the frustration and offense caused as I straddled being both "Western" researcher and potential friend. Despite providing consent, interlocutors were also invested in spending time with me because I provided a connection to a global upper-class life. Friendship rests on reciprocity, whereas being an object of research can operationalize a relationship which places the researcher in a position of supremacy.[70] There were various moments in which the "inauthenticity" of our friendship revealed itself: when I could not fulfill requests to hang out (particularly acute after I left Egypt), when I asked questions revealing an instrumental interest or took notes visibly, or when I tried to set up an informal exchange where I would "give something back" (such as help with a job application) in exchange for information. Navigating these tensions was challenging, but through openness to uncomfortable reactions I was able to forge meaningful relationships.

Many interlocutors involved me in their hopeful labor. Meeting them in a setting where they were working toward social mobility placed me in the position of potential aid. Thereafter my body came to fuel their labor of hope in myriad ways.[71] This stemmed from my social and cultural capital: some hoped I might send an invitation to migrate, find a British woman for them to marry, or help with applications. Spending time with me also provided a suggestion of social mobility as we hung out in elite spaces, had different kinds of conversation, or met other foreigners. I also incited hope by nonjudgmentally listening to employment struggles and even responding positively at the prospect of things improving out of fear of inducing disappointment. The hope vested in me was cruel as I could not significantly impact trajectories. It felt like a duty of care not to destroy the hope that enabled them to cope. But on occasion disappointment emerged as participants realized I could not make much difference. This enabled more honest conversations to emerge. Sometimes I did make a difference by giving money to help men secure visas or facilitating language exchanges with Europeans, which ended up in one participant getting engaged to a Dutch woman, with the prospect of migration suddenly on the horizon. Yet, despite the inevitable impact of my presence on the lives of these young men, their labor of hope was reproduced by a much broader terrain of objects and discourses that reflect a particular social, political, and economic context in Egypt. The remainder of this book excavates this labor.

ORGANIZATION OF THE BOOK

For the most part the book follows a linear trajectory of young Egyptian men's pursuit of a fulfilling career and durable intimacy. Each chapter, however, is designed to highlight specific aspects of their emotional labor. Chapter 1, "Selling Hope," reveals a booming labor market industry of training, recruitment, entrepreneurship, and self-help—spanning public, private, and developmental spheres—which has rapidly grown in Egypt in recent years, reflecting neoliberal moral transformations in the aftermath of the late-twentieth-century infitah. By examining encounters between university-educated youth and training courses, employment fairs, and entrepreneurship events, and conducting interviews with people managing these spaces, the chapter reveals how this industry thrives by selling a feeling of hope that rests on the extension of a neoliberal understanding of selfhood alongside a meritocratic vision of the labor market. It argues that the industry is purposely set up to profit from the production of hopeful laborers who are ready to invest in a precarious, segmented labor market. In doing so, it advances conceptual understandings of the way affect infuses spatial practices of governance and accumulation in contemporary labor markets and illuminates the commodification processes and political economy driving the labors of hope examined in the rest of the book.

Chapter 2, "The Drugs of Life," follows young male university graduates who are pursuing a private-sector career as they find work in Cairo's telecom industry, especially call centers—described as a "new kind of factory" for Egypt's youth. I trace the "emotional labor of distraction" required to keep going in jobs that induce constant frustration, boredom, and humiliation because of their inability to provide middle-class masculine respectability amid low pay, deskilling, and insecurity. Through macho joke-making, watching light television, scrolling through social media, periodically engaging in performative consumption, organizing social outings, going to the gym, and even smoking hashish and drinking alcohol, men forget the negative emotions that build up on the phones and "fuck with their heads" momentarily. Developing literature on detachment, avoidance, and deflection, I argue that these collective gendered practices constitute a form of emotional labor that enable workers to dissipate the anxieties and frustrations thrown up by low-status work and continue offering their labor power. However, the chapter also shows that the labor of distraction can reproduce anxiety through fears of permanent stagnation, which drives men into a form of emotional labor resting on hope.

Chapter 3, "Without Hope There Is No Life," follows the same group of men but instead focuses on the daily practices through which they sustain a vital sense of hope amid the structural disconnection between their career aspirations and current employment. By praying to God for guidance; recounting inspirational stories of successful friends, lessons from self-help books and religious texts, and quotes from entrepreneurs or Hollywood movies; and following these examples by attempting to work on their skills, apply for jobs, and plan their dream start-ups, men reintroduce a sense of "prospective momentum" toward a fulfilling future. Departing from literature highlighting the agentive ability of marginalized populations to navigate precarity, I argue that these practices represent an emotional labor of hope that enables laborers to survive but also legitimizes continued exploitation by keeping them invested in low-paid work and constructing a meritocratic moral economy that places emphasis for success and failure on the individual. Drawing on literature conceptualizing how consent can be retained among disaffected populations, I demonstrate how the labor of hope continues to operate despite the emergence of cynicism and disbelief.

While Chapters 2 and 3 focus on chasing careers, Chapter 4, "The Labor of Love," interrogates the vital but precarious pursuit of love. Revealing the inextricable power of love within the economy, it argues that finding intimacy represents a key form of emotional labor that enables men to forge livable lives amid conditions of precarity. While avoiding familial pressures to marry enables Egyptian men in their early twenties to sustain hope for their careers, discussing women among male friends, recollecting memories of past relations, and engaging in casual courting provides brief distraction and masculine validation in the context of demoralizing work experiences. Over time men turn their attention to longer-term love by slowly preparing a marital house and entering relationships. These practices provide self-worth, excitement, and hope, which can make up for labor market struggles and add vital impetus to keep going. However, through becoming embroiled with moral frameworks of gendered respectability and Islamic piety, as well as a moral economy which leaves love dependent on money and status, this pursuit produces immense heartache. Sustaining love and a career simultaneously, the chapter argues, requires an extremely difficult balancing act on the part of women and men—and intense emotional labor—amid a set of structural economic and cultural forces that are rendering both precarious in contemporary Egypt.

The final chapter, "The Migration of Hope," explicates the relationship between the act of migration and the labor of hope. It traces how imagining and investing time and money into the possibility of migration constitutes a crucial form of emotional labor for young Egyptian men struggling in precarious work. This labor is fueled by a migrant industry that makes money out of stimulating these hopes. It also takes great effort to overcome the disillusionment of failed attempts and doubts that plague more realistic prospects. The chapter then follows men who migrate to the Arab Gulf, Malaysia, and Europe and describes the relationship between the experience of migration and the hopes imbued in it. While sometimes enabling dramatic financial mobility invested into aspirational consumption, homes and business projects, migration is also experienced as immensely disappointing as men become stuck in low-end jobs, experience intense loneliness and everyday racism, and navigate difficult relationships. The chapter also serves to plot the temporal shifts in emotional labor as interlocutors get older, arguing that aging requires a more contingent and detached orientation to the world in order to maintain a livable life. The concluding chapter reflects on the wider application and consequences of the labor of hope. Highlighting the ruptures emerging from this labor, it examines the question of the emergence of more collective labors of hope geared toward tackling the injustices built into capitalist economies.

CHAPTER ONE

SELLING HOPE

I TRAVELED TO DOKKI, AN upper-middle-class area of Cairo on the banks of the Nile, on a hot June morning.[1] After struggling to find the building, I looked up to see a sign—in English—on the second floor of an apartment block: *Training for Jobs: Where Hope Works.* I was greeted by the receptionist and told to wait in a classroom, where I was joined by forty young men and women all dressed in suits. They sat in silence for a few minutes before a middle-aged Egyptian woman wearing jeans, a blouse, and—unlike most of the female participants—no hijab entered and introduced herself in flawless English as Wafaa, TFJ's program manager. She welcomed participants to the job-placement training program, a two-month educational scholarship designed to help unemployed university graduates find career-building work by providing the soft skills needed to succeed in Egypt's private sector. Participants were asked to introduce themselves in English by outlining their dreams, their role model, and where they see themselves in five years. One man enthusiastically announced his role model as Steve Jobs and his dream of becoming a global entrepreneur. Others described dreams of traveling abroad, working in multinational companies, and becoming governor of Egypt's Central Bank. We were then shown a video. According to the U.S. CEO on screen, TFJ "helps youth get that first job, gives them an economic advantage, a path to social mobility, and an opportunity of choice." Alumni were shown on screen wearing suits and sitting in pristine offices.

They were labeled "content associates" or "accountants," but these current jobs were crossed out and replaced with speculations of their future roles: "future commerce expert? future CEO?" After the film, participants were asked what they understood. One woman responded anxiously: "TFJ helps people who have no hope." Another student followed: "It does not just focus on customer service jobs." Wafaa agreed but added: "We think it is important to get that first job."

Wafaa began the first session on career advancement by relaying her trajectory. She had wanted to attend the American University in Cairo upon leaving school. She dreamed of becoming an economist or entrepreneur but had to give up those dreams and attend public university as her father could not afford AUC's exorbitant fees. She quickly began to tire of the poor quality, so her father paid for her to study English for two years at the British Council. Over time Wafaa developed fluency. She described the reason for that fluency as her "hard work": "I would go to the library to read books, and even listen to songs on public transport to practice." Wafaa described how English gave her "freedom" as it had been a "hot commodity" at the time. It was vital in enabling her to obtain a job as a receptionist in a multinational company, which provided a salary five times that of an engineer, she said. Wafaa kept working to improve, teaching herself Excel and even German on the job. This "attitude," she described, secured her progression to project management in Vodafone. Eventually she began training new staff, and as a result she became interested in the training field. By reaching out to her networks she heard about and applied to TFJ. The key reason for her career advancement, Wafaa stressed, was her constant drive to "work on [her] development." She told the captivated students: "You have to be passionate and believe. I have seen so many young people who are not sure what they have to gain, or how to develop themselves. The ones who want to achieve will; the only one who stops you is yourself."

The training program these graduates were about to embark on has formed part of a governmental and developmental strategy to tackle the entrenched problem of unemployment among Egypt's educated youth since 2013. The same program, or scholarship as it is labeled, is offered by multiple nonprofit organizations that obtain funding from development donors and the private sector, as well as international training companies that run corporate social

responsibility programs with government help. It sits within a broader training, recruitment, and entrepreneurship industry—stretching across state,
private, and third-sector spheres—that has rapidly grown in recent years as
a supply-side intervention to youth unemployment. This industry promises
to improve the skills of job seekers, help them locate jobs, and provide supportive "ecosystems" for budding entrepreneurs. It mirrors a global boom in
training, recruitment, and entrepreneurship that is designed to enhance the
capacities of working-age individuals and materialize and entrench meritocratic practices.[2] It thus represents an extension of neoliberal labor market
logics into an Egyptian context: constructing a "modern," "fair," meritocratic
formal private sector within which talent and skill is rewarded rather than
nepotism or prejudicial notions of where people belong. These logics map
onto a broader shift in moral responsibility in Egypt away from family, community, and state and toward the individual following processes of economic
liberalization.[3]

This infrastructure, and the discourse of meritocracy itself, has been critiqued in scholarship for operating as a governmental "technique of power"
for "making up" the ideal worker-citizen required by contemporary capitalism, while also making individuals responsible for employment outcomes and
masking structural inequalities. But in this chapter, I trace how meritocratic
logics become powerful in practice among low-status workers in the labor
market. For this I turn to conceptual work demonstrating how affect and
emotion infuses governance practices, while also adopting a nuanced notion
of neoliberal governmentality revealing how knowledges and techniques are
taken up and reworked in everyday life by their recipients. The following
chapters trace how this shifts over time within the ethical life-worlds of men
who are navigating prolonged disconnection in the labor market. But the
focus of this chapter is the encounters between aspirational educated unemployed young Egyptians and soft-skills training courses, entrepreneurship
events, and employment fairs. It argues that these industries accumulate
profit and secure funding by selling a feeling of hope. They aesthetically symbolize Egypt's exclusive international private sector, promise to provide the
missing link to it—that key skill or character trait, vital network or source
of funding, or first job—and construct success as dependent on "attitude"
(suluk al-shakhṣ). As a result, they attempt to produce—and very often suc-

ceed in producing—hopeful laborers who are ready to invest in a precarious, segmented labor market by focusing on themselves as determinants of life chances instead of structural issues creating high un- or underemployment.

TRAINING FOR JOBS

Egypt has a thriving training economy made up of universities, local and international NGOs, foreign cultural centers, and private entities ranging from international corporations to self-employed "career coaches" offering an endless array of vocational courses. This economy has emerged amid a decline in the quality of public schools and universities alongside the creation of huge youth populations struggling to locate work matching their education.[4] Each offering promises to be the gateway to success, and one's training portfolio has become a key marker of distinction among middle-class Egyptians. Indeed, Egyptians joke that Egypt has become a country of certificates. But opportunities are highly stratified. The most prestigious courses can cost thousands, lying out of reach for most. A seven-week English course (one of four per level) at the British Council cost LE2,000 (US$250) in 2014; by comparison, the average monthly salary of graduates in service and sales was LE1,500. This stratification leaves many investing in cheaper options, which means lower-quality and larger crowds.

The TFJ scholarship was targeted at university graduates most prone to unemployment. TFJ is a U.S.-based nonprofit founded in 2006 with the mission to create "economic opportunity" by "providing world-class professional and technical training that leads directly to career-building jobs" for youth in the Middle East and North Africa (MENA) region. It operates as a series of franchises across nine countries, funded by foreign government donors and international companies through corporate social responsibility programs or employment partnerships. By 2019, some 100,000 youth had graduated from its programs. In exchange for a "commitment fee" of LE150/200 (US$19/25), the job-placement training program offered to provide graduates who have been unemployed for six months with the "soft skills" they are apparently lacking in the internationalized labor market; these include business English; "essential labor market skills" like interview techniques, CV writing, and career planning; and "work values/character development" such as self-presentation, communication, teamwork, commitment, and time management.

It also offered to help graduates find "decent work," an aim upon which success is measured and continued funding rests. This led to partnerships with companies offering to employ participants, which require the teaching of specific skills.

The "soft skills" focus has international origins.[5] While vocational training has historically been associated with technical and manual labor, there has been a recent rise in attention to nontechnical skills.[6] The template used stems from the soft-skills training initiative of the International Youth Foundation (IYF), which considers these "non-technical, professional" abilities to include "communication, interpersonal and customer service skills, as well as personal traits such as integrity and responsibility." In Egypt it is widely believed that a lack of "soft life skills" rather than technical skills is holding graduates back: their "personal responsibility, adherence to common work ethic, leadership, and ability to manage conflict and criticism" in addition to "basic IT and English language skills."[7] However, this focus also stems from the employment deemed accessible to, and suitable for, public university graduates. TFJ attempts to form partnerships with or otherwise direct youth into entry-level service or sales work, for example in call centers, hotels, or shopping malls. These growing fields are looking for people with basic computer and English skills who can deal with upscale customers.

For these jobs, as Mona, a manager of another "soft skills" training organization, told me, no specific skills are required:

> You will be surprised but all they need is good communication skills, negotiation, they can present themselves, have confidence, be respectable. In Cairo they need basic computer skills and English, and that's it, they don't need any other skill. Employers tell you bluntly, bring him to me and I'll teach him everything, but at least they can be teachable, that's all I need.

Despite not requiring skills, these jobs are considered suitable for university graduates—or at least those from the "faculties of the people" who make up the majority of attendees. These graduates are labeled "without skills" by program organizers. When pressed, staff told me they had to "respond to the market," that "these are the available jobs at the moment." Yet they were presented externally as good jobs, as defined by International Labour Organization (ILO) standards of "decent work"—they are white-collar and have a contract, social insurance, and minimum salary in 2014 of LE1,000 (US$125) per month. However, they are not considered "decent" by attendees. Although some stratification exists, the Arabic-language call center work accessible to these low-end graduates is infamous for being demeaning, low-paid, and insecure. It does not provide the basis for a respectable middle-class life. Despite TFJ advertising that it helps "unemployed" youth, many participants had actually worked in call centers and left in order to enroll. One participant told me at the beginning he would "rather die than go back."

Among staff and within Egypt's development apparatus, responsibility for this misalignment is placed on youth. Salma Wahba, youth and adolescent development officer for UNICEF Egypt, made this clear in a 2014 *Guardian* interview:

> In Egypt youth still prefer to work for the government, rather than the private sector, perceiving it to be a secure job. Many people are waiting for the job that best fits their qualifications rather than actively seeking employment and accepting jobs that they think are below their level. This is a major cultural barrier among youth in Egypt.[8]

Although I found that young graduates craved prestigious private-sector work above state employment, the broader point holds. Educated youth are understood to be in "luxury unemployment" where they "choose" to wait for suitable jobs while being supported by parents.[9] Their unemployment is presented as illegitimate, a product of a classist society. TFJ staff described youth as "image-conscious" and "closed-minded," with aspirations based on what they consider "prestigious" rather than real knowledge; one staff member even told me, "Egypt is a classist society where someone would rather work as an accountant or lawyer with no opportunities to advance rather than a call center with opportunities."

Wafaa also illuded to another "issue" to resolve during one meeting:

> Youth need to be realistic. The mindset of graduates now is to finish and get the certificate, and with that it is assumed you get a job, they don't have guidance to know it doesn't work like that. I try to think where this taking culture comes from, the lazy culture of expecting things to be done for you. Maybe it was from Nasser and the government giving jobs, but I wasn't given anything.

Refusal of work becomes a personal deficiency to be solved. It is explained as a product of a socialist mindset, unsuited to a capitalist labor market in which one starts low, builds a career, and switches frequently rather than being "given" a job for life.[10] Thus, alongside teaching the soft skills required in modern private-sector jobs and application skills such as CV writing or interview techniques, breaking down this mindset emerges as a key and progressive task. Staff expressed great confidence about doing so, although they said men were more difficult to convince because they possess "stubborn" aspirations. It is to be achieved by teaching work commitment (iltizam) and "career planning." Participants are to view themselves as a bundle of skills, match them to the market, and continually engage in self-learning to "climb the ladder" in a labor market that recruits based on merit and acquirable skills.

TFJ extends a vision of a meritocratic labor market where success depends on individuals and trains participants how to achieve it. This training has faced critique in scholarship using a Foucauldian lens that views it as a "technique of power" for constructing the ideal workers required by neoliberal labor markets.[11] The same can be said about the extension of meritocratic and entrepreneurial discourses more generally that produce individualizing logics.[12] Although existing research has developed a complex discursive critique of these logics for disciplining and responsibilizing workers and legitimizing privilege and inequality, their actual influence is often assumed, with recipients given little room to interpret messages. This reflects a broader critique of overdetermining approaches to Foucauldian biopower that elide the complex ways subjects enact it.[13] We must carefully examine how dominant biopolitical techniques and knowledges interact with ordinary ethical life-worlds in order to assess their success or failure. Laurence Ralph, for example, described how "career days" are met with "scornful distain" as poor Black youth in Chicago penetrate the fantastical notion that they might one day follow in the footsteps of the Black lawyer or president who are pinned up as role models.[14] Ralph highlights how marginalized subjects can reject dominant biopolitical discourses designed to encourage aspirational citizens, but in other cases the agentive reception of messages can also make the workings of governmentality all the more powerful.

Ralph also hints at the underexplored role of affect and emotion in biopolitical projects. Moving beyond a nonrepresentational approach to affect, Ben Anderson argued that theorizations of affect need to examine how affects become both an intentional "object-target" of biopolitical techniques and an unintended medium through which they work.[15] This requires tracing how material and discursive formations produce "affective atmospheres," as well as how these atmospheres are received and reworked by people. Some literature has adopted this approach in examining how particular corporate and governmental structures operate by producing atmospheres of anxiety and hope.[16] Natasha Schüll's *Addiction by Design* provided particular stimulation for my analysis in this chapter as it demonstrates how casinos, and specifically the mechanical rhythm enacted by electronic slot machines, are arranged to pull players into a "trancelike state."[17] Stimulated by this work, I argue that employment training like TFJ's soft-skills program, and recruitment fairs and entrepreneurial events, becomes effective by producing atmospheres of hope that rest on the construction of a meritocratic narrative that career success is accessible to anyone if they implement the correct behavior. By closely following the experience of these spaces by young aspirational Egyptians who have recently entered the labor market and crave a hopeful sensibility, the chapter shows how this narrative resonates powerfully. In the context of the TFJ skills program, amid a stubborn misalignment between participants' employment aspirations and the low-skilled service jobs into which they are directed, the organization succeeds by generating hope for future mobility.

LEARNING TO HOPE

Ibrahim was born in a village in the Nile delta governate of Sharkia to secondary school teachers. In 2012 he graduated from the Faculty of Commerce (Arabic section) at Zagazig University and spent one year in the army. Upon returning, Ibrahim defied his father's expectation to take an accountancy job in 10th of Ramadan, a purpose-built industrial town that has provided employment for the region since the 1990s. Ibrahim described 10th of Ramadan as a "tomb for youth" (qabr l'al sha'b), recounting the story of his brother-in-law who had become "depressed" (mukta'ib) on a salary of LE1,500 (US$190) per month, which meant he struggled to afford family expenses. Ibrahim looked to his struggle, which also included threats of termination, and saw an inability to lead a dignified life. In university Ibrahim engaged in extracurricular activities, joining Students in Free Enterprise, a global organization designed to enhance youth entrepreneurship, and setting up an initiative called Make Your Goal to teach students CV writing, business structure, and English. These activities were like a "trip," through which Ibrahim "found himself" (laqa nafsuh) and his "entrepreneurial mind." He developed a passion to "aid the development of mankind" through entrepreneurship, following in the footsteps of his idol Steve Jobs. The idea of being an accountant filled him with dread: "You work like a robot, only working to get money, marry, and have babies." Ibrahim wanted his work to be about more:

> I am not obsessed to raise my level to get things like a car or flat, that stuff is important to get respect from others, but I just want to be comfortable. What drives me is to make a difference to the world, Steve Jobs wanted to do that.

Specifically, Ibrahim wanted to make a mobile app. Technology, he said, is "very important for progress." He distinguished his form of entrepreneurship from sellers (beʿaiyyn) in his village selling mobile accessories. They were not entrepreneurs as they did not create anything new.

Ibrahim therefore developed a disconnect between his entrepreneurial aspirations and the expected trajectory that lay before him. For a year Ibrahim searched in vain for funding for his start-up. After hearing about it from a friend who had attended, Ibrahim decided to apply for TFJ's scholarship. Other participants had similar trajectories. They too traveled to this exclusive part of Cairo from informal neighborhoods or towns across the delta and even beyond after finding out about the course through friends, on Facebook, or at employment fairs following months and sometimes years of failing to locate fulfilling jobs upon graduating. This course they hoped would change their fortunes. But first they had to attend an application day, where they were interviewed and had their English tested. During these interviews, Salma, the program coordinator, asked applicants if they were "ready to work in any job." If they replied no, or not in a call center, a negotiation ensued. Salma declared that TFJ considers the call center a good job, while also arguing it provides useful skills, saying to one aspiring lawyer: "All lawyers need to be good salespeople!" If Salma figured people would not take work after the course, they were rejected. During a break she turned to me and said, "Youth want to buy time, to do something while doing nothing. We want underprivileged youth who want a job and need money. It is bad if people take the place of others just because they want to fill time." Ibrahim later proudly told me he lied about being ready to work in customer service to secure access to the course, revealing how participants do not buy into all they are told.

Ibrahim made it into the program. The application day induced the feeling that doing so was an achievement, although it was rare that applicants were rejected based on skills. The next step was orientation day, where participants were immediately exposed to the idea that their dreams depended on them through Wafaa's narration of her career. Wafaa's ability to afford a British Council course signified an upper-middle-class background. But according to her it was her "attitude, dedication, and need to learn" that secured her progression. Her narrative produced hope for participants, most of whom quickly began describing her as an inspiration. In the days following they watched videos of Australian executives introducing themselves over work drinks and Steve Jobs giving lecturing advice, pretended to be Vodafone executives as they practiced introducing themselves in English with a teacher who studied in England, learned how to put together professional attire by wearing suits every day—which was a course requirement—and discussing the right amount of perfume to use, and studied how sales, customer service, and marketing formed different aspects of business. Scott Hurrell argued that "soft skills" often represent the dominant cultural capital held by a society's middle classes.[18] Speaking English in a non-Egyptianized accent, presenting oneself formally by wearing a suit or hijab in a modern way (if one wears one at all), introducing oneself by shaking hands, and knowledge of formal business structures are recognizable markers of Cairo's globalized economy and privately educated upper-middle classes. They are juxtaposed with the "humorous" Egyptianized English accents, "impolite" Arabic speech, dress such as a galabiyya or traditional hijab, greetings between men involving kisses on the cheek, and "informal" business practices associated with sha'by culture.

During interviews with recruiters at international companies, I was told that soft skills were vital in enabling them to distinguish whether someone was suitable. Arafa, an employee at PricewaterhouseCoopers (PwC), described them as reflective of a deeper "mentality":

I don't know how to describe it, you know when you sit with a person and he's open-minded, he talks about different topics and knows about lots of things, and you listen to someone else who doesn't know anything. It's not technicalities, what he studied, just narrow-mindedness. This is a very common interview question: what was the last film you saw, what's your favorite band, what music do you listen to, did you travel, things that have nothing to do with your education but make a huge difference, and the problem is it limits certain classes of society, it's very socially based."[19]

In TFJ these markers are presented as acquirable soft skills by upper-middle-class trainers who often described a motivation to "give back" for their success. By wearing a suit every day, speaking business English, and pretending to be company executives, participants learned not only that these forms of middle-class distinction were acquirable but that they were acquiring them. The pleasure induced was clear to see as participants attentively listened to trainers, put their hands up before trainers even finished asking a question, and asked for breaks to be delayed so they could carry on learning. Sessions were highly interactive—participants were asked to present, perform role plays, or draw out what they were learning. This was key in securing a perception of progress. On most occasions there was a rush of volunteers, but any reticence was directly combated. After one activity, the teacher told students: "The idea is to build your confidence of speaking in public, to stop you being scared and get you used to mistakes." Frequent English struggles briefly penetrated the euphoria, but trainers made sure to extend praise. They also told others to encourage those presenting, informing students that "no negative energy is allowed, you have to support each other, no one should feel embarrassed."

These activities were experienced as empowering. Participants began telling me how they felt the course was making a difference. The act of coming to TFJ—which aesthetically signified Cairo's upscale economy through its English signs and mixture of Western and upper-class Egyptian staff—represented a traversal of social worlds and provided a sense of elevation. Gamal, the man introduced in the book's opening vignette, described how the course made him feel different from people in his lower-middle-class neighborhood in northeast Cairo: "They do not think about what goes on in the outside world, they spend time talking about trivial topics like neighborhood gossip, football, fighting, girls, drugs. I prefer to talk about serious topics like work or politics." Gamal declared himself "raqy [classy] in character now, just sha'by in background." He continued demarcating this distinction after the course by wearing a suit every day as he moved around the city. Conversations like this represented a performance to me but also an exciting experience of progress. I often found myself swept up in this euphoria inside the classroom, only to be reminded of the hidden forms of privilege that enabled upper-middle-class trainers to hone these soft skills over many years. Arafa, the PwC employee, described how an "open-minded" mentality cannot be created quickly. One must be "ibn al-nas" (son of the people), from an upper-class family and area.[20] He expressed sorrow for people who take English or computer courses because "they do not make much difference." The students at TFJ would not even get an interview at most places, he said, because companies screen out public-university graduates beforehand.[21]

Back inside the classroom, participants learned how to continue honing their soft skills beyond the course. For this they needed to manage their time effectively. Time management, the teacher said, is "vital to achieving your professional goals." It involves stopping activities that are "wasting your life"—such as chatting on Facebook, sleeping long hours, or socializing—and using your time on productive activities such as studying, even during endless hours spent on Cairo's public transport. Ibrahim recognized "time-wasting" as a problem among youth. He described to me how many of his friends sit in cafés watching football and smoking. Ibrahim, on the other hand, was traveling two hours every day to Cairo to develop himself. This perspective disrupts literature on timepass by revealing the moral economies that can develop between youth who are actively and passively waiting.[22] The importance of these moral economies for the maintenance of hope will become clearer as the book unfolds, but for now what is significant is the transfer of knowledge from upper-middle-class trainers. Time management was disciplined into students through a points system. Each started with fifty points, with points deducted for being late, missing sessions, or disrupting classes, while points were awarded for performing well. If a student reached zero, they were kicked out, although this never happened during my stay.

Part of Ibrahim's self-development consisted of conducting a SWOT (strengths, weaknesses, opportunities, threats) analysis, which Wafaa explained was useful when considering career changes. It enables you to assess your weaknesses and work on them to create opportunities in your desired field. Opportunities and threats, Wafaa said, "mostly follow from your strengths and weaknesses, but sometimes from outside. If the economy is in bad shape, like now, you need a plan B in case you cannot access your desired field." This was the only time I heard teachers stress a factor beyond individual control. Otherwise, structural constraints were substituted for a focus on the individual, who in the event of failure should learn from their mistakes and keep going. Even here it was up to individuals to adapt constructively to external circumstances. Participants conducted their own SWOT analysis. Ibrahim did one for HR, with his strengths being his communication skills, passion, and ability to match people with jobs and his weaknesses English and lack of connections. Upon completion, Wafaa asked for feedback. One student excitedly said: "It gives a snapshot on me, an organized way of thinking about myself that can help me start to plan." Another welcomed learning "how not to get angry with my weaknesses, but to focus on dealing with them." This exercise instilled an empowering mindset as impenetrable barriers were converted to surmountable weaknesses.

This included the issue of *wasta*, getting a job through relatives or friends, which remains a notorious object of scorn in Egypt's labor market. When one participant sarcastically mentioned wasta during an exercise discussing tactics for job searches, the teacher was quick to interject, insisting that "nobody pays money or is just placed in jobs anymore." Instead, recruitment processes were open and dependent on one's skills, particularly in private companies, which, as Ibrahim insisted to me, "want profit so they want the best people, and only employ someone if they are skilled and efficient rather than if they know someone, so if someone knows what he wants and takes the relevant qualifications they can reach it." Wafaa described this as the "modern" way of getting jobs: acquiring skills and marketing yourself instead of being placed in a government job. Making use of social connections was a legitimate part of this strategy. Wafaa emphasized how she used her network of friends to find out about training, which prompted one participant to ask how to combat a bad network. Instead of answering, Wafaa asked others to respond. They suggested asking friends, attending conferences, taking courses, and using sites such as LinkedIn. A widely acknowledged exclusionary class-de-pendent mechanism, and source of much anger, was therefore converted into an obtainable resource, a source of hope.

Throughout the course participants were fed narratives constructing Cairo's private sector as open and meritocratic, where acquirable soft skills and perseverance are rewarded rather than illegitimate, impenetrable vectors of inequality such as money, wasta, or private education. TFJ therefore became a site that produced meritocratic logics in Egypt's labor market. Tracing their reception by underprivileged course participants reveals the affective power of these logics. Meritocracy offers the promise of reward to any individual, no matter their class, race, or gender, who acquires the right skills, charac-teristics, and connections. In the classroom, participants learned they could be the hard workers who succeed—if they continue to improve their English, tinker with their CVs, or wear the right suit. This put the future within their control, thus inducing hope. Hope was embodied in a trainer's career narra-tive, international marketing textbook, or piece of paper outlining a SWOT analysis. But this hope required action. When I suggested to Wafaa during a conversation that TFJ provides hope, she replied:

> It doesn't just give hope, it gives ideas, we are saying you have capabilities, you have to look for your talents and discover them, it is conviction. Hope is a weak word, it sounds laid back, like youth just sit at home and hope. We are talking about courage and conviction that something will come, even if the picture is mixed, that conviction that you will work on Excel, English, instead of sitting on Facebook like they all do, not learning . . . in your brain you are capable of looking to a great future, or to be like the guys in the coffee shop."

TFJ was thus providing "hope with conviction" according to Wafaa, a form of hope requiring action. Inside the classroom this action-oriented hope manifested as participants engaged their bodies in the tasks of introducing themselves in a business meeting or carrying out an interview. This hopeful affect was tightly controlled by staff, as cynicism and sadness were quickly shut down. As well as being encouraging, participants were told to "walk into class with a smile" whatever happens outside. Divisive topics like politics were forbidden, and the points system forced positive engagement with the course. This therefore became a hopeful performance that participants had little choice but to engage in. One trainer showed the way by posting inspirational quotes on Facebook every morning—"smile for life, believe in your dream, believe you can and you will." Ibrahim picked up this practice on his own profile.

One aspect of the course, however, produced a different affective reaction. Participants became frustrated as they were taught customer service vocabulary or forced to tailor CVs to call center jobs. Ibrahim said skilled graduates do not belong in call centers, and that TFJ should expand its focus and stop trying to secure workers for sponsors. One participant said he would "take what he wants" from TFJ. This demonstrated the presence of some resistance, which was openly negotiated by staff. Near the end of the course Wafaa asked which jobs participants had applied for. One student replied: a call center job "because it was the only available job." Wafaa interjected: "You shouldn't apply if you don't like it," forcing him to backtrack. She then turned to everyone: "You need to do something you love, you need to know what you love and what fits your skills." Participants were not forced into call centers. Many conversations took place between teachers and confused students who, as one participant described, were experiencing a "war inside their heads." Ibrahim sought advice about reaching his entrepreneurship goal. Wafaa told him to follow this passion but recommended he take temporary work to save money. To other students trainers emphasized, using personal stories, how in call centers they can learn valuable skills for the field they were passionate about, secure promotion to other departments by "showing themselves well," or save money for further courses. Recent alumni also played a role, with one informal chat taking place in the bathroom, where a man told students he was able to move to other departments from his call center role. Through allowing for agency, compliance for the course's aims was rendered more powerful. Participants were not giving up their dreams; rather, those dreams were pushed into the future, and the pathway to them involved the call center.[23]

For Ibrahim, TFJ's graduation was a euphoric experience, sealed by the final assignment. Participants had to come up with an imaginary start-up and present it, in English, at a ceremony in an events hall in Zamalek, Cairo's most upscale neighborhood. They were told to invite family and friends and imagine it was the "real thing" of pitching to investors. They had to come

up with a vision, an organizational structure, a target market, and projected
costs and revenue, with the stated idea to introduce participants to company
logistics. When I mentioned the juxtaposition between the project and the
employment that comes after, Wafaa replied: "It is about planting a seed, so
if you are in a call center for two years, but also working on a project . . . I'm
sure someone can find financing these days." Ibrahim became his group's
CEO. They spent days researching a start-up of hydro-powered cars, which
Wafaa said she would definitely buy. On graduation day only two participants
brought family. However, the atmosphere was one of excitement and nervous-
ness. Students sat together on the right, teachers on the left. The general manager gave a speech congratulating graduates while reminding them that only
15 percent of youth get contracts: "We place great emphasis on formal work;
the objective of the program is finding work for youth. Egypt has no confidence in customer service; you will change that." Next, groups presented a
GPS watch, a sand-manufactured microchip, and a mobile app for helping to
navigate Egyptian bureaucracy. Some forgot lines or messed up grammar, but
their embarrassment was quickly dispelled by shouts of encouragement and
applause. Each person received hugs from smiling teachers, who told them
how proud they should be. Ibrahim thanked TFJ on stage: "TFJ is not just a
training center, it's a trip in which you find your passion." Two participants
were asked if they would be filmed talking about their TFJ experience for a
promotional video.

Ibrahim brought a friend to the ceremony. Hassan's voice was hoarse and
quiet, his face visibly drained. He had graduated from TFJ two years ago
before joining a call center in the hope of obtaining a bank job. But he was
still in the call center. He described how tiring the job was: he had to speak
for three hours nonstop, and both his voice and hearing were suffering. He
had also forgotten English, lacking the time, money, or energy to maintain
it. A teacher came over to say hello, enthusiastically asking, "How are you?!"
Hassan replied, in Arabic, "Good, but the job is hard, there are no opportunities for promotion." After a brief pause, the teacher replied: "Okay, well, keep
trying, something will come." Hassan nodded and smiled, and the teacher
moved on. Hassan represented a lurking presence of potential future struggles to come. But for now, that future remained unacknowledged amid an
atmosphere of euphoric hope. Ibrahim felt sorry for Hassan but also blamed

him for letting depression overcome him. He had "surrendered" (istaslim) and stopped working on his skills. This reflected language picked up at TFJ. Ibrahim needed to criticize Hassan for the sake of his hope. Despite originally being one of the most resistant, Ibrahim made a plan to take a call center job and use it as a base to save money, expand his connections by attending events in Cairo, and learn how companies are run from the inside. He felt more emboldened than ever. Others made similar plans. Many insisted they had to be practical but also expressed confidence about the future. TFJ could therefore advertise success to donors, measured through a survey of whether participants were in "decent work" after three months, with no long-term measurement taken apart from exemplary alumni "success stories" posted on its website.[24] This success had been secured by inciting a hopeful attachment to meritocracy. Participants had not been elevated in terms of employment status. They were taking (and often retaking) low-skilled service work in the hope it would lead to social mobility. In the following section, I show how a similar extension of hope occurred in Cairo's entrepreneurship scene.

PLANNING IN HOPE

In October 2014, two months after the TFJ course, I attended a UN fair with Ibrahim and two other former students, Mahmoud and Youssef. Ibrahim had taken a job in a call center and moved into a shared flat with Hassan. Attending this fair was part of his attempts to locate funding and expand connections for his start-up. He had come across it on Facebook. It was located in the Fish Garden, also in the exclusive neighborhood of Zamalek. The park ordinarily required a LE15 entry fee and was frequented by upper/upper-middle-class Cairenes or tourists, but today it was free and open to all. The fair was designed to commemorate the successes of UN start-up beneficiaries in Egypt, thus forming a small part of the country's entrepreneurship scene. Although entrepreneurship has been a dominant ideal in Egypt for three decades, it intensified after Barack Obama's 2009 Middle East entrepreneurship initiative. It is concentrated in Cairo and incorporates donors and investors, incubators and platforms designed to provide supportive "ecosystems," co-working spaces, educational facilities teaching entrepreneurship skills, and start-ups themselves. It is focused on technology or scalable businesses. Entrepreneurship is presented as a powerful tool for decreasing youth unemployment and provides a fashionable target for development funding.[25] Promotion through training such as TFJ's course is one manifestation of this.

We arrived shortly after the two p.m. opening, entering after having our bags checked. Earlier there had been a closed event attended by government ministers, the only remnants being a tent filled with empty cocktail tables. The fair had an upscale feel owing to its location. Ibrahim himself commented on its professional look. However, there were visible separations. The people running the event and the UN stalls—outside some UN-supported microenterprises—were either from Cairo's upper-middle classes or foreigners. One stall attendant was a German roommate of mine doing a UN internship.[26] These people moved freely in front of and behind the stalls, enjoying convivial conversations. Another group, of which Ibrahim, Mahmoud, and Youssef were part, was more restricted. They moved between stalls, picking up leaflets and sometimes talking with stall attendants, in Arabic after initial attempts in English. This group had come to seek job opportunities, build connections, and learn useful information. Their communication with the upper-middle class was restricted to questions about work opportunities or project information. Stalls included UN-funded start-ups, ranging from date farmers in Upper Egypt to app developers in Cairo, information stands on UN projects, NGOs offering services like educational networking, and UN volunteering initiatives. Many crowded around the volunteering stall seeking to apply for jobs and the initiative itself, only to learn that this was not possible at the fair.

Youssef excitedly collected any leaflet he could. He said he would benefit from reading the information contained. By the end he had collected too many to carry and so he put some down, only to pick them back up after deciding he could not let them go. Among the leaflets was a monthly schedule of the U.S. embassy's Information Resource Center, on which he had marked events he wanted to attend: Business Planning for Entrepreneurs, English Conversation Club, Introduction to Project Management. I left briefly to speak with my roommate. She commented that attendees do not know how to have memorable conversations. They come and ask if there are opportunities, and if so how to apply. They do not show genuine interest. I thought about Youssef. He did not show the necessary conduct to stand out or display deep interest, performed qualities considered important. But I reminded myself that even with the correct behavior, there were other barriers preventing him from standing out compared with the privately educated UN employees. Our conversation was interrupted by Ibrahim, who called me over to listen to an "amazing story." A young man from one of Cairo's 'ashwa'yat was selling ice cream. He was ushered by an organizer to tell his story. He began, shyly, to say he had been in prison for fighting someone with a relative in the police, but since leaving had established an ice cream business with UN funding. After expressing our congratulations and buying an ice cream, we left. Ibrahim said: "Isn't that amazing, he has not done anything bad since and turned his life around . . . he shows if you do the right thing you can overcome anything."

We continued so that Ibrahim could exercise his plan. He was here to build connections and find funding for his latest start-up idea, a mobile application to help deaf people communicate. Ibrahim learned he needed to do this by attending lectures by existing entrepreneurs and coaching sessions and doing online reading. After one lecture by a locally known entrepreneur at Ibrahim's university—which Ibrahim paid to attend—he told me: "It made me so happy, it was so helpful and motivating, I learned how to follow and develop the passion inside me; that makes me feel like I am flying, it was even on TV, it was so cool!" Ibrahim was told to expand his network and search hard for the plentiful funding opportunities on offer. He also learned that entrepreneurs have passion (shaghaf), unwavering belief, and must be risk takers and hard workers. This was reflected in Ibrahim's favorite Steve Jobs quote: "Because the people who are crazy enough to think they can change the world are the ones who do." However, at the fair Ibrahim found it difficult to bring up his project, so his effort went toward obtaining business cards from stall attendants. By the end, he collected two, which he was very happy with. Following these activities, we joined the crowds at the stage to listen to the free evening concert, performed by Wust El-Balad, a band popular among middle-class youth. As we listened, thoughts of entrepreneurial dreams lingered on.

Later, I spoke to these men about the day. When I asked Youssef why youth went, he said:

Most are looking for a chance or to see how they can improve themselves,

how it can help them. They have a talent and dream. Today I told myself I
can do everything I want to. Others go there for the free concert, you can see
that, but there are others who have a goal and a dream. They take inspiration
for their own projects.

In contrast to Youssef's optimism, Mahmoud had been more skeptical.
Throughout the day he was noticeably disinterested. He also said most people
come because "they are searching for hope, motivation, and new ideas," but
he had not felt motivated: "I am fed up with speaking to people, I need actions, I am not pessimistic, but I am realistic." But for Ibrahim, like Youssef,
this event incited much hope. Hearing stories of entrepreneurial transformation and obtaining business cards ensured that the fair enacted a sense that
his own dreams were realizable too.

The UN fair, and its location, aesthetics, and upper-middle-class inhabitants—like TFJ—signified Cairo's upscale globalized economy. The inhabitation of this space by lower-middle-class Egyptians cannot be interpreted
as an exercise of belonging to the cosmopolitan upper-middle class. The difference between them and the UN employees was starkly represented in the
way they used the space and their divergent cultural capitals. It also cannot
be interpreted as a transgressive act, a traversal of spatialized class boundaries.[27] This privileges the desire to seek out resistance. Rather, I argue that the
spatial terrain of Cairo's upscale economy incites hope for lower-middle-class
Egyptians. The fair generated an atmosphere of positivity as objects such as
a UN leaflet, a U.S. embassy timetable, business cards, and ice cream symbolized successful entrepreneurship and a global knowledge economy. For
Ibrahim and Youssef, encountering these objects induced hope and a sense
of participation in Cairo's upscale economy. The practice of hearing about
inspirational projects, picking up leaflets and marking future events, and collecting business cards enacted prospective momentum toward belonging for
real. This rested again on the upscale economy discursively opening itself up
as reachable by extending meritocratic fantasies.

Nowhere is the liberal incitement to autonomy more apparent than entrepreneurship, which is presented as a tool for challenging an exclusionary
"family business model" in Egypt, with various outreach and soft-skills training programs promoting it.[28] In September 2016, I met Zahra, an employee of

a for-profit entrepreneurship platform called RiseUp that supports budding start-ups by providing "know-how, data, and talent," organizing an annual summit attracting thousands of attendees alongside regular meetups, and selling a start-up manifesto. Zahra was an AUC graduate, fluent in English and Arabic. Her father owned multiple companies. After discussing Cairo's entrepreneurship scene for an hour, I admitted skepticism that young men like Ibrahim would ever open a start-up because they lacked funds, knowledge, and connections. She immediately rebuked me, saying:

> No, there is hope, you need to be more positive, Harry! They are just doing things in the wrong order. You know they need a career coach. They just need a plan, a career plan, and they will do it, everyone can do it if they do the right things, they are just doing the wrong things.

Zahra then told me about Malcolm Gladwell, an author who had proven "scientifically" that hard work and taking the right actions can secure success.[29] His writing had inspired her. Working at the platform had also made her more positive: "I was told by my dad I would take over the company only, but here I saw more ambition, and it made me ambitious too. I saw perseverance that made me believe anything is possible." She then repeated that I was too negative. She wanted to make me more positive, so she would send me a positive thought every day; the first was "to be grateful."

As I looked around, it was easy to see why Zahra was so positive. We met in the GrEEK Campus, formerly part of AUC but now an entrepreneurial hub in the heart of Cairo—which required a membership card for entry. Here Zahra was surrounded by Egypt's most successful start-ups. Employees certainly worked hard to succeed, obtain funding, and build networks and know-how. However, conversations with people involved in entrepreneurship, all graduates of elite private universities, hinted at the class position required to succeed: the fact that "nine out of ten start-ups fail." According to Zahra, most start-ups rely on family funding in the pre-prototype phase as investors do not invest in "an idea." Both she and others also emphasized the benefit of knowing investors personally. Salma, a researcher in AUC's Center for Entrepreneurship, told me that "social capital is important in the early stages, it is facilitated through connections, of clients, the promotion of family and friends, and their resources. If you know investors it is easier too. Alone it is possible but more difficult." Ghada, Salma's boss, interjected: "You can't generalize, though; if it is a good idea people are going to reach out." These conversations revealed the reproduction of meritocratic discourse in Egypt's upscale economy, which posits that reaching its employment and lifestyles is dependent on autonomous individuals, on attitude rather than inherited privilege. Whenever a potential barrier arose, a solution was offered and positivity restored. Funding can be found because "there are so many options!" and networks can be built. The entrepreneurship "ecosystem" is designed to combat such barriers. Success becomes about characteristics: perseverance, passion, risk-taking, and hard work. This terrain has transnational origins, but many Egyptian ideologies generate individual autonomy. These ideologies are reproduced every day within the upscale economy by people performing the work, producing success.

Again, these ideologies have been much critiqued for legitimizing privilege and inequality. Egypt's entrepreneurship scene has been criticized for placing people in debt and being dominated by privileged Egyptians.[30] However, entrepreneurial narratives also have important effects on those pursuing privilege because of their hopeful quality. While inhabiting the places of Egypt's upscale entrepreneurship scene—a start-up competition, a lecture, or a UN fair—Ibrahim, a member of an excluded lower-middle-class group aspiring to upscale entrepreneurship, was repeatedly told by members of the upper-middle class that if he worked hard, took risks, and remained passionate he would reach it. Hearing these discourses and seeing proof of their success in successful bodies and acting them out produced feelings of hope, making it seem like the life he desired was within reach. This affective power was the explicit aim of such places, which made money by selling entrepreneurial hope to attendees of lectures and summits and securing development funding by promising entrepreneurial mobility. Again, Mahmoud's skepticism demonstrates that this governmental process is not automatic. The shape of the emotions induced by encounters is dependent on the "affected body's existing condition to be affected."[31] Mahmoud was slightly older than Ibrahim. He had two more years of struggle in locating a fulfilling job. He also considered entrepreneurial information intangible. This led him to other spaces that did induce hope such as the employment fair.

APPLYING IN HOPE

In November 2015 I attended two employment fairs with Mahmoud. Mahmoud grew up in the lower-class to lower-middle-class neighborhood of Faisal. When he was young his parents divorced, and during the separation he passed into the care of his mother's sister, who had remained unmarried and worked in the Giza tax office. Having begun at a private language school, Mahmoud suddenly switched to government schooling because of his aunt's low pay. He continued to see his half siblings enjoy private education. Mahmoud entered the Arabic faculty of commerce at Helwan University and subsequently had spells in numerous insecure low-skilled service jobs. By November 2015, five years after graduating and a year after the TFJ course, Mahmoud remained desperate for a fulfilling job in Egypt's private sector. Immediately after TFJ, rather than taking a call center job he borrowed money from his aunt to enroll in an English course at AUC, promising that this would finally lead to a successful job. After the course, he worked as a sales rep in a Vodafone store and in a data entry job; however, in October 2015 Mahmoud was fired without explanation.

After a period of depression and angry rails against corruption in this "daughter-of-a-whore country" (balad bint al-wiskha), Mahmoud reengaged in the job search, locating two employment fairs on the internet. Job fairs have been part of Egypt's recruitment circuit since the 1990s. They are organized by government agencies, universities, and recruitment firms with sponsorship from government, foreign embassies, and private-sector stakeholders. They represent an effort to enhance communication in the labor market, providing a transparent space for companies to locate talent and graduates to encounter employers. During my fieldwork I attended job fairs in upmarket hotels, universities, even shopping malls. The fairs I attended with Mahmoud were held in the InterContinental, a newly built upmarket hotel in the upper-middle-class neighborhood of Nasr City. On each occasion we woke up at six a.m. to travel by microbus two hours across the city. In the microbus on November 7, Mahmoud recounted how a man he had outperformed while interviewing for his banking job entered the prestigious customer service department because he was rich. Mahmoud left the bank after realizing he would be counting money as a teller all his life but now regretted it. He then told me about a trainer at another soft-skills course he had done in 2013 who had been an inspiration, getting him to feel confident speaking in public. He compared her to Dale Carnegie, a U.S. self-help guru who teaches you how to be "creative and positive." Mahmoud was shocked I had not heard of him: "These skills are so important, Harry."

Our conversation was halted by our impending arrival. Mahmoud was skeptical about this fair. He had seen that it would predominantly advertise call center jobs, but he hoped there might be other opportunities. The fair was organized by the Information Technology Industry Development Agency (ITIDA), a government body designed to develop Egypt's technology industry. It was the seventh annual fair. Upon arrival I remembered we had attended the sixth a year earlier with TFJ graduates. We were shuffled through the hotel's side entrance away from guests. Our bags and bodies were scanned and thereafter we entered a bustling function room to register. Before approaching stalls, we came across an organizer conducting an interview with the state television channel NileTV. We listened as he explained the fair's aims, in Arabic with frequent use of English words, suggesting an internationalized education:

> The aim of the fair is to present a variety of companies for young people and to improve the communication between companies and job seekers. . . . It is not just a case of youth coming here and choosing a random job, it is about tailoring yourself to the labor market, and picking the career that best suits you.

The organizer evoked a language of consumption. Like commodities in a mall, companies are presented for youth, who can pick the career that best suits them. Employment fairs represent a material manifestation of an open labor market. One can reach desirable employers in the expectation that they will judge you based on your CV or how you come across in person. They incubate the notion that recruitment is based on meritocratic principles, with those most qualified succeeding. Reem, an employee of JobMaster, a recruitment company that organizes fairs, told me during an interview that she was adamant that things like wasta were not a big problem in Egypt now. Companies recruit "the best candidates."

As we walked around, Mahmoud and I laughed about the supposed choice as we saw mostly call center companies, alongside the familiar sight of companies offering soft-skills training. I asked a representative of one about their course. After I introduced myself, he enthusiastically announced that he had studied at the University of Essex before describing how his company offered a scholarship, funded by the Ministry of Communications, to help youth get jobs. The soft-skills focus stemmed from partnerships with the call center industry. I asked how they handle graduates who do not want this work. He said that is their biggest problem: "We tell them there are opportunities to be promoted. I started in the call center and I'm in HR now." His English ability and background suggested that his call center stint constituted an upper-middle-class summer job, rather than the more permanent Arabic call center job of the lower-middle classes who cannot access English accounts. We left the stall, with Mahmoud expressing disappointment at the admission that soft skills were targeted for call centers. He also questioned the hopeful message of transfer to HR: "There are rotation shifts and it is hard to do courses outside, it's so hard to afford HR diplomas." His own experience in a call center led him to critique this hopeful narrative. Mahmoud decided to go back and ask how the man traveled to England: "Was it a scholarship?" "No, I paid for it," he replied, followed by an awkward laugh.

Mahmoud turned his attention to jobs. We approached outsourcing companies looking for English accounts, even though Mahmoud had applied multiple times and been told his accent was not good enough. One woman stressed that they had "special training" for language, but if Mahmoud did not make it, he could go into an Egyptian account. She also outlined a "steps" program that helps employees "build their dreams": "People think the call center is just a temp job, not a career, they don't know you can rise up." We found a slogan reflecting this hope at another stall: "Our today's beginners are tomorrow's leaders." Financial incentives to reproduce these narratives were laid bare as young HR reps at another company who studied in private colleges described how recruitment targets affect their bonuses. They try to "convince people to take jobs" by telling them they can apply for other positions within one or two years. But these narratives were by this stage not effective on Mahmoud. As we walked, we spoke to two other men disappointed by the call center focus. After jokingly asking if I could get them a job in England, they said they wanted bank work, but "you need wasta." One of their dads worked in a bank, but he was unable to use this wasta because he obtained only an "acceptable" grade in university. In this case, wasta could be used only with a minimum university grade; otherwise the bank would be unable to justify the recruitment. This story punctures the hopeful myth presented at the fair and revealed the marginal position of people who could not even use the social capital they held.

Some stalls did offer hope to Mahmoud. The representative of one company recruiting engineers and software developers said they also had admin jobs and asked Mahmoud for his experience. He began to respond, nervously in English, that he had worked as a sales rep, but she cut him off, asking for his university major. When he responded commerce, she put his CV on a huge pile, and he would never hear back. After Mahmoud had submitted his CV to every stall he could, we went to another room where there were various talks. One was by the CEO of Jobzella, an online employment and course aggregator also offering a self-assessment tool, career consultation, and ebook, *From Zero to Hero: Your Guide for Everything About Jobs*, to loyal users. Jobzella describes itself as "The World's First Online Career Mega Mall . . . providing a one-stop shop to all career services for job seekers and professionals to aspire to a better life," a description that does not hold back in transforming jobs into easily acquirable commodities. The CEO asked the audience about the biggest problems they faced in job searches. People responded with the prevalence of wasta, lack of experience, the difference between knowledge learned in university and that required by companies, companies advertising a job falsely, and the prevalence of call center jobs. Rather than replying, the CEO confidently described joblessness as a "communication problem":

> There are four million jobs available; you can't say there are no jobs. How you write your CV is crucial. Youth always put "I want a challenging opportunity in an international company"; they won't listen to that. You need to tell them what you are, who you are, and what you have done; you need to market yourself. Make your CV stand out from everyone else's.

According to this logic the problem lies in CV writing, an easily fixable fault. This enables people to believe in the possibility of obtaining employment currently out of reach. It shut down the negative structural barriers introduced by the audience and reinstated an atmosphere that might produce hope. I asked Mahmoud what he thought, and he replied, "I want to believe him, but the situation I have seen is different. I have applied to so many jobs and not been able to get a good one. I spent a lot of time improving my CV, I don't know if I could have done more." Mahmoud by this point was skeptical as a result of his material stagnation, but he still felt some attraction to this belief.

In September 2016 I managed to meet Jobzella's CEO and another partner in the GrEEK Campus where the start-up is based, through using Zahra, the RiseUp employee, as a contact. The CEO was motivated by "helping people and affecting lives." I described how graduates I meet feel they cannot reach their dreams because of wasta or the favoring of private education. The partner immediately responded: "No, no, I feel like these are excuses for losers. You need to invest in yourself." The CEO jumped in:

> Lots don't take it seriously; they don't show up to jobs when they are offered.
> If you don't have wasta you can build a professional network; through a web-
> site it is easy, you can connect with people and then after show your knowl-
> edge. Wasta is not needed nowadays. Look, you built your network through
> Zahra, and met me through that; they need to do the same.

In referencing my network-building, the CEO skirted over my English, class compatibility, and ethnicity, which enabled me to gain access. He then said he meets lots of young people at events who say they want to work in anything; "That is not an answer, you need to know what you want . . . youth send blanket emails to companies, but they have to put in much more effort. You can find information online, how to apply for stuff, or online courses. It goes back to the motivation of the person." Jobzella is one such website through which youth can find courses and contact people. The internet, he said, is "opening up the world," because you can find courses, contacts, and job information and not face exclusion from networks or knowledge.

Again, this highlights the narratives prevalent in labor market institutions. Success is pinned on the individual. The internet is presented as playing a key role in enabling a level playing field, despite continued hierarchies shaping whom people can access and which courses they can afford. I finally mentioned that I was doing research with graduates of the "faculties of the people." The CEO responded saying, "Oh yeah, they all work in call centers, right?," thereby displaying tacit knowledge of where people like Mahmoud and Ibrahim belong and providing insight into how they might be judged in applications. At the employment fair, however, an atmosphere of hope is sustained by HR reps who promise and embody career progression and soft-skills trainers and recruitment agents who claim to hold the solution to employment struggles. This effect is driven by accumulation—recruitment companies get revenue through footfall, training companies obtain funding by attracting participants, BPO companies and HR employees benefit monetarily by attracting workers, and online recruitment marketplaces aim for increased users. For many, interacting with this place and meritocratic discourses within it, applying to jobs, making connections, and learning how to write a CV induces hope. But Mahmoud's skepticism following years of disappointments led to frustration and confusion and to him partially laying bare the fair's real goal: an effort to funnel graduates into Cairo's call center industry. He did, however, feel a compulsion to believe in its promises again, starting to reveal the presence of an attachment to meritocratic forms of hope.

Two weeks later we were on our way to the InterContinental again, this time for a fair called Our Future in Our Country, co-organized by recruitment firm JobMaster and Egypt's branch of the Rotary Club. As we approached, Mahmoud excitedly ran through the international companies, banks, and large Egyptian companies that would be present. We went through the same arrival process, only this time Mahmoud had already filled out an application form—a means of attendee prescreening—on which he had to declare his qualifications and career goals. This was one of several attempts to prescreen attendees. Private universities held fairs exclusively for their graduates. Other fairs charged an entry fee (around LE50 [US$6.25]), which put off people like Mahmoud who struggled to afford it and criticized the idea of unemployed youth having to pay. Another format was the one applied in this fair. Prospective attendees had to send CVs, fill out applications, and await acceptance. During my interview with Reem, the JobMaster employee, she explained that the screening process is designed to target a specific caliber of graduates. For this fair, they wanted foreign-language university graduates, alongside graduates more generally. They also had their own fair focused on call centers, targeted at graduates of law and commerce.

Mahmoud had attended more prestigious fairs before. Shortly after the TFJ course, he and several other TFJ graduates went to the October University for Modern Science and Arts (MSA) employment fair. As he described it to me in a text message, his excitement was palpable:

> It was amazing, there were lots of banks, like CIB bank, Arabic African bank
> and good insource companies, even Ferrari was there, there were amazing
> vacancies actually in supply chain, HR, and sales. I really hope I get accepted
> in any of them. I applied to a supply chain job in MAC, it's an amazing
> job, I would be the guy responsible for purchasing, if I get it that would be
> amazing. Wish me luck!

At this stage, Mahmoud's interaction with the fair, its location in an elite
private university, its stalls presenting prestigious jobs and companies, and
having his CV accepted and conceivably considered enabled him to imagine
the role he would do and thereby experience a moment of hope. The material
representation of meritocracy that is intrinsic to employment fairs was crucial. These feelings reflected those that followed the practice of submitting
applications to desirable jobs in general. Every time, submission generated
an imaginary shift into a desirable future of acceptance and occupation that
produced a flash of hope.

However, months later at a similar fair Mahmoud had a different relationship. As we entered the hall, he commented on the "professional" appearance
compared with the call center fair. Attendees were noticeably higher-class;
Mahmoud could tell by their clothes. We immediately saw the multitude of
prestigious companies: Pirelli, QNB, Vodafone, Elaraby, the list went on.
Each stand was surrounded by groups of youth waiting impatiently to hand
over their CV and talk to HR representatives. Mahmoud joined the crowds,
rushing to hand out his CV, with the only consultation being to ask which
vacancies were available and whether he could leave his CV. Once the CV
had been delivered, Mahmoud moved on. "The more the better!" he said as
I questioned the speed, before feeling guilty about scrutinizing Mahmoud's
strategy. Some firms told him to apply online; some said they needed more
experience. At one stand Mahmoud inquired about HR vacancies, but after
the representative looked at his CV she wrote down "customer services." After
this Mahmoud said it was a fake fair. He became distracted by a laptop at
one of the stalls. We laughed because he was preoccupied with consumption
desires, but this reflected the alienation Mahmoud felt. On the way out, he
tried to submit his CV to the hotel after suddenly telling me he had applied

to work there seven times before, never receiving a response. They told him to return the next day, an answer he knew was a way to get rid of him. As we departed, of the fair he said: "Let's see if they call, I think these fairs are all for marketing, but let's see."

On the way home, Mahmoud recollected the MSA fair with a different affect:

> Nobody ever rings back in these fairs. We applied to every single company at MSA and got no reply. They asked us if we were MSA students, they had to put it on the CV, but for everyone else they didn't ask, I think this is corruption.

Mahmoud had concluded that fairs were marketing tools for companies and the government, advertising their efforts to help unemployed youth. This reveals how the hopeful affect of this meritocratic infrastructure shifts over time. This once hopeful space now conjured up frustration, reminding him of his exclusion. But despite his skepticism, Mahmoud had attended another fair. The continued construction of transparent employment fairs left the door open for hope to return. Mahmoud had returned, he told me, "because I have no other choice but to try, I might get lucky." The reproduction of an atmosphere of hope continued to catch the body of this young man, and secure on the surface a high footfall for the organizers, not through a clean linear influence of the subject by certain places, objects, and discourses, but the body's compulsion for hope. This compulsion will become clearer in later chapters, but the focus of this chapter has been on the industries that produce hope.

CONCLUSION: SELLING HOPE

Cairo's upscale economy is continually producing hope. Training centers, entrepreneurship events, and employment fairs repeatedly extend the logic that Egypt's contemporary labor market is open to all no matter their class background, gender, or race. This represents a new "rule of experts" in twenty-first-century Egypt, as the government, international development organizations, and members of the upper-middle classes working in recruitment, entrepreneurship, and training are attempting to discursively and materially construct a modern, fair, meritocratic labor market and destroy "backward" recruitment practices such as wasta or bribery and prejudicial notions of where people belong.[32] This is an extension of transnational educational and labor market logics, but these logics also interact with Egyptian ideologies. It is clear that meritocratic logics are providing legitimizing cover for the continued and even worsening production of class inequalities within Egypt's globalized private sector. Inequalities are hardwired into the labor market through discrepancies in access to education that have widened sharply in the last two decades—and are easily identifiable through bodily markers—and unequal access to social capital. These inequalities were on display through the close-knit upper-middle-class networks that cut across labor market industries as I navigated them. Tacit recognition of these inequalities remains beneath the surface among the upper-middle classes, but the public primacy of a language of individuality and earned privilege—as others have argued before—enables them to justify their position.[33]

But the language of meritocracy—and the material manifestation of it—carries a powerful effect for those pursuing social mobility. As un- and underemployed graduates interact with training courses, entrepreneurship events, and employment fairs—as they watch a video of Steve Jobs's lecturing advice, collect a business card from a UN employee, or obtain CV-writing advice from a recruitment company CEO—they experience a momentary flash of hope for a future of mobility. The upscale economy in Egypt and around the world discursively opens itself up to potential belonging to all. It tells people over and over again the alluring notion that their behavior and attitude will secure mobility in a labor market that responds to acquirable skills and networks. This represents a powerful technique of governance in labor markets, which operates through affect and emotion. Meritocratic industries act as a tunnel that keeps young lower-middle-class Egyptians compliant in their participation in the competitive individualized pursuit of success, by keeping their attention focused on themselves as hardworking individuals and away from structural issues that might inhibit that pursuit. The chapter has demonstrated how this compliance is secured affectively, as meritocratic narratives produce emotional shifts that sustain a sense of hope toward a desired future.

The production of hope is propelled through capitalist logics. Recruitment firms bring in revenue by setting up fairs and online marketplaces, from companies and training centers that pay for stalls in the expectation of heavy traffic, and sometimes from job applicants. Training companies and NGOs secure profit or funding by promising participants that their course will make a difference. TFJ secures continued funding by convincing young graduates of the potential of taking low-skilled service work. Entrepreneurship incubators make money by hosting network events and coaching sessions and selling start-up manifestos that promise to unlock entrepreneurial success. Finally, BPO companies—even individual HR reps—financially benefit by convincing prospective employees of the long-term potential of outsourced call center work. There are also various financial links between these industries that make them interdependent. The accumulation models of these industries are propelling the production of hopeful laborers who are ready to participate in a competitive labor market. However, this governmental process is not inevitably effective—the ways dominant biopolitical techniques interact with ethical life-worlds are complex and must be traced. Some Egyptians do not believe in the hope sold to them owing to prolonged stagnation. By and large, though, at the end of 2014 the young men I was following had bought into the hope sold to them by these industries. In the following two chapters, I trace their attempts to realize this hope in a labor market ridden with hierarchies. This will reveal both the fragility and the prolonged power of meritocratic logics by shifting focus to the daily practices—or emotional labors, as I label them—by which they carry on participating in a labor market that produces continuous precarity. This chapter has revealed the political economy that is fueling and profiting from these labors.

CHAPTER TWO

THE DRUGS OF LIFE

I MET ALI IN AN ahwa (café) on the bustling Haram Street at nine p.m. Before we sat down, he began venting about his day. He had just finished another twelve-hour shift as an outdoor salesperson (mandub) trying to sell a new brand of cheese to shops. Ali received a basic salary of LE300 (US$37.50 in 2014) per month, and an extra LE1,200 if he reached a target of selling 3,000 kilograms per month. But today he had managed only 70 percent of his daily target. Customers are obsessed with profit, he said; they don't want to pay extra for higher-quality cheese, especially in Haram: "They want to pay one dollar and get ten back." As we sat, Ali received a call from a customer asking for a discount. He had to phone his manager to check before calling back to make a counteroffer. The customer refused, so Ali rang his manager again. After relaying a final offer, the customer said he would think about it. "Motherfuckers! They always say they will think about it, and then say no," Ali lamented. "Why don't you just say you don't want it?" He expressed worry that his manager would shout at him, but a company representative accompanied him today and confirmed he was a good seller. Ali declared he was tired of sales work; he had done it for six years selling goods as varied as medical supplies and building materials—even sacrificing an unfinished commerce degree after failing two years in a row. He thought completing it would not make a difference to his prospects. What most added to his stress was the responsibility of his salary being dependent on him. This also produced angst regarding his inability to save money: "I put in so much effort, but I can't get what I want, I can't buy a house or a car, I can't get satisfaction," he said.

Ali transitioned from lamenting his daily work to his inability to move toward a satisfying life. He pays LE300 commission to customers to keep them loyal, gives his parents LE400 a month, and has daily expenses of LE15 for clothes, food, and transport. This does not leave him much savings each month. The issue of money is what agitates him most of all. He feels tense when he cannot afford things. To illustrate the importance of affording things, he pointed to the bottle of water that had been put on our table: "If you want water now and pay for it, it is much better than someone coming back in an hour and saying here is the water for free; it isn't the same. It is better to feel like you can pay for something right away, it gives you satisfaction (rida)." Now, he asserted, he could not buy anything for the next twenty days until his salary came in, only sit in the ahwa. "Everything in Egypt runs by fucking money," he exclaimed. "If you want to get a good job you have to pay money, a good education, everything. People only deal with people for benefit, they don't do something for nothing."

Suddenly two young women walked into view:

> You know that's why I hate Egyptian girls, they expect so much, they get influenced by friends with rich husbands and demand a lot: "Let's go on holiday to Copacabana!" When you go to a father he asks: Do you have a flat? Where do you live? Do you have a good job? Look, I loved a girl in the call center, but she was from a high class; I couldn't keep up with her, she had a rich dad who worked in antiques. I loved her but couldn't marry her because of stupid fucking society; they only care about how much money you have, as long as you have money you can do anything you want, you can buy a flat, get a car, get a family, and be satisfied. But if you don't you can't do anything.

The anger and frustration Ali felt was palpable. During these few minutes he shifted erratically between dissecting the pressures of his daily work and his inability to move toward a career and marriage. Feeling powerless to comfort him, I asked if the situation was worse than before, and he responded, "It was easier for my parents, there was government work, but the problem now is prices are so high." Pointing to his cigarette packet on the table, he said cigarettes were LE7 before the 2011 revolution; now they were LE17. At that moment Ali stopped talking and reached for a cigarette. He lit it, sat back, and inhaled deeply. After a ten-second silence he said, "You know, I didn't use to smoke, but I do anything these days just to fuck with my head a bit, to stop overthinking; I even smoke hashish sometimes." This prompted me to ask what else Ali did to relax. Sighing, he said he used to go on outings to different places around the city but he could not afford it anymore; the only thing he could do was sit in the ahwa and go to the gym: "In the gym I forget about my problems. I just love doing weights, building muscles, I feel powerful." Chuckling, he showed me a Facebook post he had written earlier in the year: "Happy Valentine to my partner, the gym." He related this sense of empowerment to his favorite film, *Fight Club*: "This film gives me motivation whenever I watch it, to keep surviving, keep suffering, because it is about someone trying to escape their boring routine . . . I love Tyler Durden [the character played by Brad Pitt] because he can do what he wants when he wants, he has that satisfaction."

The previous chapter revealed how industries sell a feeling of hope for career mobility to young educated underemployed Egyptians. This chapter follows a group of men as they try to convert that hope into reality in Egypt's labor market. As Ali's torments show, very quickly hope becomes supplanted by feelings of frustration, anxiety, and boredom during prolonged periods spent in low-paid, insecure, low-status service work. These feelings arise because of the day-to-day work itself and its inability to provide the foundation for middle-class masculine rida, which translates as "satisfaction" and is used to connote the fulfillment of one's desires. I trace how men experienced and articulated the anxieties of precarious, low-status work. But this chapter focuses on their dissipation of these feelings through daily practices that provide distraction and temporary relief, or "fuck with their heads" as Ali put it. These gendered, classed, moralized practices include forging friendships, joke-making, watching light television, scrolling through social media, periodically buying new clothing and engaging in performative consumption, organizing social outings, going to the gym, smoking cigarettes and hashish, and drinking alcohol. Recasting literature on how people "get by" in precarious circumstances—particularly through detachment, avoidance, and deflection—I argue that these practices of temporary distraction constitute a vital form of emotional labor that enables young Egyptian men like Ali to dissipate bad feelings and keep on investing their labor power in the labor market.

ENTERING CAIRO'S NEW "FACTORIES"

Eslam, Adel, and Mohamed all moved to Cairo in late 2014 from towns across Egypt: Eslam from Sohag in Upper Egypt, and Adel and Mohamed from Zagazig and Zifta in the delta. They graduated from Arabic sections of local public universities, Eslam in English literature and Adel and Mohamed in commerce. Adel and Mohamed spent a year in the army, but Eslam was exempt as he was the only male sibling. They were all between twenty-three and twenty-four years old when they moved. Their parents had benefited from the lifetime government employment extended to secondary school and university graduates up until the 1990s. Yet late-twentieth-century economic reforms drastically hindered the pathways for graduates growing up in Egypt's regions. Although state education continued to expand, cities like Zagazig and Sohag were especially impacted by declines in manufacturing and state jobs.[1] The jobs left for graduates—especially those graduating from faculties like commerce, humanities, and law—such as outdoor or indoor sales or small-scale low-paid accounting or legal work do not provide middle-class respectability, particularly as aspirations shifted toward globalized employment and lifestyles. Eslam actually spent two years after university trying to become a professional footballer before deciding he would not be able to support a family if he continued playing for the city's team. After searching for alternative work, he found only outdoor sales positions, a job many of his friends were doing unhappily. They struggled to afford daily expenses let alone save for marriage and had no prospects of progression to managerial positions. Eslam wanted more; he wanted a "career." After coming across TFJ's course offering to teach the professional skills needed to succeed in the private sector, he decided to come to Cairo and try it out, initially relying on parental funds and the spare bed of a cousin who was studying to survive.[2]

Cairo has long been a destination for internal migration in Egypt. Greater Cairo contains over twenty million inhabitants, one-fifth of the nation's population. Its dominance was only enhanced in the aftermath of economic liberalization, which put it at the center of new avenues of wealth creation and expenditure. As Samuli Schielke notes, for inhabitants of the provinces,

Cairo is "a place to make money, to make a career, to make things happen—it is a center of wealth, power, culture, and glamour."[3] "Everything is in Cairo" was the ubiquitous response I received from young men puzzled to be asked why they moved. It is often referred to as *Masr* (Egypt) by those outside the capital, signifying its dominance in terms of jobs, services, and administration. It houses the largest national and multinational companies as well as the best educational opportunities. Although Eslam found aspects of Cairo difficult—being away from familial support and responsibilities (according to him, the reason most people stay in Sohag) and having to navigate a stressful, alienating rhythm of life—being there meant the future was open: "In Sohag the opportunities are set, you know that your level will not change, but in Cairo opportunities could open up tomorrow." Cairo for internal movers had a powerful hopeful effect. It was a place of imagined possibility and indeterminacy, unlike other towns within which the future would be predictably difficult—some even described them as places "without a future."[4] They had become places of disconnection from the global economy, no longer fulfilling the globalized dreams of educated youth in Egypt.

After completing the TFJ course, like many graduates Eslam heeded its message and took a call center job in an outsourced Arabic-language mobile account, earning LE1400 (US$175 in 2014) per month, just above minimum wage. He did not have the defined dream of some other graduates—although he knew the call center was not a long-term option because of its temporary contracts, low pay, and reputation. He would take the job, which he needed to sustain a life in Cairo, in order to gain experience in customer service and develop language skills on the side, before looking for something better after six months. Eslam quickly met Adel and Mohamed in the call center. They had both moved to Cairo after hearing about friends who had relocated and secured jobs in multinational companies. They both had similar dreams—Adel to work as an accountant and Mohamed to work for a "big company" in which he could grow and develop a "career"—but they also settled for temporary call center jobs while looking for other opportunities and trying to develop themselves. Eslam discovered that Adel too had encountered TFJ before. He was accepted in the spring of 2014 but dropped out after one day as he struggled with the daily two-hour microbus commute from Zagazig.

These men decided to look for a flat together and found one in Faisal, a mixed neighborhood of Giza that emerged through landowner property development and inward migration.⁵ Although not part of Cairo's 'ashwa'yat (slums), this area is on the lower end in terms of socioeconomic status. When I mentioned living in Faisal, both upper- and lower-middle-class Egyptians responded with confusion and fear, commenting on the sha'by inhabitants they considered to be ignorant, rude, immoral, and violent. Adel, Eslam, and Mohamed often talked about their desire to live in a more upscale neighborhood such as Mohandiseen, as they were surrounded by symbols of sha'by culture such as uncleared rubbish, unpaved streets, and open-air vegetable markets.

The flat itself was also a source of annoyance. It contained five beds in two bedrooms, a kitchen that was dirty and unusable, a bathroom where the water often cut out, and a living room consisting of a sofa, television, fridge, and ironing board. They paid LE1,600 (US$200) a month between them and were joined at different times by friends who also came to Cairo to work or study. I joined in May 2015, five months after they moved in. Most days they arrived home from work around two a.m. and sat up for an hour or two as they ate koshary (a low-cost dish consisting of pasta, rice, lentils, fried onions, and tomato sauce) or pasta with liver bought from the street. We watched television and chatted before heading to bed. After waking up around twelve p.m., they showered, prayed, and went out to get breakfast, always bean and falafel sandwiches. Thereafter, apart from the odd occasion when they needed to run errands, we sat again in front of the television. During this time, we did the most talking, about Egypt and their current situations and future dreams, as well as more lighthearted topics of world politics, films, and football. By three p.m. they left for work, walking ten minutes to the company bus before being taken back to what Adel called the "factory," a call center in 6th of October, a city one to one and a half hours away, ready for another nine-hour stint on the headset. While they were at work, I met other men who were free in the evenings after their own work shifts.⁶ The only break to this routine came during days off, usually two days per week. Adel and Mohammed returned to their family homes every week. Eslam stayed in the flat because Sohag was nine hours away.

This daily rhythm induced frustration. Every day they returned home drained after spending hours on the headset, moving from one customer to the next without respite. As soon as they walked through the door, they began complaining about "stupid" (rikhim) customers who had phoned up complaining about being overcharged two pence when the call itself costs fifty pence, spoke in English just to prove they could, or spent one hour on the phone unable to follow basic instructions. The hardest thing to deal with was customer abuse, in the face of which agents must remain polite. One evening Adel angrily explained how a woman rang when his shift was supposed to finish. Adel told her to follow certain steps after the call to get her internet working again, but she insisted it work immediately. She ended up swearing at him, calling him a donkey. This time Adel could not help swearing back: "I don't even care if the company listens to it," he said defiantly, "I won't let arrogant people swear at me." This type of abuse was a common problem for service workers, Adel said. He had seen a YouTube video in which a woman comes to a Vodafone store in an upmarket neighborhood only to find out it was closing. She becomes angry and starts abusing one man, saying, "You are from Imbaba (a slum), you are no better than animals!" She ends up slapping him, so he gets a knife and slashes her tires. After people come to break it up, the woman approaches a police officer to complain they had harassed her. He asks which one, but she says, "All of those dogs!" The officer insists he needs one person, otherwise he cannot do anything, but she refuses and starts abusing the officer. For Adel, the worst bit of the story was her abuse of the man's class. Low-skilled service work puts people in positions where they are reminded of their class position by upper-class customers who "act like they are better than them."

These challenges also made achieving key performance indicators difficult. Adel, Mohamed, and Eslam were measured based on customer handling time, solution rate, and feedback, with a LE150 bonus, possible promotion, and keeping the job dependent on achieving them. They constantly struggled with handling time as it conflicted with solving problems and achieving customer satisfaction, which required spending long periods on the phone, especially with Egyptians who "like to tell stories in great detail," Mohamed said. They complained about the pressure this put them under, with particular anxiety induced by the threat of punishment. On one occasion Mohamed had half a day's pay deducted after he kept getting moved to broken computer stations and as a result officially clocked in late. They were also often made to stay late in response to customer rushes or employee absences, which reflected a broader frustration regarding their inability to participate in social life. They missed weddings and Ramadan celebrations—frequently having to break their fast at work or alone in their flat. But even apart from participating in celebrations, these men struggled to do anything outside work. Eslam, for example, was frustrated by his inability to do exercise, which he described as important for him feeling like he was "doing something with his life." They also struggled to meet friends, cook, and even wash clothes or shave because of shift timings and a relentless lack of energy. All three complained about a lack of balance (tawazun) in their life. Eslam explained one day as we sat on the sofa: "We are slaves to work; we go to work, sleep, get up and go to work, we take a shower if there is water, watch a bit of television, iron a shirt, and do the same again, is that acceptable? (kida yinfa'?)"

One afternoon as a Ramadan soap played on the TV, we started talking about the long-term effects of the call center. Adel began by suggesting that the job had impacted his ability to be gida' (kind/helpful) on the street:

> The problem with the job is it makes you rude when you communicate with people; it makes you not care about other people's feelings. You learn to do what customers do; they shout and abuse you, and you can't do anything, so you take it out in other situations. Like, in the microbus I used to let the driver keep twenty-five pence, but not now, I always get it back.

Mohamed also reflected on the impact of the job on his familial role:

> When you have a job you enjoy and feel satisfied with, you can have a good life outside, keeping up with friends and family. I used to be very involved with siblings; if they did something wrong I told them off. But now when I go home and they do something I don't care; I don't have energy to tell them to stop.

Literature on the subjective experience of low-skilled service work has focused on the indignity of the work itself.[7] But as these testimonies show, it also had an impact on the ability of these men to live up to the behavioral norms expected of respectable citizens on the streets or responsible older brothers. Two qualities those roles required, generosity and attentiveness, were eroded on the headset. Adel described the call center as a new kind of factory for Egypt's youth. Having worked on textile machines as a student, he said that kind of factory was hard on your body; the call center is hard on your mind.[8] He was adamant that this factory was not the place for people who had spent years in education. In it they were unable to "find themselves," as either respectable employees or respectable men. Call center work was therefore not only precarious, in that it did not provide a stable basis for family life because of low salaries and the threat of termination; it was demeaning and deskilling.

THE ONSET OF BOREDOM

Amid these struggles, as months passed a more existential feeling emerged for these men. Arriving home one day in early June, Adel described how he had been called by an English-speaking customer. He froze when she started speaking, before frantically passing her to a colleague. Eslam and Mohamed tried to turn it into a joke, but Adel exclaimed, with palpable sadness and nostalgia, that a couple of years ago he would have been able to handle the customer. The daily frustrations produced in the call center served as a constant reminder of the need for prospective movement. However, this event reminded Adel he was not moving forward. In fact, he was moving backward, losing skills he once held. Up until that point he had recollected a lesson he remembered from his one day at TFJ: a trainer said that one year in the call center was good experience, because you learn useful skills such as communication and patience. But in the days after this incident, he stopped repeating this lesson, instead lamenting how he was becoming stuck; the job and schedule were preventing him from even thinking about the future, let alone taking courses like he had hoped. He was not even saving money. Similar moments came for the others over the summer. For Eslam, in general much quieter, this led to a period of three days where he did not speak to us. He did not join in watching television, instead heading to bed. Only afterward he told me—while pointing to a television ad offering one-million-pound villas in a new gated community—that he became annoyed thinking about the future, about his career. He looked at people who had been in the call center for years and "got used to it," and feared the same happening to him.

These feelings overwhelmed many young men after spending prolonged periods in low-status, insecure, low-paid service work. Ibrahim, as described in the previous chapter, had moved to Cairo full of hope in late 2014. How-

ever, by February 2015 that hope had disappeared—he quit his job as a Vodafone customer service agent and returned home. Upon my return to Egypt in
May 2015, he described this dramatic transformation:

> I could not stay in the job, I was becoming depressed and angry all the time.
> I was not able to think about anything outside work, only how to reach the
> targets. When I went home I would keep thinking about it, and just be so
> tired from the long shifts I had to sleep. I was not able to work toward my
> goals; I was working for the company, not for myself and my dreams. It was
> a very hard time, I felt stuck, like I was not learning anything, I was not
> moving toward my dream, I was not going anywhere, it was very depressing."

Literature on the suspension of the pursuit of a good life has explicated the
temporal and emotional experiences brought forth by the inability to obtain
jobs that match classed aspirations and hegemonic age and gender norms.[9]
Young lower-middle-class Egyptian men showed how these feelings can be
invoked through mundane encounters of embarrassment or shame in a degrading job. For others, parents becoming angry about requests for money
or seeing an ad for a gated community on TV incited similar feelings. These
encounters render conscious temporal and spatial stagnation in the pursuit
of aspirational markers of adulthood, manhood, and middle-class living.
Low-status service work quickly replaced any sense of hopeful mobility with
fearful stagnation. Young men began living "day to day" instead of in preparation for a long-term goal as their jobs consumed their time and energy,
meaning they were unable to take courses, attend events, make connections,
conduct research, or apply to other jobs. They were also unable to use these
jobs to save money. They looked up to others and feared that "what was once
temporary would become permanent," as Ibrahim described to me. He referenced Hassan—who had attended TFJ's graduation—when explaining his
decision to leave his job. He feared becoming similarly depressed.

   Adel, during an afternoon in front of the television, described stagnation
as a general affliction of Egypt's youth, using an analogy with the film *Fight
Club*:

> *Fight Club* is about someone who is bored from daily routine, who can con-
> sume anything he wants, a fridge, a television, anything, but he gets bored of

that life, he wants something different and stimulating. It is like in Sweden, where they kill themselves because they have so much money that life gets boring, so they get depressed. But here in Egypt we have a different type of boredom, it comes from not being able to do anything, you cannot solve any problems here so you get bored. You can't marry or get a flat.

Adel's description reflects previous theorizations of boredom as an effect of precarity.[10] Ben Anderson describes boredom as a "malady of a body's capacity to affect and be affected," a suspension of the expectation that there is more to life than the here and now.[11] It arises not from doing nothing, or the same thing over and over, but from one's time not moving toward normative aspirational markers. For Egyptian men it arises from becoming stuck in work that cannot provide a basis for respectable middle-class manhood. But Adel makes an important additional point about boredom, alluding to a critique of capitalism's offer of fulfillment through its markers of success. In this sense, all hope could be considered cruel in Lauren Berlant's sense, in that it does not arrest what Michael Jackson labels a sense of insufficiency. For Adel, though, empathy with this boredom was difficult from his standpoint. He just desired movement.[12]

Eslam's, Adel's, and Mohamed's boredom stimulated frequent outbursts of anger from the sofa, against a lack of available jobs, the poor state of public education, government disinvestment and corruption stemming from Egypt's infitah, and the prevalence of wasta (nepotism) and class discrimination in recruitment processes. One afternoon in early July, Adel and I flicked through the television to a soap describing how Egypt had changed in the fifty years since Nasser's presidency. I asked what he thought had changed, and he said:

The middle class is finished now. There is no middle, just rich and the rest are poor. Nasser created the middle class out of providing education and jobs, but it is over now, you can't get educated and you can't get work. My parents were in the middle class, they had education and jobs. But we can't now. The infitah ruined it all. This was the beginning, where everything started to be bought from outside, so we didn't make anything ourselves, the industry was destroyed. There is no industry now. There was oil and steel. There were factories in Zagazig but not now. Corruption has ruined things too.

The government made deals with businessmen and looked after their own interests. Land was sold for very cheap and factories were closed. We were in the middle, but now in the lower-middle. I think I am poor now. I can't find decent work, can't save money. You can't get educated now too. You have to work to pay for more education.

The 2011 uprising provided multiple frames through which structural problems can be criticized in Egypt. These men had no hesitation latching onto them as they reflected on their condition. I had countless conversations diagnosing Egypt's issues, each revealing that they were not hopeful dupes disciplined by the upper-middle classes within labor market industries, only looking to their own failures to explain their plight. They penetrated the meritocratic myths on which hope relied and showed that meritocracy did not enjoy domination. Conceptually this complicates the governmental technique of producing consenting workers invested in a meritocratic labor regime. Penetration and critique do not necessarily lead to resistance or withdrawal, however.[13] Perhaps it did in early 2011. During the uprising these frames were productive of hope for a transformative future.[14] However, this was not the case among these men in 2015. Although revolutionary hope lingers on among certain activist groups, many Egyptians speak of inertia and a desire for stability after a period of turmoil.[15] Adel, Eslam, and Mohamed did attend protests in 2011 but never became involved in social movements. They considered protest pointless, referencing 2011's failure as proof. Their boredom and anger could have transformed into what Ben Anderson called a "deepened, elongated, quashing of effective action," or depression.[16] In the rest of the chapter, I examine how these men endured and continued providing their labor power through a labor of distraction, repeatedly engaging in practices that enabled them to dissipate the stresses and anxieties that built up on the headset and beyond.

SMILING IN THE FACE OF PROBLEMS

Upon returning home one evening, Adel was visibly shaken. After putting his things in his room, he sat down, took a breath, and declared that another customer had abused him. A man phoned having been told by an agent earlier in the day that his internet connection would be fixed after two days.

Adel tried to fix it but told him it could only be processed after the call. The man replied, "No, I want it fixed now!" But Adel insisted it was not possible. The man responded by calling him a "liar, son of a dog! (kadab, ibn kalb!)" Adel immediately became angry and implored the man to be respectful, but he hung up. Adel insisted he had been so close to swearing back. Eslam immediately jumped in: "If it was me, I would have said, 'Look, son of a whore (ya ibn al sharmuta).'" This instigated a vibrant conversation, interrupted by laughter, about the different insults they could hail toward the man. Adel insisted he would get revenge, gleefully exclaiming how he had noted down his information and come up with an elaborate plot. He would ring the call center on a random number but give the customer's information and ask them to change the phone's system to something irreversible, while buying an expensive internet package. Eslam and Mohamed chimed in with their own ideas, setting up a new line and charging him without him knowing or incessantly calling the man and hanging up. During the night, we returned to this topic repeatedly, intricately setting out each strategy of revenge and imagining how annoyed the customer would be when he found out. Eslam declared at one point: "Thank God for laughter!" The anger and shame Adel had returned home with felt like a distant memory.

This was a recurring pattern. Every night between two and three a.m. on the sofa of their dilapidated flat, these men ritualistically shared stories about customers they encountered during the shift. Sharing painful stories was in itself an important form of intimacy building and relief among friends. But the tone quickly shifted to laughter at the stupidity of customers who could not recite their number properly, who did not know what an identity card was, or who called to simply swear before hanging up. Conversation progressed into a defiant recounting of what they had said to these customers in their heads, what they would have said if they met them on the street, and the fantastical strategies they would use to seek revenge. Although insisting they were going to carry out these vengeful acts, they never followed through. But the activity of constructing them and talking about them together was therapeutic. Converting these chastening events into objects of laughter and discursively retaliating and correcting the wrong enabled them to dispel anger and reassert imaginary power and respect. Mohamed confirmed that they do the same with colleagues at work. This was a vital activity—permitted by team leaders—that kept them going, providing camaraderie that enabled the dissipation of annoyance and shame on the job. Over time it produced a repertoire of jokes that anyone who has experience working in call centers can partake in, with jokes circulating on Facebook or WhatsApp.

This use of dark humor—joking about a tragic event or situation—extended into the everyday frustrations of the flat itself. We often joked about a child turning the flat's water supply on when we did not need it and off again just as we were about to use it. It also enveloped discussion of Egypt's problems more generally. I often found myself sitting on the sofa or with other men at the ahwa talking seriously about the broken education system or labor market when suddenly an eruption of laughter followed a quip by one of those present. One particularly memorable joke came while discussing the prevalence of wasta with Ali and his friends. Ali was talking about how there is so much zucchini (kusa) in Egypt, when another man declared, "Even if the Nile was made of salsa, you could not cook all the zucchini in Egypt!" This was followed by much laughter, which had to be explained to me. Zucchini, eaten frequently with salsa, is a colloquial name for nepotism. Although not true, the story goes that when traders collect vegetables to take to market, those collecting zucchini can jump the queue because it rots quickly. Nepotism allows someone to do the same in jobs.

I heard many similar jokes during fieldwork: the LE30 billion used for the new Suez Canal party could have been used to marry thirty thousand youth; microbus drivers reciting poetry is a sign not that they became educated but that university graduates are now working as microbus drivers; and the president talks about preserving stability (istiqrar)—rather than improving something like other governments—but "what stability? A stability of misery." These jokes echoed a repertoire circulating on social media and among prominent comedians. One image was shared with me after Mahmoud saw it on Facebook (see Figure 2.1). "Look, people know what is really happening" was the accompanying message. It was posted on a page called Sarcasm Station and adapted from an image created in 2012 by a U.S. business professor, who created it to illustrate the difference between "equality of opportunity" and "equality of outcome" in an argument with a conservative activist.[17] This picture compares "equity" and "equality" with an Egyptian reality in which a gleeful, paternalistic army officer is standing looking over children who

FIGURE 2.1. Comparing Egypt, Equality, and Equity. Source: Facebook page "Sarcasm Station." Reprinted with permission.

cannot see. The children have puffed-up faces, which originate from a well-known GIF comic character named "Forever Alone." This character is used to express "loneliness and disappointment with life."[18]

Hangouts between men rarely remained serious, instead frequently turning into competitions of masculine, heteronormative joke-making. Conversations often involved language and topics deemed unsuitable for a female audience. They were also classed, with some men finding certain swear words vulgar or uneducated. They represented men showing off their distinctive ability to be humorous but also dissipated frustration. At first I felt discomfort in these situations, knowing the anguish produced within individuals by the issues being converted into objects of humor within groups. Adel described how older men always ask Egyptian youth how they keep laughing when they live such a "black or difficult life" (hayat suda). But youth described laughter as essential to their ability to cope: "If we did not laugh, we could not survive in Egypt; we would get depressed from the country's situation," Eslam told me. Laughter, according to Adel, is targeted at painful things: "Life is very hard for lots of people, so we need to laugh. It's a way of forgetting difficulties." Men often tell one another to afridha (smile in the face of problems).

Egyptian popular culture also has a history of satirical humor, with films, soaps, and comedy targeted at issues like corruption and government incompetence.[19] Egyptians, I was repeatedly told, pride themselves on their ability to laugh despite the difficult conditions they live in. It was a sign of strength, compared favorably against the perceived sincerity of Western culture.

There is much discussion about the political ramifications of satirical humor, which is often caught between a view of humor as a safety valve that prevents revolt and a form of training that stimulates radical action.[20] A nuanced approach recognizes humor's ambivalence by taking into account the context within which it is produced, circulated, and consumed as well as the layers of understanding needed to participate.[21] For these young men, humor represented a reclamation of respect against people or circumstances that placed them in chastening situations. While discussing Egypt's new capital city project, Adel said to me, "We laugh because the people in power think we don't understand, they think we are stupid, but we know exactly what they do." I want to argue that humor constituted a form of emotional labor that vitally dissipated negative emotions such as anger, shame, and depression that constantly emerged amid the daily grind of degrading work and amid a sense of stagnation in relation to their dreams. As the preceding testimonies describe, it is targeted at topics that induce depression and frustration. It represents a direct assault on the harmful impact of precarity and disconnection that enables a brief experience of joy, respect, and validation through constructing a joke met with the laughter of peers. Furthermore, in a precarious, degrading context that stripped away any sense of control—over abusive customers or nepotism in the labor market, for example—humor represented a practice that asserted a sense of knowingness and discursive retaliation.

Humor can be an important precursor or complement to resistant action. In Egypt a diverse repertoire of comedy emerged in the aftermath of the 2011 uprising—with prominent comedians such as Bassem Yousef gaining huge popularity. But in a context of authoritarian fear and oppression that has driven comedy underground, I argue that in maintaining a sense of respect and joy, it was vital for these low-end male service workers to keep investing their labor power in humiliating jobs and a humiliating labor market. This form of emotional labor was highly social, taking place among young men in their shared flats and in ahwas. Humor relies on the presence of others who might empathize with and validate the joke being made. It therefore rested on and reinforced the cultivation of friendship. It is also highly gendered, as women are excluded from the spaces in which this type of masculinized humor is circulated—although they develop their own forms. Finally, it is also open to processes of commodification. As Chihab El-Khachab has pointed out, there is a thriving economy produced out of satirical humor in Egypt, as Facebook groups and comedians make money out of continually producing material to be circulated.[22] In this context, I argue that this commodification is an important part of the constitution of humor as a form of emotional labor enabling low-skilled, precarious workers to cope with degrading conditions.

AVOIDING THE FUTURE

Sometimes turning objects of frustration into humor was unwelcome, however. One evening, after a particularly strenuous rush period, Mohamed and Eslam returned home in a somber mood. Mohamed tried to instigate the usual ritual by recalling a woman who kept screaming at him, but Eslam abruptly told him "leave it, leave it (fukkak, fukkak)." He wanted to forget about the shift. Instead, he insisted we talk about anything else. He sat down and began scrolling through Facebook on his phone, chuckling intermittently as he read. Mohamed switched on the television and began watching an episode of *Ramez*, a Ramadan comedy show that puts celebrities in uncomfortable situations. During the course of the evening the conversation meandered between Adel talking about the "chic" cars he had seen in an upmarket area that day—which stimulated a discussion of their favorite cars—revisiting an old argument about who is the better football player, Ronaldo or Messi, with Mohamed insisting it was Ronaldo and Adel and Eslam ridiculing his opinion for the umpteenth time since I had been in the flat, recollecting the last time Egypt was in the World Cup and reliving a famous narrow 4–3 loss against Brazil in 2009, and discussing the UK's upcoming European Union (EU) referendum, which provided an opportunity for Adel to show off his knowledge of foreign affairs.

Conversations among men covered a wide variety of topics: commodities, TV programs and films, world politics and history, Egyptian or European football, funny anecdotes, and women—a topic discussed in Chapter 4. Little serious conversation was had among friends, sometimes to the extent that some knew nothing of each other's difficulties. Instead, men loved to yihry—talk about nothing together. Often in the middle of a conversation about careers—that I sometimes instigated—they suddenly switched to discussing a film they had watched or a football match that had taken place, which I understood as necessary deflection. While call center employees enjoyed discussing the difficulties of the job, talking about one's career dissatisfactions to friends in different jobs can instill a sense of social shame. Men might face judgment or be told to stop complaining. But men also described how they steer clear of these topics to avoid stressful thoughts. Hashem, a friend of Ali who worked in a mobile phone shop but wanted to work in a bank, described this sentiment. After catching up about the "sons of a dog" (awlad kalb) customers in the shop, I asked how Ali was doing. Hashem replied that he was still the same, negative—Ali had a reputation for complaining. I asked about his thoughts on Ali's complaints. He replied: "Between you and me I don't think of tomorrow, I just live my life, because I don't want to think about something that will annoy me. If I think about it I will just think that I need lots of money to buy lots of things like a flat for marriage and I don't have it right now." After giving this answer, we swiftly switched to talking about his favorite Egyptian music—Mohamed Hamaki, Tamer Hosny, Assala Nasri, Sherine, not sha'by music as it has no meaning and people who listen to it "are on drugs"—and setting out a list of places he wished to travel, starting with Dubai, Turkey, and France.

Conversations between men therefore provided an opportunity to focus on other things and forget the daily stresses of work and careers. But topics also embodied the type of young, modern, cosmopolitan, pious, macho men they wished to be. Talking about these things with friends enabled men to experience pride and respect, by showing off one's knowledge of world affairs, opinions on Islamic codes and norms, awareness of various commodities and the best places to buy them, "deep" ('amiq) taste in Egyptian music or foreign films, strategies for building muscle in the gym, the domination of one's football team, or an exciting trip to the Red Sea. This was often accompanied by photos shown on the phone of one's holiday or desired commodity. Usually, it was people who were doing relatively successfully who brought up careers within groups. Certain members were also a target for mockery because of the football team they supported, their lack of muscles, or being effeminate. I was often incorporated into this casual competition through attempts to compare the cooperation and humor of Egyptians against the sincerity and individualism of Western culture or to ridicule my supposed lack of masculinity. These conversations therefore provided an opportunity, although not a surefooted one, for men to locate a fleeting sense of status and power—by demonstrating a humorous, trendy, educated, knowledgeable, moral self.

Transferring attention from job struggles was also achieved through solitary activities. Every night Eslam, Mohamed, and Adel made sure to spend time watching television in the flat. Eslam also lay in bed either watching a film on his laptop, reading about football or flicking through Facebook on his phone, or reading a book. He described this as an attempt to ensure that his life was more than just work. All he had to look forward to the next day was work, so he wanted to sit and enjoy some time in which he was not imminently heading back. Eslam tried to watch or read something light (khafif), avoiding pessimistic or serious material because, he explained, "There is enough negativity in life, like all of the stuff you talk about in your research, careers and marriage, you need to cut that out of your activities. I don't want to read or watch something negative because the environment is difficult already." He picked out one film in particular, Sa'a wi Nuss (An Hour and a Half), as being too negative in its portrayal of the difficulties faced by youth. It tells the story of the 2002 Al Ayyat train accident from the perspective of several riders: a graduate who could not find work and wanders around train carriages selling love stories, two friends who traveled to Libya but returned after their money was stolen, and a railway watchman who earns so little he cannot support his daughter in marriage or provide medication for his sick wife. Instead Eslam watched football matches of his beloved Al Ahly if his schedule allowed; Ramadan soaps such as Al-Kabir Awi, a comedy about a stereotypical man from Upper Egypt and his brother who grows up in the United States but returns to claim his inheritance; and Egyptian and foreign films. Eslam also began reading a book called Sarcasm (sukhriyya), which describes funny situations that happen every day in Egypt's streets, in transport, or when dealing with government bureaucracy.

Others only watched foreign films because they considered Egyptian cinema low quality and too sexualized—although they criticized the common portrayal of Arabs as violent in Hollywood movies.²³ Again, this material often embodied an aspirational sense of self. Films such as *Fight Club*—which Ali mentioned in the introduction—and *The Wolf of Wall Street* that embodied powerful masculinity were attractive. TV, laptop, and mobile phone screens—as well as stimulating reminders of a lower-class status as I described earlier—also provided light relief for men, enabling them to transport themselves into a higher-status dreamworld and dissipate anxiety. Activities like smoking cigarettes or hashish and drinking alcohol were much rarer as they did not conform to the middle-class piety of many young men—they were often described as symbols of sha'by living—but some, like Ali, did slip into them at different times. In this context, repetitive activities such as watching television, flicking through social media, engaging in light conversation, and having a cigarette served a similar purpose. They enabled young men to briefly divert attention from the daily stresses of work, dissipating negative feelings. They also represented an effort to reclaim control over one's time and be oneself in the context of work that stripped these privileges away. They therefore formed a vital form of emotional labor, which was again highly gendered as they reflected how men avoid talking about problems with each other.

Beyond these mundane activities, the timing of Eslam's, Adel's, and Mohamed's shifts meant it was difficult to do much else outside work. As male call center employees, they got put on evening shifts because of the need for female colleagues to be home before nightfall. This meant missing out on watching football matches, hanging out in the ahwa, and meeting the few friends they knew in Cairo. Eslam, as mentioned earlier, complained about a lack of balance in his life. "If you sort out your work, religion, sports, and humor you will live a happy life," he said. In lieu of being able to afford the gym—which provided an important form of relief for other men who described it as their "second home" or substitute marriage—Eslam tried to plan to see a friend or go on an outing as Adel and Mohamed left for their family homes on days off. This was his attempt to "change the atmosphere" and break his daily routine. More infrequently, I went with him to buy a new item of clothing, usually a fake or old branded item from shops in the neighborhood. Eslam described this as a small reward (mukafa'a) for himself, comparing it to a mother buying something for a child who does good things to ensure that they carry on doing so. However, for these three young men, time and monetary constraints meant they were extremely limited in the leisure pursuits they could engage in. Indeed, this is one of the major complaints of call center work. As a result, they often talked about planning activities without actually doing so. For several weeks, we talked again and again about a day trip to Ain Sokhna, a cheap resort town one and a half hours away, intricately setting out what we would do and how we would get there. But it never happened because we could not coordinate days in which the whole group was free.

YALLA NUKHRUG SAWA

Others were able to plan group outings (kharuga) during days off. I went on several outings with a mixed group from TFJ in the months after the program. We traveled to different areas—Islamic Cairo, Downtown, Sayeda Zeinab, Coptic Cairo, Zamalek, Maadi, and Nasr City—which represented either authentic Egyptian, historic elite, or new cosmopolitan upper-middle-class culture. During these outings we visited famous balady (local) or raqy (classy) restaurants, tourist sites, cultural spaces and concerts, and even the opera house for a free Ramadan party. More infrequently, we traveled on day trips to Alexandria or Ain Sokhna on the Gulf of Suez, and on one occasion a multiday holiday to the Red Sea resort of Sharm el-Sheikh. I was often used as a means to provide company on these outings, and for them to meet other foreigners. Planning outings with friends for days and weeks in advance—often starting with the WhatsApp message "yalla nukhrug sawa (come on, let's go out together)" provided something exciting to focus on, with some citing upcoming outings as essential for helping them get through the week. During outings serious topics were off the table. Instead, these outings felt like temporary sanctuaries, with much laughter filling the air, followed by sadness when they came to an end. Outings again reflected the gendered, classed, and moralized religious selves attendees aspired to be. We often went to raqy spaces in the city, but this sometimes produced anxiety among men who did not have money. This was gendered as well. A group of men alone preferred to eat at a balady restaurant, or even from the street, but if women were present they needed to find somewhere "clean." Men competed with one another to decide which place was best, direct the group, and make sure to pay for metro tickets or food. While most avoided alcohol, some wanted to go to a bar to drink a beer—especially with me as a foreigner—and on one occasion I accompanied a group to a rooftop to smoke hashish in the middle of Ramadan. These acts represented a show of defiance, providing a momentary sense of empowerment against a difficult set of circumstances.

For the most part as little money as possible was spent—apart from the odd occasion when people blew their salary on a "new experience" such as eating sushi, or the Red Sea holiday where there was a gluttonous rush to engage in all the activities we possibly could to make it a trip to remember. One activity they could engage in, and which filled much time, was taking selfies. Every few minutes while walking in a tourist site or upscale neighborhood someone took out their phone and suggested taking a group selfie or asked for a photo to be taken of themselves in a model-like pose. These photos required multiple takes before people were satisfied to move on, only for the next opportunity to be found in a matter of meters. At times the taking of selfies—for example, in tourist sites or the opera house—received disapproving glares. These glares were met with annoyance, but they did little to puncture enthusiasm. By the end of the day, hundreds of photos had been captured. The majority were not actually used, but sometimes they were sent immediately on group chats to show others where we were, followed by a restless check on who had responded with envy. A select few might end up on Facebook—possibly becoming a new profile picture. Selfies were used to provide a memory of the day and often shown during recollections of that outing at a later date or scrolled through privately when bored at home. Selfies were kept to provide memories of the day, I was told; it was all they had in the absence of other consumption. But the act of actually taking the selfie felt as important as keeping them. It announces that you are part of a group, at that place, at that time and asserts your presence in that aspirational space. It is also a humorous activity that occupies time.[24]

One of the most common outings was to the shopping mall. During my fieldwork I visited several malls, which act as a vivid signifier of upper-middle-class consumer lifestyles and Cairo's global transformation.[25] One of the biggest fans was Mahmoud, the man introduced in the previous chapter who lived with his aunt. Mahmoud used trips to malls, alongside an incessant focus on consumption more broadly, to cope with the continual anguish experienced in the labor market. This can be best illustrated by recounting one of our trips. It was November 2015, three months into another period of unemployment. I met Mahmoud at nine a.m. to make the long journey to Nasr City to meet his uncle's friend who owned a publishing house, as Mahmoud had heard he might have a job. In the microbus Mahmoud told me about a job he just applied for: a "box boy" for a supermarket. He arrived to find "uneducated" people applying and was told by the manager he was overqualified—Mahmoud would find it embarrassing to work for tips. In the middle of the story, I pointed out a closed-off tunnel in the street, asking what it was. Mahmoud replied in a frustrated voice: "It is supposed to cross over to the other side of the road. They want us all killed instead." Mahmoud then started telling the story of when he tried to find his father when he was sixteen. He packed his clothes and traveled to Imbaba, where his father had a house. He knocked on the door but there was no response. A neighbor told him they had moved. He gave the neighbor his clothes because he could not carry them back to his house. He walked around for a while, thinking what to do, before getting a call from his father, who told him to never come looking for him again. Mahmoud had no money to get back home, so he had to walk the three-hour journey. With tears in his eyes, he said: "I just want to ask my father why?"

Before meeting his uncle's friend, Mahmoud wanted to visit a training center where he had done another soft-skills course two years before TFJ. As we walked, he recollected how he had loved coming here every day. There was an amazing teacher called Layla, a graduate of AUC who refused to speak Arabic. Mahmoud wanted to see her again. He told me not to tell her he was unemployed, though, because she would be disappointed, so he asked me to put the CV he was carrying inside my bag. When we arrived, Mahmoud asked the receptionist if Layla was there but was told she had long since left the organization. Mahmoud then asked how much a normal course cost; LE800 (US$100) per level was the reply. He could never afford that. When we got outside Mahmoud received a call. His face suddenly went red with anger, but he kept calm and polite, saying, "No problem, sir," over and over. After he put the phone down, Mahmoud exclaimed, "Motherfucker!" His uncle's friend had canceled fifteen minutes before they were supposed to meet. He told Mahmoud to come on Sunday, and then said no, Monday, then again no, Tuesday. He finally told him to call before to confirm. Mahmoud was angry and humiliated. He exclaimed, "I am cursed!" I said I was sorry, but he replied, "I am used to it now, this disappointment, it's not new." After a few moments of silence, Mahmoud suggested we go to the CityStars shopping mall close by.

On the way Mahmoud cried out that he just wanted to do his own project. He recounted the entrepreneurship project they did at the soft-skills course; he still kept his group's business plan for a GPS watch on his phone. He wished they had established the company for real, but others thought it was a risk: "I think in life if you don't take risks you never get anywhere; Bill Gates started from nothing and look where he is now." Mahmoud switched to talking about another project he had been working on recently, a restaurant called Big Ben Burger. As he talked, he saw a plane flying overhead and shouted, "Can't you take me with you?" When we arrived at the mall, Mahmoud knew the shop he wanted to find: Virgin Megastore. He had been there many times before. On the way he excitedly commented how fancy the mall was. Walking past one shop, he pointed out, "One day I hope I get money to buy clothes here" (coats were LE15,000 [US$1,875]). We entered Virgin and headed straight for the high-definition flat screens. The average price was LE20,000—Mahmoud's highest salary to date had been LE1,400 per month. As we stood, Mahmoud began to smile and laugh to himself, before saying, "Doesn't this feel so good"—followed by a brief pause—"just the thought of one day having it, it makes me very happy." I questioned whether this was really a satisfying or frustrating experience. He responded, "It depends if you are positive or negative. If you are negative, you will find it frustrating that you will never have these things. But if you are positive, it will give you hope that one day you can afford it. That something will happen to help you do it. The key is thinking positive, Harry." We entered a couple more shops and took selfies to send to the TFJ WhatsApp group before deciding to get food. I wanted to treat Mahmoud to food inside the mall, but he refused. He could not afford it, so he wanted to eat on the street. As we were leaving, Mahmoud saw a gumball machine and asked if I wanted a gumball; "It is the only thing I can afford," he remarked while laughing. Upon exiting, Mahmoud claimed he would come back one day and buy everything.

This experience represents a snapshot of Mahmoud's attempts to dissi-

pate feelings of shame and frustration within Cairo's labor market. Very frequently, when I was spending time with him, he suddenly switched from
confiding in me about a chastening employment experience to discussing
a product—shoes, wine, laptops, watches, bags, home appliances, glasses,
razors—that he had researched and planned to buy once his next paycheck
(or paychecks) came in—or when he got a job. He entered these products
into a mobile app that keeps track of the stuff one needs to buy and calculates
the money coming in and out—although when I saw it he had entered in
expenditures with no money coming in. On countless occasions we went to
locate these products. At times this was stuff he could immediately afford—
which provided an opportunity for him to showcase his knowledge of where
to find good value for money. But on other occasions we went just to look at
products—preferably ones that might be affordable at some stage. Mahmoud
described this as a motivational exercise, enabling him to visualize a target to
aim for, either when his next paycheck came in or further into the future. It
was the only thing he had to look forward to while working in low-end jobs.
Justifying his constant spending, he repeated an oft-heard phrase: "There are
no pockets in the shroud!" (mafish giyub fi al-kafan). Spending provided
immediate status by showing off his chic new items.[26]

This exercise took Mahmoud to Cairo's malls, where he walked around
the glitzy corridors, entered his favorite shops to get a closer look, and either
discussed products with me or spoke to a shop assistant about the item's speci-
fications, thereby adding it to his "wish list." Cairo's malls are exclusive places.
Security guards keep out lower-class men imagined as a threat to upper/mid-
dle-class women. However, they are open to more than those who can afford
products. In the social sciences, malls have long been conceptualized as hy-
perreal, theatrical places that offer up "transitory participatory pleasure" to
those who inhabit them.[27] In different contexts, researchers have noted how
poor people frequent malls to hang out in a modern, sanitized place, with this
activity conceptualized as an act of transgression.[28] However, as I accompanied Mahmoud this did not seem an appropriate reading. Mona Abaza, writing about poor people's inhabitation of Cairo's malls, stated that malls "might
encourage a feeling that one can participate in a better world, even if merely
by window-shopping."[29] Aesthetically, the mall's cleanliness, cool tempera-
ture, and vacant walkways form a blunt juxtaposition to Cairo's dirty, sti-

fling, overcrowded streets. The mall is also emblematic of an intensification of consumption as a class signifier. It therefore generates an atmosphere of possibility by offering aspirational objects for viewing. For Mahmoud and many others, the aesthetics of the mall, and looking and commenting on the commodities therein, enabled them to imaginatively transport themselves into a future dream-world in which consumption and lifestyle desires would be realized. Mahmoud described how the mall helps him release the frustration that builds up in his life, "because I can distract myself from everything by looking at the products I want to buy." It provides a feeling of intense satisfaction, reintroducing momentarily a feeling of hope for something to look forward to and desire, to a present and future in which—he was perpetually reminded—there was nothing to wait for.

Outside malls, however, Mahmoud expressed the knowledge that many of the items he longed for were not within reach: "I just like to pretend I'll buy it, I'm a sick person, it's like motivation . . . I only like to mess around, it's about feelings," he said to me. The precariousness of this activity always threatened to come to the surface. While looking for laptops, Mahmoud frequently encountered the disappointment of discovering prices way beyond reach, which produced complaints about the fact that Egypt does not make anything itself. At other times, Mahmoud's attempts to transport himself into a future dreamworld were ruptured by others. One afternoon, as we were walking along the Nile in central Cairo with Ibrahim, Mahmoud was imagining, with a broad smile on his face, buying a five-million-pound villa on the riverbank. Ibrahim swiftly told him that will never happen, to which Mahmoud frustratingly responded: "Why can't you let me just pretend for a minute!" This practice of distraction was therefore imminently fragile as it was tied to the need for monetary success. Indeed, this alludes to a broader fragility inherent to the emotional labor of distraction described in this chapter, a fragility I will expand on by way of concluding.

CONCLUSION: THE DRUGS OF LIFE

The everyday attempts of young Egyptian men to alleviate monotony and stress reflect those of workers in many contexts. They speak to existing work on detachment, avoidance, and deflection as responses to depression and anxiety.[30] They add an important corrective by revealing how these affective responses can go hand in hand with and actively support continued labor market engagement. The need for distraction among Egyptians has garnered particular attention in the context of postrevolutionary trauma. It invited much discussion during the 2018 World Cup.[31] Macho humor, light television, social media, exercise and the gym, socializing, cigarettes and alcohol, and novel consumption enable vital bodily shifts to take place, dissipating the anxieties and frustrations thrown up by precarious, low-status labor by providing a moment of relief and joy, but also reintroducing short-term hope through having something to look forward to. As Ali described in the introduction, these activities "fuck with [one's] head" by enabling the forgetting of struggles that come with low-status work: both everyday shame and frustration and anxieties that arise from not moving toward normative aspirational markers. But these activities represented more than distraction. They were also an effort to reclaim control over one's time and a sense of self in the context of jobs that stripped them away. They therefore embodied the type of young, modern, middle-class Muslim men people wished to be in those moments. Alongside the feelings of boredom and frustration that fueled them, they were highly gendered. Middle-class women also experience socioeconomic frustration and stagnation, and their ways of escaping those feelings require research.

While some forms of distraction represent solitary activities, creating humor, talking about mundane topics, and organizing outings rely on and cultivate friendship—which in itself becomes a crucial form of endurance. This friendship did not provide or depend on serious empathy or comfort, for the most part. Rather it enabled the temporary trivialization of difficult emotions. The focus on practices of distraction also introduces the question of politics. Withdrawal from the race for labor market success among educated unemployed youth has been understood as a form of nonparticipatory resistance.[32] Yet although satirical humor demonstrates the survival of revolutionary possibilities as Alexei Yurchak argued, recreational activities are promoted, and capitalized on, by the narrative that they facilitate relaxation, mental well-being, happiness, and mindfulness.[33] They can constitute a form of pacification, an offering of "self-evidently transient pleasures" by neoliberal regimes that place moral responsibility on the individual for self-care.[34] The question of politics must be attentive to the specific context in which withdrawal is mobilized. In the case of young Egyptian men, engaging in transient withdrawal provides the affective relief that enables them to return to low-end work in Egypt's precarious labor market. I argue therefore that it constitutes a masculinized emotional labor that maintains the psychic capacity of low-end workers. This emotional labor is open to commodification processes—whether that be comics circulating humorous memes, producers of aspirational commodities, or social media and television companies. It also has a gendered politics as it impinges upon Egyptian women, a problem that will intensify after marriage if men keep engaging in practices of distraction instead of supporting reproductive labor.

However, the emotional labor of distraction amid prolonged disconnection is also "cruel" in Lauren Berlant's sense. Berlant argued that optimistic attachments become cruel if the objects actually become an impairment to one's flourishing.[35] For my participants this labor deferred only temporarily the anxieties produced by the stagnant pursuit of dignity and mobility in the realm of jobs. They had multiple moments of realization about this cruelty. One evening in the flat, Eslam suddenly announced he wastes too much time on Facebook. When he wakes up, he is supposed to get up, have a shower, eat, and do "useful" things like study. For others, the realization came at various points—and often repeatedly—that spending time and importantly money on new clothes, going to nice places, watching football, and hanging out in the ahwa were distracting them from finding better jobs. They looked to friends or colleagues who had become permanently distracted and given up finding a career. They also observed people who were doing the opposite, spending time and money trying to build their future rather than buying stuff or hanging out in ahwas. Mahmoud described these activities as the "drugs of life." They allow you to forget your labor market struggles momentarily, but they do not solve them or banish the feelings. Alcohol and drugs in particular were perceived as securing permanent distraction from important duties, as Adel explained: "If you need to do something, pay money to get something done, and you drink alcohol, you could forget all about it, so it doesn't help you solve the problems in your life, you just forget them." I half-jokingly said television might allow you to do the same. Adel agreed, saying it allows you to disconnect, but, importantly, "you can switch it off." Among young Egyptian men, these activities do not reflect permanent withdrawal. Through repetition they can cause a similar affective reaction to experiences that induce anxiety, intensifying a sense of disconnection. This was again gender-, class-, and age-specific. My interlocutors argued that, as men, they faced more pressure to find good jobs and not get distracted. They also had limited time as youth to locate a career. The anxiety of becoming permanently distracted also took place within a moral economy that placed the future within their hands. This therefore drove many young men into another form of emotional labor, which I explore in the next chapter, resting on sustaining a feeling of hope for future mobility.

CHAPTER THREE

WITHOUT HOPE
THERE IS NO LIFE

"EGYPTIANS ARE EXPERTS IN HOPING for unhopeful things, aspiring for things which can't be aspired after. If we didn't do that, we would die." This quote comes from Mahmoud, in the aftermath of yet another job application he had submitted. It represented a pessimistic assertion about his chances at this stage of his pursuit of a stable career but also reveals a powerful attachment to a feeling of hope prevalent within both him and other young un- and underemployed graduates I met in Egypt. In Egypt, and particularly among its lower-middle classes, "without hope there is no life" (min ghir al 'amal mafish hayat) is a common phrase. The presence of hope, or the sense that one's future will live up to one's expectations or desires, is considered essential for a viable life. A life without hope is considered akin to "death." As Samuli Schielke has argued, middle-class Egyptians are chasing grand schemes in a way that requires an "aspirational sense of existence, where one must always reach for more than what one has, a sensibility that is essentially dependent on its being dynamic and growing."[1] But for many, the pursuit of middle-class adulthood—and therefore their ability to sustain a vital sense of hope—has been rendered extremely uncertain in the twenty-first century as they develop lofty dreams for internationalized private-sector employment and globalized lifestyles while being pushed into low-status, precarious cycles of employment.

The previous chapter revealed how, in the context of prolonged periods navigating the daily stresses of low-skilled, precarious service work, the hopeful momentum extended by labor market industries ebbs away, to be replaced by frustration, anxiety, and boredom. It also traced how young men dissipate these negative emotions by engaging in practices that provide relief and distraction. But distraction and relief are temporary. They do not provide a permanent fix to an absence of hope for a desired future and can even reinforce the anxiety emerging out of the tormented pursuit of existential mobility. In this chapter then I switch attention to the ways un- and underemployed Egyptian men attempt to hang on to the hope that they will find desired jobs in the future. I show how they kept investing in a labor market that disconnected them from dignity and satisfaction by repeatedly bringing to life a meritocratic moral economy that placed responsibility for success or failure on the individual. By praying to God; recounting stories of successful friends, lessons from self-help books and Islamic texts, and quotes from entrepreneurs and films; and following these examples by attempting to continuously work on their skills, apply for jobs, and plan their dream start-ups, men managed to keep at bay anxiety and frustration that kept emerging and reintroduce a sense of hope for future mobility—even as belief in the meritocratic promise waned.

By delving into daily practice, the chapter demonstrates how hope represents a moral ideal and construction among Egyptians themselves, rather than simply an affect extended from above by labor market industries. They develop creative forms of sociality—job-seeking, skill development, religious piety—to induce and sustain hope. However, the chapter also intimately demonstrates how a labor market, despite producing disconnections between what people aspire to and what they can get, can continue to motivate people to pursue their normative good-life fantasies. It therefore speaks against a dominant literature in recent years that has concentrated on locating and celebrating transformative, postcapitalist forms of hope among marginalized communities. Instead, I argue how the everyday maintenance of hope can represent a vital form of emotional labor. This is an emotional labor required to keep giving one's body to a precarious labor regime, and an emotional labor that sustains the—albeit fragile—legitimacy of that regime.

YOU CAN MAKE IT ON YOUR OWN, WITH GOD'S HELP

One afternoon in early summer while waiting for another shift to begin, Adel started telling me about a colleague. Tarek had been in the company for three years and knew everything. He applied for a team leader job, which was, unlike the agent job, a permanent contract. However, Tarek was rejected, first being told he was "overqualified," which everyone found ridiculous, and then that he could not be accepted because he was from a sha'by area (residential neighborhood is written on ID cards). I questioned whether they would actually say that directly, but Eslam—who was ironing his shirt—insisted it was true and introduced a similar story from a different branch. Two applicants had the same qualifications, but one was rejected because he was from a sha'by area, while the other was accepted because he was from the upscale neighborhood of Mohandiseen. "It is not easy to change where you live!" Eslam proclaimed with anguish. Adel jumped in again, relaying with exasperation how the current team leaders know nothing and always ask people to do things for them. They must have gotten the jobs through wasta (nepotism) because they were not qualified. This instigated a discussion of whether Adel and Eslam would use wasta if they could. Adel insisted he would not, nor would he lie about where he was from. He wanted to succeed through his own effort. Eslam disagreed. He had spoken to a graduate of Cairo's Islamic university, Al-Azhar, who told him you must use what is given to you because the environment is so tough. Adel again objected, asserting that if a better job came through wasta and another like his current job, he would take the latter because he wanted to earn it.[2]

Eslam turned to me again: "This type of rejection gives you such depression, what will I do! I am from Sohag, they won't even call me for an interview!" But Adel avowed that class prejudice like this does not happen everywhere in Egypt's private sector:

> It is hard to get rich here doing the right thing; the rich are those who do bad, cheat their way to the top, and get rich from bad industries like weapons or drugs. But you can get there; you can struggle and succeed. They are not all people who cheat and use wasta; some people use effort and make it.

To back this up he introduced the story of a friend from Zagazig who graduated from the same faculty. He had done an interview several times for an accountant position with a Saudi company in Cairo, each time being rejected. He studied the questions after every interview and in the end succeeded because he knew exactly what they would ask. Adel insisted this was proof you can make it fairly, on your own, without the help of wasta.

Whether true or not, this story superseded the other. It proved that the labor market remained open to perseverant youth from a similar background. It therefore discursively reintroduced hope. To use Hirokazu Miyazaki's language, it "reoriented knowledge" away from future classed exclusion and stagnation toward the prospect of mobility by placing the future back within these men's control.[3] Later, when Eslam had gone to watch a film, Adel referenced his own situation. Being in the call center had made him suffer a lot, but he thought he had been "lazy" since starting. He had not been proactive in looking for another job or developing his skills. Instead, he spent time watching TV and sleeping. Adel claimed he had a legacy of laziness. In university he would "sleep for two days in a row"—although he worked hard at the beginning only to receive bad grades. He stayed home for a year after university not doing much, in the process losing his accountancy and English skills. Adel's decision to come to Cairo formed part of his efforts to renew hard work, but he was now being lazy again. He made a vow to look for English and accountancy courses after Ramadan.

Although these men expressed acute awareness of structural barriers of educational inequality, wasta or class prejudice, or a lack of available jobs in Egypt's economy, they also frequently emphasized how these barriers could be overcome. A poor-quality education can be mitigated through "self-development," wasta and prejudice are not everywhere—particularly in the private sector, which hires the most qualified people because companies care about profit—and there are jobs available, in Cairo at least. These declarations discursively kept open the possibility of hardworking individuals navigating these barriers. In Chapter 1 I demonstrated how these meritocratic logics—which have become more widespread in the aftermath of economic liberalization—are extended by training companies, entrepreneurship infrastructure, and recruitment agencies. But they are also brought to life through rumor and success stories shared among lower-middle-class men. This logic legitimizes privilege, placing blame on an "undeserving poor."[4] Yet it also contains a hopeful quality, offering up the promise of reward to anyone who works to acquire certain skills and characteristics. It fosters a moral economy between individuals who work hard and those who do not, while structural inequalities are rendered invisible.⁵ In this case, Adel injured himself through self-blame. But this self-blame enabled a reintroduction of hope by providing a blueprint to be different.

Eslam achieved a similar reorientation by calling on the power of God. During his period of anxious silence, in which he was "overthinking" about career struggles, he posted on Facebook: "None has the right to be worshipped by You [Allah], Glorified are You. Truly, I have been of the wrong-doers" (la illaha illa anta subhanak inny kunt min al-zalemiyyn). This Qur'anic verse represents a symbolic repentance for past sins that have caused present difficulties. It also reflects a vow to be better to secure future reward. This public declaration—accompanied by private prayer in which he asked God to "make the situation easier and help him" (yafrigha min 'anduh wi yisa' dny)—helped recover calmness (hudu'). It reminded him that God is looking after him and would never let him down, and that present difficulties were part of a broader plan. Explaining this afterward, he said:

> You need to have patience, and faith [that] you will be rewarded by God. You have faith [that] you will get a good job, marry, have kids. I have confidence those things will happen. Something will happen to make it okay. These conditions are a test. You need to live in a good way to keep a good relationship with God, not because of getting rewards, though. But he will look after you."

This Islamic practice—known as tawakkul—represents what Miyazaki termed an "abeyance of agency," whereby future events are placed in the hands of God.⁶ When men wrestled with negative emotions regarding present difficulties, they actively returned to God through the performative, visceral act of prayer. This took much discipline and effort—Eslam always made sure to go to the mosque for Friday prayers, and all three made time for prayer before going to their shifts. Others also watched popular revivalist Islamic preachers such as Amr Khaled and Mustafa Hosni on YouTube. By doing so they reinterpreted their struggles as part of a plan, their destiny, or a test of faith and patience.⁷ Often when they were talking about difficulties, men paused to declare, "Thanks be to God, God make it easy" (al-hamdulillah, rabbina yisahhil). This—alongside other similar phrases—represented a discursive way of relieving stressful thoughts in that moment.

Enduring the test, as Eslam describes, requires "living in a good way," albeit not with the instrumental expectation of securing God's reward. Disavowing notions of Islam or religion as paralyzing, this returns agency to the individual. Eslam was certain that living in a good way would secure God's reward as it was proven before. After the TFJ program he was running out of money. A friend called him by coincidence to say he was going to an interview at Orange and suggested he join. Eslam was not enthusiastic and needed convincing but ended up going and getting the job: "This was God looking after me, making sure I was okay because if I didn't get the job I would have run out of money." Securing God's reward includes staying close through prayer, but also working hard in one's career, as Adel explained:

> There is a story from the time after the prophet. There were two brothers, one who prayed all the time and nothing else, and one who worked to look after his family. God told them the one who worked was more devoted. So it is not just about praying all the time; you have to look after your life, family, and yourself, and do things for your life and work.

It also includes a host of moralized and classed practices in other settings: not consuming "harmful" substances, refusing bribes or wasta, being gidaʻ (kind/helpful) with others, volunteering, even promising to give to poor people when rich.

Amr's story reveals how intricately connected the realms of morality and career are. He grew up in Boulaq al Dakrour, one of Cairo's poorest neighborhoods, and worked in an upmarket restaurant, spending his spare time in the streets. In his words, he acted like a "thug" (arbagy)—smoking cigarettes and hashish, using swear words, and verbally harassing women—in those days. He did not think about the future. But one day in the restaurant, two Egyptian women he was serving switched to speaking English, which he could not understand at the time. In that moment he thought he wanted a better life, which he associated with speaking English, so he set about learning it. Simultaneously he said he began changing his behavior: quitting smoking and swearing, being "respectful" to women, and no longer hanging out with his friends because of their "bad habits." For Amr, performing broader morality was an essential part of improving his socioeconomic situation, symbolizing a transition away from his neighborhood into a respectable career.

Scholars have argued that modern revivalist Islamic belief increasingly places emphasis on individual morality.[8] Muslims are required to repetitively cultivate a moral selfhood to secure God's satisfaction and reward. This responsibility is summed up in the phrase "You need to do what is on you, and God will do the rest" (lazim ta'mil illy aliyyk, we rabbina heya'mil al baqy), which I heard countless times during fieldwork. It means, as Adel explained:

> God will look after you if you do your part, if you struggle hard. I believe I will find a way because I am doing the right thing. Some people do not try; I know some and that convinces me to stay here. They are staying in their place and accepting; I am trying to change the situation.

Men picked particular stories, verses, and phrases that emphasized individual over communal responsibility—and masculine responsibility in terms of work—because these words provided hope for their own future by putting it back under their control. The writings enabled men to both blame themselves for "going far from God" during a period of struggle and establish a blueprint to be different—as Eslam had done by repenting for past sins—or congratulate themselves for "doing what one is supposed to" in difficult conditions in the expectation of eventual reward. The enactment of this religious moral economy demonstrates how Islam can work to reinforce neoliberal subjectivities that enact and sustain hope. For these men it formed an integral emotional labor that enabled them to keep invested in low-paid work. Alongside emphasizing the presence of meritocratic norms, calling on faith discursively set up a world in which they might succeed, if they exercised the correct behavior. It helped them overcome the overwhelming experience of anxiety and frustration at various moments in their daily lives.

I AM A "MUKAFIH"

After Ramadan ended in July, Eslam, Adel, and Mohamed set about trying to be more active. All three searched for English courses to take alongside work. Eslam and Mohamed completed placement tests in a low-cost center nearby, only to be told there were only afternoon classes. Adel was placed in a nine a.m. class. For two sessions he got up in time, excitedly recalling afterward the phrases he was learning. For the third he failed to wake up, having gone to bed at three a.m. This quickly punctured any newfound momentum while also revealing the structural barriers faced in pursuing self-development. These men could not leave their jobs because of financial constraints or take courses because of their shift work.[9] However, Adel felt bad. He reiterated that he thought he was lazy, using his inability to wake up as proof. I said his schedule made it difficult, but he maintained he should have done it:

> I need to put myself in uncomfortable situations for my future; you have done it, you came here, away from family and friends. But you enjoy it, you enjoy the new experience even though it is hard. I need to do the same. You know Bill Gates said four things you need to do to be successful, the first one is never get lazy, always keep trying . . . I can't remember the others. I need to take the opportunity I have in Cairo. I came here to develop myself and work hard. It is a very important time but I am not making the most of it. I am getting stuck. I need to work hard now.

Rather than focusing on his job schedule or lack of money that meant he could not leave it, Adel again blamed himself. To back this up, he reintroduced a meritocratic moral economy by pointing to me and hazily recollected lessons from an international entrepreneurial icon that "prove" success is down to attitude. I felt the urge to outline my privilege—and the inherited privilege of Bill Gates—but realized it would not be heard. Focusing on structural limitations was useless, depression-inducing in this context. Lauren Berlant argued in the U.S. context that people living in crisis form an optimistic attachment to promises defining liberal-democratic ideas of the good life, such as meritocracy, despite their continual breakdown because it is the only way for people to maintain "continuity of the subject's sense of what it means to keep on living on and to look forward to being in the world."[10] Her argument, alongside literature on neoliberal legitimacy, largely remains Western-centric. In this Egyptian context, it was becoming clear to me that men were developing an emotional attachment to meritocratic narratives. While legitimizing stagnation and harming well-being through self-blame, these narratives renewed hope by enabling the men to perceive that they might change.

Bill Gates was not the only entrepreneur to provide inspiration. When I came across Ibrahim's Facebook post beginning "#we need other Jobs in our life," I thought it was a frustrated cry for better employment. However, he was talking about Jobs the man. What followed was a declaration of his importance in Ibrahim's life:

> Steve Jobs, the person who always inspire me. The person who always give me hope and power to feel everything will be good one day. I always look to his eyes and see hope, power and enthusiasm. His eyes always tell me not to give up on my dreams and there is always a way, and one day all dreams will came true. His eyes always tell me to be crazy enough to show others that everything is possible [sic]

For young Egyptians, Steve Jobs's story is powerful. He was the adopted child of a Syrian father and did not have university education. Despite a "disadvantaged" upbringing, he proved that success is about one's "brain and attitude." He stands in contrast to Egyptian elites who make money by "stealing, giving bribes, and utilizing wasta," and he "added value to the world" rather than just making money. This morality was reflected in his actions as an entrepreneur. Whereas Egyptians are obsessed with "appearance, place of birth and study, and social level," Jobs, Ibrahim argued, selected applicants based on "smartness" (zaka'). His nonjudgmental attitude was materialized in the simple blue jeans and black turtleneck he wore. Steve Jobs therefore personified the antithesis to what held these men back: overcoming disadvantage through passion, smartness, hard work, and belief. These qualities could be cultivated and performed. Young men like Ibrahim returned to Jobs's story and quotes in difficult moments and attempted to identify themselves as similarly "crazy," "passionate," or "entrepreneurial."

Adel, Eslam, and Mohamed soon made new plans. Adel asked me to ask friends about accountancy courses. I knew a PwC employee—an upper-middle-class man with private education. He said the only course that made a difference was the Certified Management Accountant course, which cost LE10,000 (US$1,250). I reluctantly told Adel, who knew it was beyond his means. Instead, after talking about it for a while, he bought a laptop and internet stick with his savings to study English and accountancy and look for courses and jobs. It was an exciting moment; not only was he buying a new commodity, it materialized hope for an ensuing period of mobility. Eslam brought a laptop from Sohag to do the same. Every night after work, he spent half an hour watching English films and writing down words he did not know before looking up their meaning. Adel set up a makeshift desk and wrote words from videos of Saudi women speaking English obtained from a friend working in Saudi Arabia. He also insisted we speak English. One day he showed me a film he had downloaded so I could translate something. It was *The Pursuit of Happyness*. This film was "an inspiration to Egyptians, they are used to these problems, they feel them, Will Smith struggles a lot, he is close to homelessness, but he is successful in the end through hard work," Adel said. It was circulated and referenced by many men. It involves a black male protagonist in the United States, a victim of poverty, homelessness, and institutional racism, who, through continual struggle, manages to prove that he is qualified for Wall Street. It emphasizes the defiant individual, as demonstrated by the film's key quote from Will Smith to his son, which is the section Adel asked me to translate, and the section posted on Facebook numerous times:

> Don't ever let somebody tell you . . . You can't do something. Not even me . . . You got a dream . . . You gotta protect it. People can't do somethin' themselves, they wanna tell you you can't do it. If you want somethin', go get it. Period.

During this period these men used objects available to them—a laptop, a desk, a pirated Hollywood film—to sustain an atmosphere of hope that a painful present would not last. Others used a language course, an Excel spreadsheet setting out expenditures and revenues of a future start-up, or suit trousers and a buttoned shirt. These objects all materialized a merito-cratic terrain—with epistemological origins in a variety of globalized entre-preneurial narratives—that rewards perseverance, as well as a cosmopolitan upper-middle-class status. Using and interacting with them enabled men to perceive they were moving toward a better life. As a result, they could assert themselves as "mukafehin" (strugglers) and "raqy" (classy). These activities could be interpreted as "shrewd improvisation," with these men making the most of what they had.[11] But this reading neglects their politics. Men construct a meritocratic terrain that promises that these activities will make a difference. But some people's improvisation leads to more success than others.

Indeed, hope never lasted long. It took continuous work for these men to keep positioning themselves on the pathway toward success as a result of structural barriers that kept resurfacing. Adel and Eslam oscillated in and out of activity. Adel admitted he was struggling for motivation: "It is hard studying on your own, I don't know what to do, you learn Arabic here, not in England," thus alluding to the structural inequalities between us. But most of the time he returned to his own failings. One afternoon I came home to him eagerly waiting to say he had woken up early because he did not want to be lazy. This instigated another discussion:

> I am fed up with the water and the heat in the flat. I could live in Zagazig and be comfortable, but what work would I do? There are guys who work in small shops, one in a small accountancy job, but I want more. Everyone who has good work came to Cairo. Like my friend who works for the Saudi company. He struggled for a long time to get into his field; he applied again and again to companies, and memorized the questions, and in the end was accepted. He was good in English. He took a course while we were in university called New Horizons; it was for English, presentation skills, stuff like that. I was rejected because you needed to speak English. I was really bad; they asked me to describe myself and I was like, "What?!" This course would have been amazing; if I had taken it I would have been good. He is successful now through hard work; I could have done that.

Adel then referenced another friend who worked in a bank after doing accountancy and English courses. I suggested that this friend might have had money to take courses. "Yes, maybe; but he had the motivation, he would not accept the shit jobs we are in." Adel reiterated that he was lazy in comparison but trying to change: "That's why I got up early!" He restated—almost telling himself—that he had come to Cairo to put himself in a tough situation. He was not like the people in his hometown who accepted their fate. He reiterated the core lesson from *The Pursuit of Happyness*: "The conditions suck here, but at the start of that film there was a homeless guy who just sleeps, accepts his lot, and gives up, but Will Smith doesn't, he struggles and doesn't give up, and is eventually rewarded." This conversation brought forth palpable déjà vu. By returning to the stories of successful friends and the cinematic success of Will Smith, Adel was wrestling with his predicament and attempting to position himself as one of them. He knew he had been lazy in the past, and he regretted this, but he was now struggling. Two days later Adel was surer of his status after spotting my copy of Samuli Schielke's *Egypt in the Future Tense*. On the cover is a picture of a man leaning against a wall holding a cigarette. "Who is that sarsagi?" Adel asked. "Is that how you are representing Egypt? He is doing drugs, not doing anything useful."[12] Adel knew people in Zagazig like this who had surrendered, whereas he was working to develop himself: being a mukafih.[13]

Adel was not alone in this wrestling act. Others struggled daily with positioning themselves on the pathway toward success. It is an emotional labor that many who are desperately struggling to locate mobility need to enact. It requires mentally sidelining structural barriers preventing the pursuit of mobility and emphasizing what they can control. While an application was being developed, or while awaiting a reply, men constructed the notion that they stood a good chance of acceptance. In the aftermath of rejection, following outbursts against corruption, they disciplined themselves into focusing on what they might do better next time, or what other opportunities they could find. During prolonged periods spent in difficult jobs, they tried to focus on the positives or engage in activities outside work that induced the perception of movement. This mindset required a numbing of one's emotional responses, as Gamal, who was doing unpaid work in a legal office for several months, explained:

> You can't be emotional here; you need to keep your emotions under control. If you think about how you are exploited, you will get annoyed. You can't think of that. Recently I was depressed at work and didn't want to do anything; I didn't want to meet clients or do reports. I was depressed because I wasn't receiving a salary. That is what may prevent me now: my own emotions and negative feelings. I try to deal with it by thinking of the positives of the situation.

Sustaining this positive mindset is not easy. It required returning to God or the stories of entrepreneurial success found in movies. It also sometimes required the advice of others. During Ibrahim's period in the call center in Cairo, he posted on Facebook tagging friends:

Asking for an advice:

If you work in a temporary job and you work for money. You need money to develop yourself and hold a diploma or a specific course which will give you an opportunity to catch your dream job, but unfortunately when you have the money you spent it quickly. And you find yourself unowned, you have no single plan, just you have passion and you didn't follow it yet. But you know from deep in your heart that you wanna do it. But the problem is you didn't till now.

It's too late, too late cause every day which I lose, is an opportunity which I haven't catch.

So how could I start!! It's not a shame to ask for advice, but the shame is to be such a failure person.

Please, I need your helpful criticism.

#Advise_me

The post received a mixture of empathetic replies from people experiencing the same problem, suggestions to enter a gama'iyya (savings scheme), and "do what you love first and money will come later"—another Steve Jobs quote. The most powerful response came from a career coach Ibrahim met in Sharkia. He praised Ibrahim for completing 50 percent of the journey by asking for help, before advising him to "define a goal to achieve after 3–5 years and write down what you need to do, learn and achieve to achieve this goal. Develop a plan and keep money aside every month to achieve your plan, make a yearly budget for your development and start bold and fast." This advice, coming from a figure of apparent success, renewed Ibrahim's hope.

This demonstrates how the labor of hope is not only an individual pursuit. At times it also becomes a collective endeavor that involves reaching out for and relying on the empathetic encouragement of friends, family, and acquaintances. This was also the case in the flat, as Adel, Eslam, and Mohamed came up with strategies and plans and vented frustrations with each other. However, as I suggested in previous chapters, it was extremely common for men to refrain from talking about their career struggles with family—whom they considered to be unaware about the nature of modern elongated employment trajectories—and with friends who might be judgmental about career ambitions or too much complaining. I was often used as an avenue of encouragement in the realm of careers because I listened with a nonjudgmental attitude and even found myself reacting positively about the prospect of things working out in order to banish negative feelings.

I witnessed a judgmental moral economy toward others on numerous occasions. Men told stories of friends who had never tried or stopped trying to improve their situations. They sat in ahwas, smoked hashish or cigarettes, played PlayStation, gossiped, spent money on new stuff, and complained about the prevalence of wasta or corruption. For Gamal, even though complaints about structure were valid, it remained incumbent upon the individual to not give up: "Even if there are many things you cannot control in reality, you must try and try until you achieve your goals." This moral economy also made its way into the flat. One evening Gamal visited and asked Eslam if he was taking courses, before suggesting the very expensive AUC. Eslam said he could not take courses because of his work schedule. "You should leave then," Gamal insisted, but Eslam shot back, tentatively, saying he could not afford to. Gamal asked if Eslam was at least saving money, forcing him to admit he was not. This exchange felt like a brutal dissection of Eslam's stagnation by returning the emphasis to him. Afterward Gamal told me this practice could be useful: "If I blame people it will help them be positive, it will help them think they didn't do enough, that they are not qualified enough, and can control it so they can change it." However, he also admitted worry about becoming judgmental: "I am scared to become plastic if I get rich, so I will not feel the pain of others. But I also want to be proud of myself and recognize my achievements." What Gamal illuminates here is the relationship between the meritocratic moral economy and the maintenance of hope. These men kept emphasizing the moral responsibility of the individual, both themselves and others, because it enabled them to sustain hope and experience a sense of status. It was vital to their emotional labor.

I SAID IT WOULD BE DIFFERENT

When I left Cairo in August 2015, Adel, Eslam, and Mohamed felt positive about their trajectories. Adel insisted that when I returned in October, he would have left the call center and taken an accountancy course. But when

I returned, Adel had neither left the job nor done an accountancy course: "I said I would be in a different place, but it is so hard, taking a course takes money." He admitted struggling to find an affordable course but declared he would leave the call center to look properly: "You can earn LE20,000 as an accountant!" he exclaimed. Adel had finally taken the English course, but the lack of improvement punctured any euphoria. The classroom was over-crowded, so he did not have a chance to speak. He showed me an old Charles Dickens book he had brought from home: "I am still trying, God make it easy, we need to do what is on us (rabbina yisahhil, lazim na'mil illy 'alina)." In this moment of anguish and regret at his immobility, Adel called on God to smooth his passage. He was trying to do his duty in return. But Adel was upset with himself. After lamenting how much money Egyptians need for everything nowadays, he again focused on his laziness: "If I wasn't lazy I would have left the job and looked for other work already, I could have found it and saved money for a course." Adel then told me about a self-help book he downloaded by Zig Ziglar, an American guru who helped Egyptians "keep positive and not get fed up with trying." He was shocked I did not know him: "He is an inspiration to youth, you should ask, they will all know him." He described his favorite passage:

> Two guys are trying to get water from a well, it is really hard to do, and the guy was struggling when it got near the top, and wanted to give up. But if you let go you have to start over again. So it is a metaphor for life that you shouldn't let go, you should keep struggling until you reach your goal.

Adel then told me about an Egyptian guru, Ibrahim al-Fiky, who had written books in Arabic. He started as a waiter and ended up owning a chain of restaurants. One of his best lessons was that the worst thing to do is "talking only, talking about your goals and not doing them." Adel recognized himself in this. He was lazy, talking about doing accountancy courses, changing jobs, or learning English, but never doing them.

Once again Adel reoriented consciousness away from structural bar-riers. This time he referenced U.S. and Egyptian self-help books, spread through friends, which have increased in popularity since Egypt's eco-nomic liberalization.[14] This industry, alongside Hollywood film, profits from the promotion of the hopeful promise of rags-to-riches mobility. The

narratives extended by self-help are affective because they easily relate—
Adel had talked repeatedly about his goals without reaching them. His
lack of money, education, and connections in a weak labor market ensured
this. All he could do was talk, plan, and plan again.[15] However, self-help
directs people away from structural issues, submitting them to individual
character faults. They become powerful because people keep investing in
them. Adel actively sustained an injurious meritocratic moral economy
between successful and failing individuals because it enabled him to hope
he might change, again. His attachment becomes "cruel," as Lauren Berlant argues, because he cannot detach from the meritocratic terrain. It is
the only way to maintain his ability to engage with the world.[16] The alternative of letting go is too much to bear. This requires constant deferral
of the relief that might be enabled by the object that is hoped for, in this
case a fulfilling job.

Two days before my departure in November, I found Adel on the sofa
in the morning studying from a battered Arabic accountancy book. It was a
first-year university textbook that he had brought from home. However, he
was struggling to remember the material, and in any case needed to learn accountancy in English. On this day, another roommate joined. Mostafa used
to work in the call center but had been fired because of an injury layoff. He
spent six months looking for a call center job with regular daytime shifts so
he could take an evening HR course, which he was now doing. His long-term
ambition was to travel abroad to do a master's on a scholarship, for which
he had applied and been rejected several times. Each time rejection came he
became dejected for a few days before searching for the next opportunity and
considering how he could be more competitive. This time, he thought his
HR course would make the difference. Mostafa also took advantage of my
presence, asking me to find a language-exchange partner who could teach
him English. During intense conversations in these two days, despite acute
awareness of the structural barriers facing Egypt's youth, Mostafa expressed
optimism that he would make it:

> Allah has promised if you make a certain amount of effort, he will make
> sure you have something in return. So you have to work hard and you can
> make it. I regret only that I didn't develop myself sooner, I regret that I will

arrive at my goal late, but I will get there; I am working hard to make sure that happens.

When I asked why Mostafa felt regret when he knew the barriers facing Egypt's youth, he replied: "I have to blame myself; if I just look at the hard circumstances, I would not be able to keep my goal alive." He described how there are two kinds of people in Egypt: those who have it easy, and those who need to struggle to achieve success. Of those who struggle, there are those who sit and complain about the conditions and those who believe they can make it through hard work. Some get fed up with trying and give up, and others keep going. Mostafa was someone who keeps going: "You have to go out and search, go out into the streets, not just stay in your house and watch TV and expect something to come, you have to go into the streets and grab it, that's how God will reward you." He quoted Thomas Edison as evidence of the ability of individuals to overcome failure:

> It took him 1,000 attempts to find the right answer for the lightbulb. People saw his 999 previous attempts as failed attempts, but he said no, they were vital to learning and reaching the successful last attempt; even if I go through lots of failure I can reach it eventually. I have had bad experiences which have returned me back to the start of the journey. But I am ready to keep going.

Adel looked to Mostafa with jealousy, perceiving that he was marching toward success. His presence stimulated more regretful lamentations regarding Adel's perseverant friend in the Saudi company and his rejection from the New Horizons training course long ago. I asked Adel why he could not leave the job and do courses for a while. He replied: "I wish they would make me leave, fire me, so I am pushed into doing something!" After I pushed further, he reluctantly admitted this would cause financial problems.

Adel struggled to admit his structural predicament. Instead, he cried out to be fired. This is the destructive cry of those who have no choice but to endure stagnation. I then reminded Adel that he previously said he was lazy. "Yes, I am," he replied. I said I did not agree with the idea that youth are lazy. He agreed, asserting that he knew that youth work hard, before pondering: "I am unsure if people are lazy, or if it is the conditions here." This exchange demonstrates the cracking of the meritocratic myth and an acknowledgment of the overwhelming structural barriers facing young men like Adel in the pursuit of dignified work. But Adel always shifted back toward individualizing narratives. On my final evening, he asked what piece of advice I would give him from my research. I struggled to answer, not wanting to fuel the meritocratic moral economy. After saying I did not really know, I let out in a comical voice: "Find wasta or money, or travel!" This was not enough for Adel: "That's all you have out of your research?!" I scrambled and said he should look for a job with fixed shifts so he could take courses like Mostafa. This answer was better received. It reintroduced hope.

I left the flat in November 2015. Over the previous six months these men had worked tirelessly not only in the call center but also to sustain a precarious sense of hope that their journeys would not end there. This labor entailed praying to God for guidance; repeatedly returning to stories of successful friends, lessons from self-help books and religious texts, and quotes from entrepreneurs and movies; and following these examples by doing what they could to work on their skills and find courses and jobs. This labor took place before and after shifts at work. It was both individual and at times highly social, requiring the support of others. This emotional labor enabled them to keep going to shifts. It relied on the notion that the individual can control the future. In doing so, it had the effect of legitimizing the structural barriers continuing to hold these lower-middle-class men in place. However, as Adel's psychological struggles show, this labor was imminently precarious, with the façade of individual power in danger of collapsing under the weight of structural constraint. I will now demonstrate how some men stopped entrusting in the meritocratic promise in the face of repeated failure to secure movement, with cynicism and despair overwhelming them.

THE BRINK OF "DEATH'

By 2015, Mahmoud had tried for six years to locate a stable job that would enable him to lead a desirable middle-class life. He had stints working in a kebab shop and as an accountant assistant, a bank teller, a call center agent, and a Vodafone sales rep, leaving each due to insecurity, low status, and low pay. He also spent a year working in Dubai before returning after a governmental decree stating that his job had to be done by an Emirati national. Over the years, Mahmoud also made countless efforts to develop himself, investing money in soft-skills and English courses and engaging in endless self-study. Each time, doing these activities provided a sense of expectation that he had finally found the missing link. But he had applied in vain for countless more-prestigious jobs in Cairo and innumerable jobs abroad and searched for funding opportunities for a start-up. Each rejection or prolonged period in a difficult job induced intense frustration—especially since he had been exposed multiple times to the workings of wasta in recruitment processes and the need to already have money to obtain business loans. Especially hurtful were the events that took away his dreams just as he felt closest to them, when he even felt brief confidence. The hurt often brought back feelings of abandonment and distrust he felt in relation to his parents, who had abandoned him as a child. But after each disappointment, Mahmoud picked himself up by rewatching inspirational self-help videos of Ibrahim al-Fiky, focusing on the next application or course that might improve his chances next time, and replanning his entrepreneurship project.

This cycle reflects the labor of hope described so far. But it was ruptured in August 2015. Mahmoud had been working for two months in data entry for a kitchen appliance firm. Even though it was temporary, Mahmoud again let himself believe he had found stability. He told his manager how happy he was because he could "finally plan for the future, for a car and family." His manager ominously urged caution, but Mahmoud did not listen. His excitement was uncontainable. He talked every day about the job. One day he had been sent on a factory tour in a private car accompanied by an engineer. The other temporary employees were all jealous, and the engineer told Mahmoud he was asking all the right questions. This coincided with frequent praise from his manager for being a "fast learner" and "creative." Just two days after the tour, Mahmoud was called into the HR office. Mahmoud thought this was finally it, his efforts were being rewarded with a permanent contract. But when he got there, they told him he was being laid off: "I thought they were joking until they made me sign resignation papers," he said. Mahmoud asked why. They simply said they don't need him anymore. On his way out, an HR employee asked why he was being fired: "Your file looks good." Mahmoud said he had no idea. The employee replied, if he had to guess, that it was either so they could bring a relative in, or that Mahmoud was overqualified. They thought he would not stay.

When I saw Mahmoud two days later, his voice trembled as he told me the story. "Why did they do it?" he cried out. Wasta was not a reason, because it was such a "shit" job. If they thought he was overqualified, they should have told him: "I would have said to them they are not right, I will stay in the job." Mahmoud pointed to a car in the street: "Look, I would have bought a small car like this if I had kept the job." Mahmoud decided he could not tell his aunt because she would be so disappointed. He continued to get dressed and leave the house at six thirty a.m., going to the library to sit at a computer instead of work.[17] As we walked near his home, Mahmoud began lamenting the plight of Egypt's educated youth. He had seen a young woman selling perfume on the street the other day and could tell by her clothes she was educated. He felt sorry for her because he understood her difficulty: "We have worse prospects than the uneducated here; you work so hard to educate yourself and can't get a job after." He then turned to me: "In Europe you get a chance to live, to build a decent life, but not here."

In the days and weeks following, Mahmoud became extremely negative and inactive. Every time I met him, he spent time expressing deep frustration with Egypt's labor market and rigged economy, the prevalence of wasta, the preference for those with private education, and the corruption of the rich. He started sending me satirical pictures he had found on Facebook—a plat-form on which Mahmoud had previously shared hopeful quotes and images. Having previously watched self-help videos, Mahmoud now scolded anyone who still believed in self-help stories, or even that God would make sure things turned out okay: "People do these things just so they can create hope in their lives, because they need it. But it is bullshit and fake; it only enslaves youth in fake positivity." While some people rely on believing that God will make everything okay, and others find inspiration in the stories of people like Steve Jobs, Mahmoud said he had become the "third kind" who has had enough of both. When I asked why he no longer believed in these things, he responded dismissively: "After six years of unemployment I have seen the real world, Harry."

Mahmoud at this point was judged by others for the pessimism he exuded. But moments like this came for many in the aftermath of events shattering their own momentum. It happened repeatedly. In 2016, a year later, Mahmoud experienced the same ripping away of his dream when a Lebanese company suddenly closed because of liquidation shortages as he held a three-month probationary job as an import specialist. Mahmoud did not speak to me for months after. On these occasions, men were stripped of that vital component of a meaningful life, the sense that "there is more to life than what exists for us in the here and now."[18] This underpins one's impetus to carry on acting in the world. In 2015 Mahmoud became inactive for weeks, not leaving home for days at a time. Late one evening he messaged me: "I'm so sad and angry, I'm reviewing my life from my shitty country to my shitty parents . . . to be honest I still doubt, maybe God is there, and it frightens me every time I think about killing myself. If I was sure that there is nothing on the other side, I would do it." Later in the conversation Mahmoud told me not to worry, he was just "thinking aloud." But this signifies the emotional state he had reached. A combination of childhood abandonment and a pro-longed inability to secure work brought forth moments of intense ikti'ab, which translates as depression or despair but differs from the more clinical definition in Anglo-American contexts. When I met Mahmoud the next day, I tried to tell him he could still find a job. But he shot back:

> I don't live as a human, Harry. When we let our dreams go, we never get something back, even our simple rights to live as a human. What kind of human can live with less than US$150 in a month [the salary in a call center], even your pets need more money. Harry, I'm twenty-seven years old, I have nothing, I can't afford myself, do you think I enjoy that, I cry every single day of my life, I am so sad, so upset, I can't even do anything.

Mahmoud saw a future in which he would remain in his area, in low-end work that meant difficulties in getting married, let alone looking after a family. This would lead to a reproduction of his class status in his children. From his experience, it would bring only darkness, struggle (niḍal), and "death." Death was a common term used by men to describe their condition in diffi-cult moments. Reflecting previous discussions of social death, for them death meant living a life within which they would give up their dreams and accept their present social level.[19] It meant living a life stripped of a sense of hope, of movement toward a desired future.

In periods like this, young men experienced what Ann Cvetkovich la-beled an impasse, a state of not being able to figure out what to do or why to do it, that emerges from the "frequent fallout of the dreams that are bred by capitalist culture"—in this Egyptian middle-class male context, an inability to find dignified work.[20] In these moments, they were far from dupes invested in meritocratic notions of mobility. They displayed fervent and radical critique of these narratives—with some even questioning their religious faith—as they latched on to long-circulating discursive frames critiquing structural inequalities. It may be tempting to position these forms of withdrawal and collective social consciousness as the grounds for radical action against the tendency of contemporary labor markets to produce a falling out of line of aspirations and chances.[21] But in a dejected postrevolutionary environment that saw a swift return of a repressive security apparatus, there were high levels of fatigue and fear. These men were in any case not exposed to activist groups or frames. Their parents expected them to get on with their lives rather than engaging in protest. Protest would also not negate the expectation to pursue a career. In the absence of alternatives, and an inability to adapt their aspirations, I show how men dispersed depressive feelings by practicing a form of hopeless labor. They reengaged with the same objects and discourses of atomized hope that generated their depression, not because they retained belief in their promises but because it was the only means by which they could sustain continuity. It is in this way, through affect, I argue, that continued compliance was secured.

HOPELESS LABOR

In November 2015 I returned to Cairo to find Mahmoud still unemployed. But he was back on the hunt for employment opportunities. During this month I accompanied him on multiple outings to Nasr City, an upper-middle-class neighborhood two hours from his home (see Chapter 1). On November 23 we traveled because the General Authority for Investment and Free Trade Zones had released two hundred government jobs. He wanted to submit his CV for one of seventy accountant positions. When we met, Mahmoud immediately suggested he had no chance: "There will be an army of people there!" He told a story about the state water company, which had advertised two accountant positions a year before: "Two million people applied for them!" The LE20 application fee made Mahmoud think it was a scam to make money. In the microbus we discussed jobs more generally. Mahmoud complained about call center jobs because of their nonfixed salaries and hours. He refused to take

another temporary job. Government jobs at least provided fixed shifts and job
security even though salaries were weak. This security was exemplified by his
uncle who had traveled to work in the Gulf for ten years but still managed
to keep his job. Interrupting this story, Mahmoud suddenly said defiantly:
"I think I'll do something illegal to get money, maybe smuggling, I won't
do anything that hurts anyone, but I want to do something illegal." After a
brief pause, he continued: "I need to travel, at least I'll be rich. I can't feed
myself here. I am twenty-six and take money from my aunt, it's humiliating."
As we reached the building it was nine a.m. Mahmoud looked up to a plane
overhead and said, "I want to grab on to one, can't they just take me away?"

We switched our attention to the application process. Mahmoud was told
to take a ticket and wait outside the gates along with around two hundred
others. He took ticket 850 for the day. The application was open for ten days,
suggesting many thousands would be applying. Other applicants had traveled
similarly long distances from inside and outside Cairo. Mahmoud helped one
who could not read work out what positions were available. However, he
had not come with a CV or photos, so Mahmoud informed him he would
have to return tomorrow. While we sat on the wall waiting for Mahmoud's
number to be called, we got talking to other applicants. Some were working
as self-employed lawyers or in small shops, and all longed for the stability that
would come with a government job. Everyone expressed, however, that they
had no chance of acceptance. Many made jokes about the jobs having already
been decided through wasta. The application process was administered to
project an image that the government was helping unemployed youth. One
man asked if I worked. "I am still a student," I replied. I told him I get a
scholarship to do research. He then quipped: "In your country they give you
money, in ours they slap us on the back of our necks like donkeys!"

In response to the air of hopelessness that followed these conversations,
each shrugged and said, "We have to do our duty" (lazim na'mil illy 'aliyyna).
After we had waited more than an hour, Mahmoud's block was called in.
He came out five minutes later, having submitted his CV. Immediately after
we left, Mahmoud said he was proud he had come, and that he felt hopeful,
before going on to note: "If I get this, Harry, I will convert to Christianity,
so pray to God to help me, it would be amazing." Mahmoud expressed happiness that he had come, as well as excitement at the prospect of acceptance,

even though he thought he had no chance. I asked him why people come despite thinking the process was already concluded by wasta. "They come because they hope," Mahmoud replied, "they need to hope. Egyptians are experts in hoping for unhopeful things, aspiring for things which can't be aspired after. If we didn't do that we would die." He then repeated that he would actually kill himself but remained scared of God's punishment.

Leaving the area, we walked past a Pepsico factory. Mahmoud wondered if he could submit his CV, but security swiftly told him to apply online. Mahmoud angrily cried out: "Why don't they just let us apply here?" We then walked through this upper-middle-class area. Mahmoud wanted to live here. He noted that they collect the rubbish unlike in his neighborhood. He pointed to a flat with a wide balcony and said, "I want to live there," before seeing what looked like a teenager driving a car. "That's crazy!" he exclaimed. We walked past an empty plot being used as a dumping ground. Mahmoud bellowed: "Why don't they build a building on that and give me a small flat!" As we walked, Mahmoud again began telling me about the project he had been working on for a while, a restaurant called Big Ben Burger (see Figure 3.1):

> It would serve the same burgers I made you for LE14.50, and then cheaper burgers for LE4; the more expensive is handmade and better-quality meat. It will be cheap, so sha'by people will come, but it will be different from what is there already. A mix of people will come. I will have hot dogs too. People now just think about making money quickly, but I won't think about that for the first year, I will make LE1, but I will build customer loyalty and after that I will start to make money. I have done very precise plans for it.

Mahmoud got out his comprehensive business plan, an Excel spreadsheet working through expected expenditures and revenues that he kept on his phone. We then went to get a microbus home. Mahmoud suggested going for a beer, but I had to meet someone else.

During November, I spent many days with Mahmoud like this. On six occasions we made the journey to Nasr City: twice to his uncle's publishing house, twice to employment fairs in upmarket hotels, the government recruitment day, and an overseas volunteering event for AIESEC (a global youth volunteering organization). Moving around the city, away from his house and

FIGURE 3.1. Mahmoud's British-inspired company logo. Source: Mahmoud. Printed with permission.

local area to upmarket spaces, rekindled his imagination of a better future. He was actively seeking out experiences, spaces, and topics that might fill him with what Kathleen Stewart labeled a "surge of vitality," a rush of hope and excitement.[22] But this surge was volatile. During these days Mahmoud's emotions oscillated wildly between extreme pleasure and frustrated despair. He flipped erratically—often in response to certain spaces and objects he encountered—between radically lamenting his plight, the state of Egypt, the past hurt he had been through with family, intimacy, and work, and the marketized pleasures of imagining a future start-up or job, international mobility, and consumptive desires. It felt like a highly condensed version of the oscillation experienced in previous years.

The nature of this oscillation was intensely cruel in Berlant's sense. Mahmoud was returning to the "objects of his desire," which materialized the promise for future mobility and gratification. But these objects sustained the ikti'ab that engulfed him as a result of their absence. One afternoon I asked Mahmoud why he was doing this, and he replied:

> Imagine you are in an isolated desert, with no food or water; you'll die for sure by the end of the day. And you find a map to a well, but it's too far and you will never make it. But you don't have anything else to do but wait for

death and think about that. Instead of waiting for death and hurting yourself
with negative thoughts, you decide to keep yourself busy, you decide to take
the trip to the well, although you know you will never make it, but the feeling of doing this trip and the feeling of drinking water from the well is much
better than the feeling of waiting for death. In both ways you are going to
die, but it's all about feelings. The hope of the hopeless, it's not about achieving anything, it's just how it makes you feel.

Mahmoud expressed acute awareness of the cruelty of these objects. He kept
applying for jobs and planning his start-up because the feeling this provided
was better than "waiting for death." He could not bring himself to adapt to
low-end jobs. Despite acute awareness of the fallacy of this emotional labor
by this point, he kept going back to by-now-shattered objects because of the
visceral bodily shifts affected within him. In the moment he was able to
defy doubt and enjoy feelings of renewed hope and excitement. At the General Authority, Mahmoud called on religious divination to enjoy the act of
submitting his CV. When planning his start-up, he tried "to imagine ways
money might come." His compulsion for the feeling enabled him to disavow
cynicism and keep coming back. These activities turned into a way of coping,
of carrying on and releasing the ikti'ab he now felt. Mahmoud described
hope as a drug, which allowed the "hopeless like him" to carry on. Echoing
Berlant, Mahmoud continued to hold on to this cruel form of hope because
the alternative of letting go of the "scenes of his desire" was too much to bear.

   Mahmoud's ability to describe the instrumental nature of these activities undermined his hope. At times, he struggled to expel doubt and locate
pleasure, and thus engaging in this labor made him feel worse as it reminded
him of his stagnation. Mahmoud declared he was not good at being hopeful.
Others were better at "lying to themselves." It is true that others expressed far
less reflexivity regarding the futility of their attempts to sustain hope. This
would have destroyed the pleasure of hope itself. However, the same drive to
perpetually recreate possibility acted upon many young men. Mostafa, briefly
introduced earlier as he entered the flat during my final days, revealed this
attachment as I asked him why he kept applying to foreign master's scholarships despite many rejections:

It's like when someone falls into a deep hole and is trying to reach the top to get out. Every time you get near the edge you fall again, so I think what is better for me, to keep trying or to stay in the hole? I decided to not stop trying because one time I might succeed to get out. If I stay still I will kill myself. . . . I don't mean kill myself literally, but when you live without a goal or target, or hope, you will live like a dead person. I cannot imagine myself to live like an animal, to eat, drink, and sleep, or like most sha'by people, that's all they do. So I search for a source every time to find inspiration again. A source means hope, anything that can make me dream and therefore renews the hope inside me.

Mostafa's decision to carry on investing time and money represented an attempt to sustain the bodily feeling of hope rather than a deep belief that he would make it. He had developed an attachment not to the meritocratic promise but to the feeling that it stimulated. To secure this feeling, Mostafa reengaged each time in self-blame and created a privatized space of hope by no longer telling friends or family who were increasingly responding with "depressing words" (kalam muhbat) about his chances. This feeling enabled Mostafa to continue engaging with the world and avoid "death." The prospect of adapting was world-shattering at this stage, too much to bear. He, alongside many others, therefore had no choice but to keep returning to the same objects that had produced so much pain.

CONCLUSION: HOPE AS LABOR

By tracing the everyday practices of young precariously employed men, this chapter has argued that, despite the production of a disconnect between people's aspirations and chances of realizing them, people continue to participate in Egypt's labor market by practicing a labor of hope. I have focused on the labor that goes into producing hope for future mobility beyond the wage relation. But it is integral to workers' ability to continue investing their labor power in low-paid, insecure, low-status work, and therefore integral to the ability of employers to extract value from that labor. It is constituted by a series of practices that bring to life a meritocratic moral economy that places responsibility for success or failure on the individual. As Chapter 1 demonstrated, this moral economy is extended and sold by a set of training, entrepreneurship, and recruitment industries. But it is also constructed and maintained by low-status Egyptian workers who valorize hope as a form of social creativity.

Men recount the stories of successful friends, lessons from self-help books and religious texts, and quotes from inspirational entrepreneurs and movies that apparently prove that success is possible for anyone who exercises enough perseverance and struggle. These narratives have a complex geography, involving Western entrepreneurs, self-help gurus, and Hollywood movies, which are circulated globally through pirated platforms and social media, alongside more localized revivalist Islamic belief in destiny and moral responsibility. Men also attempt to follow these examples by continuously working on their skills and character, applying and reapplying for jobs and scholarships, and planning their dream start-up. Practicing this labor of hope enables men to keep at bay the anxiety and frustration that emerge as a result of remaining stuck in cycles of precarious work and reintroduce a sense of momentum toward stability and success. But it also cruelly enables a labor market that actively produces precarity and inequality to continue operating, by sustaining a focus and moral judgment on individuals instead of structural issues such as corruption, nepotism, educational inequality, and employment supply.

Maintaining the labor of hope is immensely difficult. It requires continuous work to see oneself on the pathway toward success within a system that does not provide the necessary grounds to do so by encouraging high aspiration at the same time as pushing people into precarity. This work is often an individual endeavor because there exists a high degree of fear regarding potential judgment and discouragement; however, it also at important moments relies on the empathetic intervention of friends and family. But over time this emotional labor begins to fray. People go through periods of disaffection and withdrawal, sometimes lasting minutes, sometimes weeks, where they no longer trust in the meritocratic promise or the moral economy it introduces. But what the accounts of these young men demonstrate is how precarious labor markets can retain compliance despite encroaching disaffection.[23]

A loss of trust in meritocratic logics might lead people to a Bourdieusian-style adaptation to the social position and employment they are able to reach.[24] I discuss in the next chapter how this happens as men get older in the face of the pressure to settle down and prepare for marriage. However, at this stage of their mid- to late twenties, men find adapting too hard to bear. Refusing to adapt is an act of gendered defiance against a system that promises so much but delivers so little. This defiance stems from emotional compulsion, an inability to live with current reality, in a state of "death." This does leave open the possibility of more collective or resistant forms of hope-making emerging. Scholarship has demonstrated how the stubborn pursuit of aspiration can act as a stimulus for collective claims-making.[25] Yet in this postrevolutionary middle-class Egyptian context, and possibly in the case of many engaged in the everyday pursuit of capitalist livelihoods around the world, people recoil back into the atomized labor of meritocratic hope. Anger and ikti'ab is dispelled by returning again and again to the same practices and objects of hope that sustain exclusion. This produces continued participation in the labor market, not out of a disciplined belief in it but because of an inability to bear the loss of the feeling that the "scene of one's desires" provides. It is therefore an affective attachment that produces continued participation and compliance.[26] This form of compliance signifies starkly the affective power of meritocratic capitalism. But it also highlights its fragility. People navigating precarious labor markets are not duped. They know the system is often rigged against them. Without structural changes, the anger resulting from a disconnect between aspirations and realities will continue bubbling up to the surface again and again.

CHAPTER FOUR

THE LABOR OF LOVE

IN LATE 2015 I ASKED Mahmoud on Facebook how he holds on to hope for his future. To my surprise, considering what we had talked about throughout the previous eighteen months, he did not reply with thoughts of commodities or jobs: "I think about the things I love the most, love, family, and friendship." I asked what he meant exactly: "I think about how someday I might find love and establish a family, or my father will come and get in touch with me, or about friends and the good time we can have together." When I admitted my surprise that he did not reference his consumption desires or employment dreams, he shot back: "I'm talking about the hope of life, not the aim of shitty work." Thinking about desired commodities was a way for him to forget the "shitty" life he has now, but the real source of hope was love and friendship. At this point, he asked if I was sitting close to my partner: "If you are you should do this, buy some flowers and chocolate and sing this song to her"—he forwarded a link for a song by Francesco Yates called "Nobody Like You"—"and then shake her with all your passion." I asked Mahmoud why love is more important than being rich or having a good job, to which he replied: "Because if you have true love money would not be important. A good job is part of happiness, but love, god mate, for love you can leave everything else." I reminded Mahmoud he had previously told me money can bring love, and he replied: "No, money can bring girls not love, also a source of money would be good to maintain love after you find it, to look after your family's needs. But love is more important, you do everything in your life to make the people you love happy."

For precariously employed young Egyptian men, the pursuit of a successful career formed only one aspect of their efforts to sustain hope for a livable future over the years. Something that also consumed much of their attention—and sometimes took on greater importance—was the quest for intimacy, relationships, and marriage. As Mahmoud suggests, this can be summed up under the umbrella label of *hub*, love in Arabic, which in contemporary Egypt has come to encompass all kinds of intimate connection: "romantic and erotic attraction, sexual intimacy, obsessive longing, sympathy and liking, companionate marriage, parental and family affection, friendship, religious devotion, and a general sense of human compassion."[1] This chapter follows the attempts of lower-middle-class Egyptian men to locate, sustain, and stay away from love, and the feelings associated with it, across different registers in their twenties and early thirties.

In literature on the lives of marginalized youth—especially those of young men—the pursuit of love often gets left out of accounts in favor of a focus on the realm of employment. This is in part because it is assumed that men especially achieve fulfillment and self-worth more through their public status. However, in recent years there has been growing interest in the affective dimensions of gender, sexual, and marital relations.[2] This has responded to the dramatic impact of global cultural flows, changing gender relations, economic transformations, religious reformism, and state policies on reshaping intimate life around the world. While romantic love has long been an aspirational pursuit and is not simply a Western invention spread by globalization, the promises of modernity—whereby the ideal of a love-based nuclear family emerged as an essential element of modern subjectivity, and practices of consumption transformed courtship and marriage—have meant that romantic love has taken on a new more urgent quality.

Vitally, this literature has shown that affairs of the heart are as important as the pursuit of economic success as a powerful driving force in the lives of men and women around the world. But at the same time that romantic love has become a powerful yearning, it has also been rendered more uncertain and difficult to attain. As an aspirational category pursued in everyday life, love becomes embroiled with competing moral frameworks that throw it off course.[3] While love has long had a relationship with the economic, it is increasingly tied to economic power as a result of rising consumptive expectations around marriage and courtship. The pushing of vast populations into conditions of economic instability has made meeting those expectations more difficult. Love itself has then become a precarious aspirational pursuit. Literature focused on intimate life has shown that the economic marginality of young men has huge consequences beyond the economy, rendering them unable to realize aspirations and conform to hegemonic norms of masculinity in the realms of love and family.[4]

These global transformations have been felt in Egypt. During the twentieth century, processes of globalization and modernization placed the nuclear family based on companionate marriage and romantic love at the center of society and as a symbol of modernity, with the expectation that couples marry soon after economic stability is secured.[5] Samuli Schielke describes romantic love as one of the grand schemes—alongside middle-class respectability, religious commitment, and political ideology—which acts as an aspirational frame through which middle-class Egyptians orient their lives. It is an unrealized potential of "absolute passion and sacrifice," alongside a "practical guideline of life and marriage" confined to the volatile realms of the reflective, ethical, and experimental as it interacts with other moral and material concerns.[6] Even though marriage in Egypt has long involved significant financial commitments on the part of men, the onset of late-twentieth-century economic liberalization, which had the dual effects of inducing labor precarity and rising consumer expectations, has made this aspirational ideal harder to achieve in recent years.[7]

In this chapter I want to examine the impact of economic precarity on intimate relations in contemporary Egypt. Not much is known about the premarital relations of young men in Egypt and the wider Middle East, in part because these relations are kept under a high degree of secrecy to maintain norms of respectability.[8] By delving into these relations among educated un- and underemployed young Egyptian men, I want to develop insights on the pursuit of love amid conditions of economic precarity more generally. The questions driving the chapter are as follows: How do people pursue love and the feelings associated with it in the context of economic precarity? And how does the pursuit of love in turn interact with and shape the pursuit of a career?

In answering these questions, I argue that the pursuit of love represents a key form of emotional labor that enables people to forge livable lives amid conditions of precarity. So far, I have established an expanded definition of emotional labor that incorporates the practices that go into maintaining the emotional states of workers. In this chapter I explore how pursuing love and intimacy represents a vital but tumultuous part.[9] In the context of extended job insecurity and ramped-up marital expectations, many Egyptian men in their early to midtwenties view love as a symbol of social stagnation. Avoiding serious relationships and familial pressures to marry and focusing on work acts as a method to sustain hope for prospective mobility in their careers. However, while they are engaged in this difficult pursuit of jobs, love and intimacy act as fleeting feelings to pursue by discussing women they see on the street, at work, or on TV among friends, recollecting memories of past relations, and engaging in casual courting and sexual relations. These practices provide brief distraction and masculine validation in the context of demoralizing and undignified daily work experiences, but they can also induce disappointment and insecurity.

As men reach their later twenties, the pursuit of longer-term love—or marriage, which is not necessarily dependent on love—takes on heightened importance. This initially involves slowly preparing the marital house, alongside forging more solidified relationships and getting ready for engagement and marriage. These practices can provide a vital form of masculine validation, status, and hope for the future, which can make up for labor market struggles and add vital impetus to keep going. However, by becoming embroiled in sometimes competing moral frameworks of gendered respectability and Islamic piety, as well as a moral economy that leaves love and marriage dependent on money and status, this pursuit frequently produces immense disappointment and heartache and a questioning of self-worth that can be dramatically paralyzing and call into doubt the pursuit of a career. Overcoming these feelings and relocating the hope for future love requires intense work.

Overall, the chapter reveals the inextricable power of love within the economy and labor market. Even as it often exists at a structural disadvantage compared to employment considerations, it can act as a powerful legitimizing force for continued labor participation by providing a key foundation for self-validation, while also throwing it into question if it is lost. Sustaining the pursuit of love and a career simultaneously requires an extremely difficult and sometimes impossible balancing act—in other words, intense emotional labor—especially amid a set of structural economic and cultural forces that are rendering both extremely precarious in the contemporary world.

AVOIDING LOVE

On October 30, 2015, I met Saami at his family home in a small town to the south of Giza. Today was a big day. His younger brother, an undergraduate student of commerce at Cairo University, was getting engaged to a woman in his program. The family had splashed out on a large ceremony with relatives, friends, and neighbors to mark the occasion. When I arrived at the house, even though a celebratory atmosphere filled the air, I found Saami alone and distracted in the still-undecorated flat his parents had built for his marriage. This was a significant day for him too. Late in the evening he would be leaving the party prematurely to go to the airport to take a flight to Malaysia. This represented the culmination of years of attempts to leave Egypt. To finance his trip, Saami was using money his parents had saved for his marriage. Even though they had not blocked his decision, until today they were pleading with him to stay and get married. In fact, whenever anybody from his family found out about his travel, they inquired as to why he was not preparing for marriage. They believed he had a stable job and a high enough salary to do so. Saami, by this point twenty-eight years old, knew that the fact that he was not married was becoming a subject of gossip—something his parents had to negotiate. If he was not married by thirty, he told me, it could become difficult because women might be considered too young for him.

But Saami was adamant about his plan. It was the only way to ensure that his future—and that of forthcoming children—was not full of the struggles he had endured—relying on low-quality public education, utilities, and transport and unable to secure a prestigious job. A period abroad would enable him to find better or return to Egypt to start a business and raise his social level. He looked to his older brother, who worked as a low-paid government employee and struggled to afford daily expenses for his wife and child. He also knew that many Egyptian men—including in his town—often ended up regretting marrying before establishing themselves in a solid career.

Once married it is tough to leave one's family and travel abroad. Saami did not speak to these men about his ambitions, though, as they would just tell him, "Well, everyone is dissatisfied." Saami told his younger brother he was making a mistake getting engaged and would come to regret it. Particularly as a commerce graduate, he would struggle to find decent work and therefore needed to invest resources into developing his skills. Getting engaged would divert them into marriage. He worried that his brother would take any job following his final two years of university and army service to get married quickly—only coming to regret it later when he struggled to take care of a family. Saami's brother, however, was optimistic. According to Saami, he was also blinded by love—Saami admitted he might have made a different decision about his migration had he met a girl he had fallen in love with.

We were taken to the engagement party by Saami's cousin (see Figure 4.1). In the car he asked why he was traveling. Saami replied that he wanted to develop himself before he married. "You are doing it right," his cousin asserted before insisting that he would also not marry yet: "Girls just want so much, I am not ready for it yet. You need to build yourself first; what will you live on, love?" To prove his point, he introduced the story of a graduate who realized he needed to educate himself further after university and earned a diploma at the American University in Cairo. He subsequently got an internship in KPMG and managed to travel to Qatar and then on to Dallas, where he now lives. This proved that focusing on one's career for a few years after university rather than love was beneficial. However, during the ceremony Saami's brother was the center of attention. The act of engagement gave him status within the community, especially among older generations. At the party Saami faced further inquisitions about his decision not to marry. He had placed his reputation in the neighborhood in some jeopardy. At around ten p.m. he snuck off to take the metro to the airport—dramatically escaping the pressure on him. However, he left steadfast in the conviction he was doing the right thing. Traveling induced a powerful sense of hope for future social mobility, which in his eyes would enable him to properly take care of a family when financially ready.

A common assertion about Arab men—and un- and underemployed youth around the world—is that difficulties affording marriage produce intense frustration. I sat with young educated underemployed Egyptian men

FIGURE 4.1. The engagement party of Saami's cousin. Source: Author.

countless times as they lambasted the huge outlays involved. Estimates ranged from LE200,000 to LE600,000 (US$25,000 to US$75,000 in 2015)—which included getting a (preferably owned) furnished flat, buying the gold (shabka), paying the dowry (mahr), and funding a wedding. Affording this without parents contributing significantly is impossible. It is often the case that parents prepare the skeleton of a flat, but they are left skeletal with men unable to set money aside for furnishings (tashdiyyb). Men frequently reject further support, as they see it as their responsibility. With a monthly salary of LE2,000—which most participants were earning, if not less—it would take five years to save LE50,000—"You do the math," I was dejectedly told. Aside from money, many complained that they did not have suitable jobs to secure acceptance. The salary was certainly an issue in terms of affording a family—some estimated that this would require at least LE5,000 per month. But precarity was a bigger issue, as one man who worked as a customer service agent in an Orange store explained: "They could fire me at any time. I had to sign my resignation paper before I started. When I get old, they will tell me thank you very much, we don't need you anymore, they want young people so I will be out of a job. It's not a career." Aside from instability, the low-level service work in which men were stuck offered no promotion opportunities and did not reflect a recognized field like accounting or law. Negotiation on these conditions might have been possible among poorer groups, but not for middle-class men.

"In other countries marriage is a right; in Egypt it is a dream." To prove this, men recounted tragic stories of friends—or indeed themselves—who had been rejected or who halted the process because of the bride's family demands. One of these rejections took place on the back of the TFJ course. Tamer, a man who grew up in a notorious sha'by neighborhood, started courting Mona, a woman from a higher-class family. After several months Tamer approached Mona's father but was swiftly rejected. According to Mahmoud, Mona's father was right: "Fathers would rather keep girls safe than let them marry someone who might make her live in tough conditions. He will not marry Mona; he won't be able to prove that he is [at] a high enough level, or get the things they require, especially not [at] Vodafone." But these stories also led to outbursts against the link between love and money in Egypt. "There is no love without money here" was a response I heard numerous times to questions about marriage. Ibrahim explained how marriage had become embroiled in the issue of money:

> It is hard for youth because in the society we look for money as a sign of status. You will go to a father and he will first ask, where do you work? What is your salary? Where do you live? Do you have a flat? The second day you will come back and he will ask, do you have a car? I think you should have a car. You need modern furniture, and nice gold. It gets crazy. It is not just the father, girls now expect a lot because they see rich people on TV, or friends hang out together and boast about what they had bought for them.

Although marriage has long involved financial outlay for Egyptian men, Ibrahim speaks to rising consumer expectations—and the role of global media in fostering them—which is making it difficult to shoulder, especially amid male labor precarity. Ibrahim recognized this shift: "It used to be the case that if you love someone you can marry them, it did not matter if you have money. My father married at twenty-one; he got hired easily by the government. They did not focus on money more than the person; if you are a good person you will marry. Nowadays it is more complicated; you need to work to save for a long time. There is no difference between a good or bad person; if you have money you can marry."

In other contexts, scholars have found that men's inability to perform as breadwinner leads them to critique the notion of love depending on money and instead hold up an idealized form of romantic or "clean love."[10] In these cases, the relationship between love and material exchange has not changed, but rather the difficulty men have affording it. This is also happening among Egyptian men. Ibrahim understood that fathers want daughters to be looked after, and daughters want the best for themselves, but he asserted that there were lots of unmarried women as a result. It also went against religious teachings: "Religion teaches us we should not need money to marry. The Prophet told a poor man who wanted to marry that he should marry, it does not matter that he is poor. Your mind is important, whether you have respect and morals, not money." The relationship between love and money also became an object of satirical joke-making. This often was targeted at women, with images sent among men critiquing how women only looked for money and tallying up tasks men did in relation to marriage, alongside videos of U.S. social media experiments supposedly demonstrating how women only respond to male approaches in the street if they have nice cars (see Figure 4.2). Circulating this material provides men with an avenue to release the frustration that builds up as a result of the expense of marriage, experience a sense of solidarity with other men in the same boat, and feel a sense of moral superiority.

Amid immense difficulties in getting married and job precarity, many Egyptian men, like Saami, in their early to midtwenties actively avoid thinking about it and focus solely on their careers. Even those who can afford it actively resist pressure from parents who married in their early twenties. Marriage is constructed as a symbol of stagnation and immobility rather than mobility and respectability at this stage of their lives. Beginning the process can secure undesirable social (and spatial) positions by diverting resources and concentration away from career development. It might ensure that they remain in undesirable jobs and lead undignified lifestyles—living in bad areas and struggling to afford good-quality education and amenities.

FIGURE 4.2. A satirical joke about women's approach to money. Translation: "The biggest four things women like in men: (from top left) chic and takes care of himself; has a good sense of humor; has a beard; disciplined and responsible." Source: Facebook page "Memes and Comics Fresh, Expressive and True."

To prove this, men look to older brothers and friends who have married and now struggle to look after families or develop careers: "It is common in Egypt that people who are married get a salary and spend it in the first ten days of the month," one man told me. "After [that] they have to borrow money to survive, and at the beginning of the next month they pay it back again." Hearing about these struggles, as well as the increasing stories of divorce due to financial trouble, leads young middle-class Egyptian men to stave off beginning marital preparations.

As Saami's brother and Saami himself intimate, meeting someone can change this stance—thus signifying the power of romantic love. But this is rare and often ends in disappointment due to finances. Those who marry or attempt to are the object of much judgment. Tamer, for example, was labeled "lazy" for not working to locate a better job than his Vodafone role before trying to get engaged. Adel knew older call center colleagues who had married and had kids. He could not understand them, though. He knew they might be worried about getting too old as they waited endlessly for career improvement, but he was scared about getting to that stage: "What will they do when the call center says bye, they will not be able to work because they want young employees with energy." Others were more equivocal in their judgment, announcing that Egyptian men are stupid and have no patience: "They only think of marriage, and getting money to be married; they don't think of their career." They may start with ambitions of working in a high position, but over time their dreams get smaller and smaller. Eventually they start to focus on opening a house and accept where they are. This often means instrumentally locating any work and a flat in a lower-class area, as Gamal explained when talking about people in his neighborhood:

> Most of these people just think of tomorrow, they don't think of a long-term plan. They only plan for the next day, their dreams become very limited, they become stuck to the area, maybe they want to open a shop. They just care for money and marriage; they do simple jobs for LE2,000 and don't aim for more. People accept work not in their field; they give up and don't use their degree. I don't want to live life planning for the next day only.

The act of avoiding marital pressures and working on one's career becomes a way for young precariously employed men to distinguish themselves as socially mobile. For many this comes with moving away from their areas—either to Cairo as Eslam, Adel, and Mohamed did, or out of Egypt entirely like Saami. This keeps the future open and sustains hope for social mobility, with resources set aside for marriage often used to cover the cost of courses or travel. Avoiding love therefore becomes a practice that keeps hope alive. It enables men to concentrate time, energy, and resources on developing themselves and incites the feeling that they will succeed in comparison to others who have supposedly surrendered. This challenges existing understandings of youth waithood that assume that the inability to marry induces frustration alone.[11] Instead, delaying marriage in precarious contexts can be a strategy to sustain hope in the realm of career. Although this masculine career-centered labor of hope may appear targeted at the individual pursuit of a career alone, it is also justified by securing the future needs of spouses and children. It ensures that wives will not have to work and children will have a decent lifestyle: a private education, a car, a flat in a respectable area, or help with their marital costs. However, for Egyptian women this avoidance has the consequence of prolonging their stagnation as they are unable to start a home.[12] This conflict will become clearer as I describe how men navigate relationships with women who want to marry while men want to continue building careers.

THE FLEETING DISTRACTION OF LOVE

The huge difficulty in getting married, alongside men's attempts to delay amid extended labor precarity, is stretching out premarital periods in Egypt. This is leaving space for casual relations to emerge.[13] While avoiding serious relationships, young Egyptian men often turn attention to girls (banat) in daily life.[14] When I was living with Adel, Eslam, and Mohamed, girls were frequently a topic of conversation. As we hung out on the sofa after a shift, they jubilantly recollected encounters they had with muzas (pretty girls), shabhan (ghosts), makanas (machines), or lahma (meat) at work. They joked about the disappointment of not being paired with girls in team tasks and gloated about getting to go home with them on the company bus because they had done the early shift. We also had conversations about which cities in Egypt have the most beautiful women, with widespread associations of beauty with whiteness showing through. According to these men, women in Mansoura are well-known for their beauty because French soldiers had been based there. Adel described how a friend who had returned from working in Saudi Arabia for a holiday traveled to Mansoura to look at the girls, and he joked about doing the same. According to Mohamed, the girls in Mit Ghamr near his home are also beautiful because of the historic location of a British army base. They joked about marrying someone from either place. Beyond Egypt, Eslam asserted that Syrians were the most beautiful women in the Arab world. He said if you want to see Syrians you have to go to 6th of October—"There are muzas everywhere!" According to Adel, English women are beautiful but cold. German girls are the best, from what he had seen on television.

As men spend time together in homes or coffee shops, switching attention to beautiful women seen at work, on the street, on television, or on holidays enables them to express desires together, feel the excitement of fleeting attraction, and assert a sense of dominance over women who are portrayed sexually. In Egypt, there is a fraught politics around sexual harassment on the street, where men hurl remarks at or grope women.[15] Although I did not see this directly, it is undoubtedly common. Middle-class men often publicly declare avoiding talk about women's bodies because it is a haram practice associated with sha'by culture. My interlocutors got into moralistic discussions about Egyptian or Western women, declaring their disapproval of music videos in which women are too promiscuous or stories circulating on Facebook in which women commit suicide because they think they are not as beautiful as their friends. But the same men talk about women on other occasions. As others have noted, it is common for these seemingly contradictory moral frameworks of masculine respectability and potency and desire to coexist.[16] I would develop that argument to consider the role of emotional attachments in driving moral ambivalence. Men want to feel both sexual potency and desire and that they are respectable men. These moral frameworks also stimulate teasing in groups—with some men made fun of or ridiculed for being effeminate or shimal (literally "left," but a colloquial term for "gay").[17]

Despite men enjoying speaking about women, most insist they engage in "words only" (kilam bas) because it is haram to engage in sexual relations outside marriage. This moral assertion also becomes an object of teasing. On one occasion Adel recalled how he had gone to pray during a break at work and bumped into an attractive female employee. I asked if he said anything to her, but he shook his head: "I may talk about girls but I don't hang out with them, I am not like that." Mohamed began making fun, repeating, "He does, you know." This threatening of Adel's respectability immediately upset him. Adel told Mohamed to shut up, warning him he "fights quickly," before Eslam interjected to calm things down. Men express judgment of openness in the West. It is suggested that refraining from sexual relations until marriage as Egyptians do proves that your relationship is based on love rather than attraction. Others make jokes about how Egyptian men only marry to have sex. In the absence of actual interaction, men access intimacy and desire by talking about beautiful women, watching pornography in their homes, or listening to love songs and declaring the beauty of love on social media. I was sometimes asked questions about sex, especially whether porn was representative. There are always hushed suggestions and veiled jokes within groups that certain members do engage in intimate relations. But for the most part, men are reticent to share details in large groups. But over time I began to hear more.

When I spent time with one man—whom I will not name—the conversation frequently turned to his casual pursuit of intimacy. This man was experiencing extreme dissatisfaction in his career and, often in the middle of laments, suddenly switched to discussing women. One time as we hung out in his bedroom talking about a recent firing that had deeply affected him, he broke off to show me an old twenty-five-qirsh (LE0.25) banknote he kept in his wallet, alongside a small passport-sized picture of a woman. On the banknote was scribbled the phrase "if I have the chance to love someone, I would choose you," followed by the signature of Heba. Heba was a Nubian woman he had fallen in love with during university. His face lit up as he recollected her soft lips and the "sex" they had enjoyed—"I would give my life to have sex with her again."[18] He then played a song they had enjoyed together. Afterward his face became pained as he recollected how Heba's parents had rejected his proposal, not because of financial or status reasons—which he would have understood—but because they wanted Heba to marry a Nubian man. "They ruined my life," he declared; "if I had married her, I would be in a better position, I would be in a more powerful position to fight, more motivated to find a job to look after her, and even if I didn't have money or a good job, I would have love and passion so I would be happy." Heba was now married to someone less educated, and also had a baby. He had even dreamed about the name she gave her baby before she had given birth.

A version of this story is common among young Egyptian men, whereby they recollect ruined love from university or school, in most cases due to monetary reasons rather than race. But I want to focus on the act of remembrance itself. This was one of several occasions when this man recollected intimacy with Heba. As difficult feelings overwhelmed him, he took out the banknote or picture—and sometimes kissed it—before happily recollecting the intimacy they had shared. This nostalgic practice was not restricted to Heba. He frequently recollected, often in great detail, secretive sexual encounters and intimate connections he enjoyed with women at university, training scholarships, or work in the past. These encounters involved eluding his family by arranging for women to come to his house when they were at work. To evade a suspicious doorman, women entered his building alone in a niqab and he followed fifteen minutes later. He boasted how one woman let him take photos, which he kept on his phone in a password-encrypted folder and flicked through when bored at home. Recollecting these encounters provided this man with a momentary reminder of excitement and validation, and an opportunity to assert sexual and masculine virility, especially amid a set of career circumstances that stripped him of self-worth. They led to boasts about his above-average penis size, manly hands, favorite types of women, sexual positions and acts, and ability to please. Other men were often made fun of in comparison for their lack of virility—I was asked if I was a virgin due to my reticence to talk about my own experiences or desires.[19]

These public performances may suggest a superficial or abusive sexual engagement. But as Caroline Osella and Filippo Osella argued in relation to flirting in India, men can embody both "assertive aggression" and "supplicant tenderness" when interacting with women.[20] I was surprised seeing WhatsApp exchanges with women talked about in sexual terms, which revealed a desperation for intimate connection through messages such as "I need to marry you" and "I just want to hold you tight." Sexual boasts thus clothed a frailty and attachment to intimacy and the validation that accompanies it—a frailty often hidden in groups. But as we spent time together, this man's recollections produced expressions of heartache regarding the ruination and absence of intimacy. He recalled lost chances—like his failure to act on flirtations because a girl had a car—which revealed his vulnerability in terms of social status and decried how difficult it was to meet women. To overcome this frustration, we discussed endless strategies for how he might meet women. Sex, he declared, could provide a good distraction from career struggles. He fantastically asked me where he might find an "orgy," and entered imaginations of being Leonardo DiCaprio in *The Wolf of Wall Street*, or a porn star: "I could get paid for doing something I love, I'm good at it, all the girls said I make them feel good." One time he recalled a woman in college who had a reputation for being "dirty," briefly floating the idea of phoning the guy who had told him about her before deciding it would be weird. We also discussed how to approach women in the street without it being interpreted as harassment, and he optimistically tried a dating app for Muslims but deleted it after he did not get any interest.

This man's attempts to pursue intimate relations constantly produced oscillation between excitement and validation, and disappointment and self-doubt. Nowhere was this more on show than a WhatsApp exchange with a woman he met at work. They began communicating after he bought printers from her, but he wanted to make it a personal relationship. He began by saying he was in Sharm el-Sheikh with me on holiday, but after sending the message, he declared she was out of his league. A few minutes later he found renewed hope as she had liked an old Facebook post, which meant she must have scrolled through his profile. He tried to take a selfie to send her by the pool but immediately said, "I look ugly," and deleted it. He reiterated that she was out of his league, using the fact that she had a car as proof. Moments later, though, he smiled while declaring that we should come back to Sharm on a double date. He smiled every time his phone went off and attempted to flirt. But he frequently expressed insecurity, telling me she only responded so he would buy more stuff. That evening he asked me if he should ask her out: "I'm never what they expect I am, they don't know my background." He said one woman blocked him when she found out. The next day he asked me again. "Life is too short!" he declared, before doubting himself by asserting that she probably thought he was rich. He finally texted her, asking, "How are you today?" before checking her Facebook. She had posted a video of a beautiful island. He thought it might be a reference to him being in Sharm. But the song in the video was about a past lover. This might have been a sign that it was about a previous boyfriend.

Later that day he declared she had friendzoned him after telling him, "You need to get married soon!" when he told her his age. He quickly got over this thought and mustered up the courage to ask for her number in a personal capacity. She replied that she just wanted to sleep, which felt like rejection. But two minutes later there was another text saying, "You have it, take it as a personal number as well." As we went out to Sharm's shopping district, he showed me texts where she had sent a flowers emoji. He took this as a good sign and decided to buy her a gift. We spent that evening searching (see Figure 4.3). He originally wanted to buy an expensive lamp before seeing a dream catcher, a handmade willow hoop, which he loved because of its "hidden meaning." I said it might be intense, so he settled on incense. On the bus back to the hotel, he boldly sent a message saying, "Each of your profile pictures looks better than the last, you are making it so hard for me." She replied sending a blushing emoji. We discussed how he might ask her out: "Maybe I can ask if she is going out with friends, and if not if she is free for coffee. I will take her to a fancy place." Back in Cairo, he finally texted: "What will you do on holiday?" to which she replied, "Not sure, I'll sleep." He then asked if she wanted to get coffee by referencing a famous Egyptian story of a man harassing a woman by asking her for coffee repeatedly. She rejected him, however, replying that she was quite busy. When I next saw the man, he looked dejected as he declared: "She is right, she sees I'm a failure." A couple of days later, she texted to ask if he needed more printers. He decided to work with her and see what prices she had but not try to ask her out again.

Despite this painful rejection, during certain periods of my fieldwork this man had casual relations with women in Egypt and abroad. He told me about a Mexican woman he met on Facebook through a film fan page by asking her if they really use guns in Mexico like the movies show, to which she replied: "So are you all terrorists in Egypt?" After discovering she was a woman, he started flirting and they began video calling. He described how she had done "dirty things," but often they just talked—"We make each other happy," he said; "if she was in Egypt, we would have the best sex." He told me later this woman had a child and her husband had left her, but he did not know why. She and her mother had pleaded with him to come to Mexico, but he said no because he would not know how to look after himself. After a while their video calling slowed down. He also sometimes met me gleefully declaring how that day he had been with a woman. This produced more detailed descriptions of the "sex" they had enjoyed. On some occasions, his efforts were stifled by the sudden emergence of a family member at his house. These interactions often fizzled out because they got bored of each other, or because the woman wanted him to "make it official" by going to her father, which he could not do because of his employment situation.

By describing these intimate pursuits in detail, I suggest that they play an important role in helping young Egyptian men cope amid a difficult and lonely career pursuit. Talking about beautiful women among friends after

FIGURE 4.3. Choosing presents for a love interest. Source: Author.

work, recollecting past experiences of intimacy and imagining current desires, receiving promising WhatsApp messages, having a video call, and engaging in casual courting all provide a rush of masculine validation and excitement. Although I am not arguing that these activities are stimulated by employment struggles, they do provide—as men describe themselves—important distraction and brief acceptance and power amid a career pursuit that constantly produces feelings of rejection, humiliation, and self-questioning. They enable men to temporarily feel better about themselves and have something exciting to focus on. In these circumstances, these practices constitute an emotional labor that is crucial for men to keep going in their elongated chase for career success. However, this is highly unstable in an Egyptian context, where religious codes render sexual intimacy taboo and casual courting challenging, class inequalities mediate the possibilities of attraction, and locating romantic attraction becomes an inevitable roller coaster. But these instabilities may sustain the intoxicating feeling that accompanies intimacy and ensure that men exert so much energy into securing it. In any case, thinking about and engaging in casual intimacy—similarly to the practices described in Chapter 2—was described as a "drug of life" by men. It is a temporary fix. It does not solve the longer-term need to build career success and locate more permanent intimacy. This requires another labor of love geared toward the future.

BUILDING LOVE AND MARRIAGE

When I lived with Adel, Eslam, and Mohamed in 2014–2016, marriage was not on their minds. Like many men in their midtwenties, where they could they saved money to spend on materials that might help their careers. This provided vital hope for mobility, and directing money toward marriage would have threatened that. But when I returned for visits in 2018 and 2019, much had changed. They were no longer together. Mohamed had moved to Saudi Arabia. Adel and Eslam had not seen him since but heard he was engaged. Adel finally quit the call center and returned to Zagazig. Between 2016 and 2019 he had worked in three jobs: as an accountant in Zagazig, a salesperson in an insurance company in Cairo, and now as an accountant in the industrial town of 10th of Ramadan on a salary of LE3,000 (US$185 in 2019) per month. Eslam was the only one left in Cairo. He managed to at least find a job with set shifts as a salesperson in an Orange mobile shop, earning LE2,500. When

FIGURE 4.4. The existing bedroom in Eslam's marital flat. Source: Author.

we met, he and Adel satirically joked about how little money they had left at the end of every month. As a result of inflation and currency devaluation over the years, their salary increases meant little.[21] Eslam had, however, made progress in another realm of life. With parental help he bought a flat in Faisal on the ninth floor of an apartment block, which he lived in himself. The flat was under an "old rent law" contract—a law introduced by Nasser to enforce a cap on rents and ensure that tenants could keep a property under a fixed price, despite inflation, for two generations or fifty-nine years. It was in poor shape, though, with no working kitchen, no running water in the bathroom, and little electricity (see Figures 4.4 and 4.5).

Over many months Eslam managed with parental help to fix the electricity and fit a kitchen and new bathroom. There was still a long way to go, though, and this, coupled with reliance on his parents to get this far, meant he continued to avoid thinking about engagement. However, this signified a shift in emphasis of Eslam's attention outside work. Rather than investing time and money into training courses as before, he was steadily building his future in the realm of family. Eslam was not alone. At the beginning of the

FIGURE 4.5. The future reception room. Source: Author.

chapter, I argued that men avoid directing resources and time into marriage and instead focus solely on careers. But as they reach their later twenties, more and more begin getting started with the most arduous part of "opening a house" (yiftah bayt). For those in rural areas, this means building on top of their parents' house, whereas those in Cairo—or those who wish to live in Cairo or a more upmarket area—must buy. For men in low-paid work, this relies on unconventional solutions such as obtaining a flat through old rent laws or getting help from parents or older brothers. The alternative is paying a lump-sum deposit and monthly installments to a housing company or government loan scheme. Deposits are sometimes afforded by participating in a gamaʿiyya, a community savings scheme in which people in a family, friendship group, or neighborhood commit to paying a specific amount every month for a set period and each receives the total sum of contributions at monthly intervals.[22] Once the flat is secured, it requires decorating and furnishing. This process is long and notoriously difficult, with complaints about unexpected costs common, especially with pressure to conform to modern tastes.

For many, switching resources to a flat constitutes a difficult and painful decision that involves sacrificing the urgent chase of a better job or living in better areas. However, it can also secure status. Sayed and Ramy grew up in the lower-class to lower-middle-class neighborhood of Helwan. After graduating, Sayed struggled in extremely low-paid tour guide work, in the hope of building experience and establishing his own agency. Ramy, on the other hand, did not have a set career plan and took a call center job for Emirati mobile phone clients, earning four times the salary. Ramy told me there are two types of people in Egypt: those who care about immediate money and those who care about building a future. Ramy was someone who cared about money and liked to spend it. Every time we met he had a new commodity to show off: a branded item of clothing, a watch, a tablet, or videos from an upmarket concert he attended. Sayed was the second type of person. He did not have new commodities to show off and teased Ramy for being deep ('amiq) in his tastes. But Sayed was building a career while also preparing another aspect of his future by redecorating the flat his parents had lived in after they moved into the flat where his grandparents had lived. Every time we met, mirroring Ramy's consumption updates, Sayed relayed news of what he had managed to fix: replacing a water pipe, redoing old tiles with stylish new ones, fixing the electricity. This was accompanied by frequent complaints about the expense and speed of progress, but also expressions of pride about how far he had gotten. While not thinking about engagement because of the need for a better job and salary, at least he was making progress with the flat.

When middle-class Egyptian men are in their early to midtwenties, those who redirect resources toward marriage are judged for the career stagnation this may cause. But over time this moral economy starts to shift. In Ramy's eyes, Sayed seemed to have a plan for career *and* marriage. Despite his consumptive prowess, he expressed insecurity about his relative future—his current job would not provide a career, and he was not making progress with a flat. However, for some men, preparing for marriage starts to take precedence over career mobility, and those who keep trying to chase a career at the expense of marriage face judgment. This is illustrated by a reunion between Mahmoud and an old university friend in 2016. Omar was six years Mahmoud's senior because he had attended a technical institute before university. He was working night shifts as a cashier in a pharmacy, earning LE1,400

(US$175 in 2015) per month, while also providing a minibus service for school children for an extra LE300. With this tiring schedule, Omar was trying desperately to save money for marriage. He managed LE500 a month, which added up to LE10,000. His brother, who worked for an Iraqi oil company, helped him out by buying and decorating a flat, with Omar now slowly paying him back. Omar said he had been close to marriage recently but broke it off because of "emotional issues." Mahmoud, on the other hand, was still avoiding marriage. He remained desperate to alter his trajectory by searching for opportunities in prestigious companies or abroad.

On the day of the meeting, Mahmoud attended an event for an AIESAC scholarship to work abroad, only to be told his English was not good enough. When Mahmoud told Omar, he responded: "See! After all those courses it is still not enough!" This proved to Omar that he had chosen the right path. In his mind Mahmoud was stagnant. He lambasted him for not settling in a job and working toward marriage. He suggested that Mahmoud take an accountant job close to his home and begin saving, referencing friends who had done the same and were now married—even managing to send children to private schools by entering a gama'iyya. Omar asserted value out of his progression toward respectable manhood through marriage. He also suggested that he did not need a relationship based on love—what was important was the act of marriage and opening a home.[23] Ramy positioned himself as a mukafih (struggler) who was doing what was upon him to secure God's reward by working hard and being a good Muslim. Mahmoud, conversely, was remaining a "crazy dreamer," refusing to settle, build his future, and make his transition into manhood. But Mahmoud in turn judged Omar. He had become a "cow in a farm." Afterward he told me how Omar used to talk endlessly about ambitious dreams of travel. He had also been saying for one and a half years he would become the pharmacy's accountant and complained frequently about his manager. Mahmoud viewed Omar's job, tiring schedule, failed marriage—which he thought was due to financial issues—and newfound "closed-minded" sha'by behaviors as proof that *he* was making the right choice. On the microbus home, Mahmoud saw a billboard with an advertisement for a gated compound: "I need that one day," he said. When I attempted to say he did not, he replied:

Yes I do, Harry; if I bring up children they need to be surrounded by good people and be sent to good schools. If I accepted what Omar accepted they would continue to exist in the same shitty situation as me and I would regret I had them, and then their children would be the same, it is a cycle. I refuse to be part of that and give up like Omar. I would rather die trying than give up now and accept a shit future. The private schools Omar talked about are shit, they are just there because there is not enough space in public schools now, they are not international. I will never give up though. He works two jobs for LE1,700, he can't afford anything with that.

Mahmoud still held on to a labor of hope that rested on career mobility. But Omar demonstrates how for lower-middle-class men, as they get older and continue being unable to locate the jobs they crave, the way in which they establish value and hope for the future can shift from career progression toward the realm of love and family. Even Mahmoud admitted he might think differently in a few years—because he did not want to "die alone." Working toward marriage—which does not necessarily require feelings of love—by getting a flat and slowly decorating comes to constitute a form of masculinized emotional labor that compensates for career stagnation and provides a foundation for respectable masculinity. This labor again places the spotlight on the individual to cope and adjust within a system which continues to make both the achievement of a successful career and marriage difficult to reach. Indeed, there was no guarantee that Omar, Sayed, or Eslam would even reach marriage as they remained in low-paid jobs. But what is important is the striking power of love and family in enabling men to cope with labor precarity as they get older. This power becomes even more significant once love has been located.

FINDING LOVE

Amid Ibrahim's drawn-out attempts to become a successful entrepreneur, in early 2015 he announced that he had begun dating Noura, a cousin on his mother's side. Every time we met, he no longer talked of entrepreneurship, rather gleefully describing how he and Noura spoke on the phone for hours every day about her university studies, entrepreneurship ideas for her father's antique business, and plans for outings and for the future—including marriage. Through those conversations Ibrahim discovered they were a perfect match: "Whenever I point out that I like something, it turns out she loves it too!" On one occasion he relayed a love story Noura had sent to him about a man who fell in love with a younger woman. Their union was not accepted by their families, but they carried on anyway. The woman then had an accident that left her blind and told the man: "I'm not worthy; you deserve more than a blind girl." The man retorted: "No, I love you and will stay with you." Ibrahim, who was twenty-five, and Noura, who was eighteen, had a similar story. She entered university but left for a year because of problems with her legs. She was sick like the woman in the story, and Ibrahim stayed with her. They frequently met in secret at her family home since her father was in Italy working. Afterward they walked in the city window-shopping and imaginatively decorating their future flat. Ibrahim also arranged outings to Cairo: to the pyramids, Islamic Cairo, or the markets of Attaba. These outings provided him with an opportunity to showcase his status as a generous, caring partner by constantly checking on Noura, buying her things, and paying for the group. On outings without Noura, Ibrahim often turned attention to buying her and her younger brother presents.

In their mid- to late twenties, many men enter serious relationships. In rural settings it remains the norm to meet women through extended family. In Cairo there are opportunities for couples to meet in different settings. Training courses like TFJ have become sites of couple creation—providing a rare legitimate space for men and women from a similar social status to converse and flirt. During my time in TFJ, two couples formed out of interactions within the classroom and outings afterward. Relationships in the early stages provide much joy and validation for men and can become a preferred focus of attention over jobs—even as they are kept discreet. They enable men to experience desire and excitement and assert themselves as caring, generous, attractive, or romantic by arranging dates, buying presents, and sometimes engaging in secretive intimate acts. Men often describe relationships as vital in enabling them to endure difficult career pursuits, as Ibrahim articulated when talking about Noura: "She gives me power. If we are together, we will tackle everything together; I want to do everything I can to look after her." Relationships can also provide the allure of social mobility themselves, by dating European women as two participants did.[24] Gamal, for example, met

Elena, an Italian woman working in Cairo, after being encouraged to approach foreigners on the street as part of an English-language course. He
was adamant that dating Elena was not about the prospect of migration but
admitted he was attracted by the chance to practice English and experience a
cosmopolitan life in Cairo.

Maintaining the intoxicating validation and satisfaction provided by romantic love requires much effort on the part of men and women. Egyptian
men spend much time anxiously discussing how to satisfy their girlfriends'
desires: which upscale café to choose for a date, which presents to buy, or
whether it is rude to take women on a microbus. Sex provides an important
focus of attention for men in long-term relationships. Although relationships
can involve intimacy—sometimes under cover of urfi marriages—many do
not.[25] This does not stop men from talking with partners about sex or discussing with friends how to improve sexual performance in preparation for
marriage. To my surprise, for one man this preparation involved proclaimed
use of a prostitute. Introducing this as we hung out in an ahwa, he said he did
it to gain experience that would help him satisfy his current girlfriend when
he eventually marries her—while maintaining her respectability. He met the
woman at the disused house his grandparents used to live in and boasted how
she told him he had satisfied her, despite being shy at first. His friend was
adamant this man was lying and actually talking about having "sex" with his
girlfriend. But he insisted he would never do that, and if he did his relationship would be ruined. He pleaded with me to believe him.

It is difficult to know what version of this story is true. But it reflects how
Egyptian men are afforded more openness regarding sexual activities.[26] It also
demonstrates the delicate balancing act—especially amid extended premarital periods—required in early relationships. Men and women must find ways
to satisfy the desires of romantic love while maintaining gendered respectability and Islamic piety. As a result, the validation and satisfaction provided
is rendered fragile. Men often complained about the way their girlfriends
dressed and communicated—with jealousies emerging if they wore tight
clothing or did not say they were going out with friends. In turn, women
got annoyed when men interacted with other women, both online and in the
street. Initially Ibrahim insisted he and Noura would never fight. But one
day he met me in Cairo during Ramadan looking devastated. Two nights

previously they had been hanging out during the fasting period when he tried to kiss her. This was not the first time. Ibrahim had kissed Noura before: "I can't help it," he told me, "she is so attractive." But this time Noura got angry and asked him to leave—refusing to talk for the rest of the day. When they finally spoke she said they had been doing haram things for too long: "You have forgotten God, we are like animals." While forgiving him eventually, Noura insisted Ibrahim seek forgiveness from God. Ibrahim was shaken by this event. He feared that Noura would think he did not love her because he used her body and disrespected her. "I have forgotten God," he said; "I have not been praying lately and bad things happened. This is a sign; God took her away because I did haram things, I need to return to God." Ibrahim cried a lot and prayed for forgiveness.

This reveals the fragility of the fulfillment that comes with young romantic love as it wrestles with moral norms. Overcoming this requires intense emotional work for both men and women. It also reveals the attachment that men develop to love amid job struggles. Despite conflict, men found it difficult to end relationships—with one constantly getting back in touch with his girlfriend because he felt lonely. This attachment was even more acute in Gamal's case. Several times Elena declared her desire to return to Italy, which she finally did in early 2015 after announcing she still had feelings for her ex-boyfriend and secured a better job. Gamal was devastated. Months later Elena returned and suggested getting back together. Gamal insisted he would not, despite being desperate for a girlfriend, saying to me: "She left when I needed her most, when I was losing my job. I thought we would build a life together; I trusted her. My mistake was to depend on someone; you cannot do that, you need to depend on yourself to achieve what you want." But when Elena arrived, Gamal met her and confessed his desire to get back together. He told me he hoped he was not doing it for revenge: "I mean that I get back with her to get to Italy, not for love." However, despite being forward at first, in their second meeting Elena left after ten minutes and kept asking if he had money: "She would be more interested if I was rich," Gamal declared. After he thought it was over, two days later they met again and kissed. Gamal expressed confusion but insisted he could separate his career ambitions from his emotions for her. He was considering getting back together, but I warned Gamal she might hurt him again. This reveals the emotional attachment men can develop to love, in this case made more acute by Elena's association with (globalized) social mobility. However, it also starts to reveal how money and class threaten the labor of love, something that only becomes more acute as men work toward marriage.

TURNING LOVE INTO MARRIAGE

The passionate love that defines the early stages of a relationship comes face-to-face with formidable forces during marriage preparations. As Samuli Schielke described, in marital arrangements "issues of class, reputation, descent, income, alliances, and enmities between families, furniture, housing, religiosity and political views matter."[27] These issues can become more important than and even usurp the requirement for love as they are seen as a more stable basis for longevity. They emerge immediately when choosing a wife, which often takes place in a formalized way through mothers suggesting suitors. Middle-class men expressed the need to find a woman who is not from a higher class because they face the prospect of rejection, while also not lower-class because they might lack "ambition" and be "closed-minded."[28] While most men want women to be ambitious rather than waiting for marriage, they want women to stop working—or at least work part time—after marriage.[29] Once a couple decide they are right for each other, they must take the arduous road to marriage, which is where pursuing a successful career dramatically reacquires significance. Ibrahim and Noura's plan to marry once Noura finished her studies depended on Ibrahim traveling to the Emirates to take a job in a building firm his uncle had secured for him. This represented a new plan after the disappointment of returning from Cairo, having failed to find start-up funding. Although he had resisted the labeling, familial wasta—and money from his parents for architecture courses—had helped. Despite initially being hesitant to leave behind his entrepreneurial dream, he told himself he could save money abroad and start a project later, while also emphasizing how crucial traveling was for him marrying Noura. This again highlights how the pursuit of love comes to compensate for as well as drive hope in one's career pursuit. Ibrahim had been obsessed with his entrepreneurial dreams when he was younger, but his career now played a more facilitative role.

During this period Ibrahim declared he was in stage two of a three-stage plan for marriage. Stage one involved "finding a connection," stage two "understanding you cannot live without her," and stage three "making her your wife." He estimated he needed LE90,000 to LE100,000 (US$11,250 to US$12,500) to get to stage three, which did not include a fully furnished flat because they would live in Dubai. Noura had also shown flexibility in her desires. They had agreed to forgo "unnecessary" things, such as the nish, a large box of crockery and kitchen utensils, or a big party. This proved to Ibrahim that Noura was open-minded.[30] But agreements between couples can also be derailed when families get involved. Although their mothers knew and approved, Ibrahim and Noura did not tell their fathers about their romance. When Ibrahim's father found out, he said he would not support the marriage. The problem was Noura's father, who drank wine and displayed his wealth in a "vulgar" way. Ibrahim's father, a teacher in an Islamic school, could not get along with him. Ibrahim got annoyed, defiantly insisting they would marry with or without his father's approval. He did not tell Noura, to prevent worry, but spent a few days venting frustration through angry Facebook posts railing against people who enter the lives of others. He overcame this anger through similar techniques to his career pursuit, posting on Facebook "never lose hope, new day, new opportunities #hope #believe" and rereading a slide show he had made a few years previously and posted on slideshare. net setting out nine ways people can find hope: "action; love (seeking advice from others); education; gratitude; giving to others; belief; passion; letting go of fear, sadness, and anxiety; and surrounding yourself with optimism." "Nobody will take me away from the path I want," he declared to me; "I will kidnap her. Things will be different when I travel; I will save money and be independent."

Ibrahim was, however, worried about Noura's father as well: not regarding his morality but his wealth. He thought her father might perceive him as lower-class or expect a lot in terms of the wedding and lifestyle he wanted for Noura. He also heard that her father was not supportive of marrying within the family, as it might cause conflict. Ibrahim's fears were reinforced when he heard that his cousin's family had rejected a potential suitor despite him being a civil engineer because they judged his family to be of a lower class. His cousin was left devastated, while Ibrahim complained: "Should it work like that? If you love each other, you should not be prevented from marrying because of money." Noura insisted that she and Ibrahim would be able to convince her father. He just needed to focus on traveling and saving money, and his cousin's suitor needed to do the same. Vital here is that Ibrahim—alongside Noura—was investing much emotional labor into sustaining a sense of hope for the future before him, even relying on the same inspirational quotes described in Chapter 3. But this emotional labor was directed toward overcoming the hurdles of class and money in the realm of love rather than career. Working hard in his career was a vital component, and it was his pursuit of love-marriage that provided a powerful incentive for Ibrahim to do so.

However, two months before Ibrahim was due to travel to Dubai in early 2016, the position his uncle had secured for him fell through. He was left devastated. When I next saw him in September, he felt like a different person from the one I had known. Although he had previously exuded positivity and optimism, as we stood on the roof of his still-unfinished flat, he lit up a cigarette—which he had previously chastised as a symbol of surrender—and declared that his friends had been right, there was no hope. After previously rejecting them as excuses, he railed against the wasta and corruption that turned powerful, creative youth like him into "slaves who walk in a whirlpool [mashiyyn fi duwama]," and relayed stories that proved it:

> I heard a story about a boy who loved a girl. He was a graduate of commerce. He had very good grades. His friend got a pass. Both applied to Bank of Egypt. His friend had wasta and got accepted even though he was worse. He then stole the girl [that the boy] loved. The boy is now working as a garage keeper. There is no hope . . . the only way to achieve a good life is to have wasta or leave Egypt.

This event had destroyed the hope for migration and marriage that provided Ibrahim with impetus to keep going. He even said he and Noura did not talk like before. Yet again, Ibrahim had to reconstruct hope in the face of economic instability. He did so by revisiting entrepreneurship narratives, doing an advice session for university students about how to build a start-up, that helped renew his own hope by reminding him of the "good days when [he] was active and enthusiastic about things." Thus, cruelly, Ibrahim's pursuit of affective solace turned him into a reproducer of meritocratic narratives for others.[31]

When I next saw Ibrahim in June 2018, he was engaged to Noura. His father had stepped in to buy the shabka and assist in preparation of his flat. Noura's father also helped by suggesting that Ibrahim run his small clothing business. This did not reflect Ibrahim's dreams of entrepreneurship and upward mobility, which induced pain, but his values and hopes began to shift to reflect this new reality. Ibrahim had changed in the interim. He dressed differently, wearing a galabiyya more, and talked about his new hobby of collecting antiques, which his grandfather had done. Ibrahim emphasized how difficult life would have been had he traveled, preventing him from being a good father and husband, which required being present. He also talked up the benefits of village life—how clean the air was, how beautiful the nature, and how he was able to do things outside work. Sacrificing these things was not worth the pursuit of money alone. Ibrahim thus dramatically reconstructed the direction of his hope again. It rested on the pursuit of respectability through love, family, and tradition and the sacrifice of the cosmopolitan mobility he once desired. This could be interpreted as an adaptation to the surroundings he found himself in, an adaptation made easier by marriage. But this labor of love relied on significant help and flexibility from his and his fiancée's family—which is becoming more common in contemporary Egypt.

While Ibrahim shifted his future orientation toward marriage and family, other men continued to make a different decision amid economic precarity. Mahmoud met Amina in the TFJ course. After they had dated a while, Amina began putting pressure on him to proceed with marriage. Like Omar suggested, she wanted him to accept a low-end job and start saving. She stressed that her lower-class parents' demands were not high—her father was a bus driver. Many Egyptians tolerate tough conditions, she said repeatedly. She even began looking for jobs for him—her sister's husband worked in a call center and could put in a recommendation. But Mahmoud refused. He could not let go of his dreams. Furthermore, he insisted this job would prevent him from being able to afford marital costs, and even if he somehow managed to do so, he refused to put a wife and children in this environment. Mahmoud therefore looked to migration as the solution. Having worked in Dubai briefly before, he knew he could earn money. He therefore decided that travel would enable him to raise his standard of living, and he eventually convinced Amina to wait for him to secure savings and the prospect of a better lifestyle for them. In the context of no parental help, Mahmoud's labor of love stimulated his chase of a career across international borders. In the next and final chapter, I trace how migration impacts such labors of hope exercised by young Egyptian men.

CONCLUSION: LOVE AS LABOR

In this chapter I have demonstrated how influential love is on the labors that enable young Egyptian men to cope with economic instability. But what does it mean to say pursuing love is a form of (emotional) labor? In the introduction I fleshed out a broader concept of labor, encompassing practices—reaching across "productive" and "reproductive" realms—that sustain life and "make it worth living." But this life-sustaining activity becomes labor only if abducted into "the aim of the expansion of money value."[32] Love often gets written out of accounts of the livelihood strategies of un- and underemployed youth, especially men, which are geared toward economic activity. However, I have shown how practices in the realm of love can facilitate, drive, legitimize, and call into question economic participation.

This may take place through the active avoidance of longer-term love, which acts as a way of distinguishing oneself as socially mobile among middle-class Egyptian men. This has the consequence of prolonging women's waithood, especially as they are more dependent on marriage, while also opening new—albeit circumscribed—possibilities for middle-class women to chase careers in Egypt. But chasing short-term feelings of intimacy and desire by discussing women among friends, recollecting memories of past relations, and engaging in secretive sexual activities can provide important forms of distraction, excitement, and validation amid the solitary and often chastening pursuit of a career for young men. This chase—although highly unstable because of religious codes rendering premarital intimacy taboo and class inequalities mediating the possibility of attraction—becomes an important emotional labor enabling men to overcome difficult emotions that emerge and feel good about themselves on a daily basis.

As men get older, the pursuit of longer-term love and marriage can overtake career mobility as a source of self-validation and status. Practices such as steadily preparing flats and instigating and maintaining durable relationships provide powerful senses of hope and pride that can compensate for and keep men engaged in stagnant careers. Yet it takes continuous work to navigate competing moral frameworks of gendered respectability and Islamic piety and the inextricable dependence of love and marriage on money. This requires refocused emphasis on the pursuit of a career, as well as substantial familial financial help and flexibility from women and their families. Overall, this chapter has shown how powerful love can be within the economy and labor market. Pursuing love represents a key form of emotional labor that enables men to forge livable lives. It sometimes coexists with, sometimes takes on heightened importance to, and sometimes drives the chase for careers. The pursuit of love and career are interdependent. Sustaining both requires a difficult and sometimes impossible balancing act amid a set of structural forces that are rendering them extremely precarious.

CHAPTER FIVE

THE MIGRATION
OF HOPE

IN JUNE 2015 AN ARTICLE was published in Egyptian newspaper *Al-Ahram* titled "Dreaming of Liberland." It was about the self-declaration of the micronation of the Free Republic of Liberland on a seven-square-kilometer piece of disputed land on the west bank of the Danube between Croatia and Serbia. Liberland was proclaimed by Czech libertarian politician and activist Vít Jedlicka on April 13, 2015, and immediately began seeking applications for citizenship and donations. Apparently only communists, Nazis, extremists, and people with a criminal past would be rejected. Within weeks, Liberland had received more than 330,000 applications. The greatest number—25 percent—came from Egypt. The interest shown by Egyptians even prompted the Foreign Ministry to issue a statement warning youth not to be "manipulated" by "specialized gangs" who want to "seize their financial entitlements" and to seek information from the Ministry rather than social media before traveling abroad.[1] Many Egyptians joked about Liberland on social media—suggesting Egyptians would still be denied a visa from this imaginary state or flock there hoping to escape only to find more Egyptians. But this did not stop many from taking this chance seriously. In that very month I was traveling with Ibrahim to his village in Sharkia to stay for the weekend. In the middle of a conversation about the employment struggles of his friend in a call center, he got out his phone to gleefully show me an email confirming his application for citizenship to the Free Republic of Liberland. For Ibrahim, this represented just one more potential opportunity to migrate. In my immediate state of surprise, I told him I thought it might well be fake, to which he replied: "Well, why not, I might as well try." He had heard about this "opportunity" to travel from Mahmoud, who had seen it on social media and also applied. The emailed response told these men their application would be processed in a matter of weeks. But to this date they have never heard anything else.

While some might pass this off as a comical episode, it does reflect something important about the collective psyche of Egyptians and their relationship to the act of migration. This psyche has developed over decades. Under the presidency of Gamal Abdel Nasser, emigration was restricted to secure sufficient labor for the nationalist economic project.[2] But when Sadat (1970–1981) took power, followed by Mubarak (1981–2011), migration became a key form of social and financial mobility for Egyptians. At the same time that many in Egypt's middle class were experiencing heightened economic insecurity in the context of structural adjustment policies, restrictions on emigration were eased. While European countries by the 1980s had begun to limit labor migration, the oil boom created a seemingly endless demand for migrant labor in oil-producing Arab countries. Within a few years, more than a million Egyptian men moved to work in countries like Libya, Iraq, Saudi Arabia, and Kuwait to finance marriage, provide for wives and children (who often stayed in Egypt), and enjoy modern comforts back in Egypt.[3] Migration, often alongside property or commercial investment in Egypt, enabled many to experience rapid mobility. Although the flow of workers slowed significantly when oil prices dropped in the 1980s, until today migration to wealthy Arab countries—alongside European countries for some—remains a major source of promise for aspiring young men to overcome a sense of disconnection overwhelming them inside Egypt.[4] A 2017 census found that one out of eleven Egyptians currently resides abroad, with two-thirds in Arab countries and other notable diasporas in the United States, Canada, and Italy.[5]

In this final chapter I want to explicate the relationship between the act of migration and the labor of hope, which enables people to sustain a sense that life is worth living. In recent years literature has begun to interrogate the relationship between migration and hope.[6] Interrogating the nexus of transnational mobility regimes and migrants' everyday practices has revealed how migration represents a promising spatial fix to existential immobility for millions around the world. But this hopeful promise is often disappointed by visa regimes that prevent movement, alongside exclusionary labor and citizenship regimes that require great effort to endure. In these accounts, which are generally restricted to a particular time or place, there is little room for oscillation, the back-and-forth actually experienced by migrants in reality, between what Craig Jeffrey calls a "sense of purposeful waiting to a purposeless inertia and back again," between fleeting feelings of hope as new visions for the future arise, or frustration as people hit new blockages.[7] By following young lower-middle-class Egyptian men across different spacetimes of migration—as they invest time and money into creating the possibility of travel, dispel doubts that arise about imperfect opportunities, or come to terms with the reality of life abroad—this chapter argues that migration, like the chase of careers and love more generally, traps people in continuous oscillation between hope, excitement, doubt, and disappointment as a result of international migrant and labor regimes that manufacture an optimistic attachment to migration as a way to move forward in life, while inhibiting the means of doing so for many.[8] This requires an intense and incessant emotional labor to navigate.

THE LABOR OF MIGRATING

In early 2015, after completing the TFJ course, Saami printed out a piece of paper and stuck it to his bedroom wall to establish a plan to achieve his dream, as trainers had advised. It set out a four-stage strategy. The first involved obtaining a job in an English-language call center so he could improve his language skills. This would help secure acceptance to the prestigious Fulbright scholarship, following which he would apply to Berea College, a university offering a no-tuition fee pledge in exchange for ten hours of work each week. He needed this arrangement because he could not afford the exorbitant U.S. undergraduate fees. The final stage contained a picture of New York City, the symbol of a future life in the United States. This piece of paper illustrates a sensibility many young Egyptian men develop as they begin navigating a precarious labor market. It entails coming to see barra (the outside) as the only solution to achieving one's dreams. Ghassan Hage previously described how "we engage in the kind of physical mobility that defines us as migrants because we feel another geographical space is a better launching pad for our existential selves. We move physically so we can feel that we are existentially on the move again."⁹ After repeated attempts to secure mobility within Egypt, young men look beyond the country to fulfill their aspirations for a career, marriage, and an upscale lifestyle.¹⁰ Hardly a day went by during fieldwork when the possibility of migrating was not mentioned. Countless times men cried out to escape Egypt and compared their stagnation to an imagined life of mobility abroad. These ruminations were often stimulated by harrowing events that foreclosed the future such as a job rejection or firing, but also by more mundane happenings such as a plane flying overhead, news stories about the dearth of work available or statistics that showed that 80 percent of Egyptians who migrate are better off, and "inspirational" films about Egyptians who travel abroad and find success. In these conversations, Egypt is described as a place where "dreams are killed," a place where it is impossible to find satisfaction (rida).

But as others have described, barra is not a uniform category. For the vast majority, their first-choice destination is the West—Europe or North America. Although often critical of Western foreign policy and aspects of its culture such as Islamophobia or individualism, Egyptians imagine it as a place that enables people to fulfill their dreams. This is demonstrated by a conversation with Mahmoud about the Egyptian film *Hamam fi Amsterdam*. It was about a "young man like me who had a lot of problems in Egypt, lost his love, and had to travel abroad to Holland to achieve his dreams." I asked Mahmoud if he thought it was easy to succeed in Holland, to which he replied: "At least they let you try hard to succeed but here they don't even give you the chance, they want you dead." For Egyptian men, the attachment to meritocratic ideals that I described in Chapter 3 over time gets displaced onto other places. Although they come to realize that Egypt is full of barriers that hold people back, the West is constructed as a place that rewards people who work hard. This is apparently ensured by equitable access to world-class education, high-quality public services, and a decent supply of jobs. As proof, Mahmoud forwarded me the Egyptian Nestlé website alongside the German one. While there were 1,385 vacancies in Germany, the Egyptian page was closed: "I will never forget this number," he said; "it shows everything you need to know about Egypt." Beyond the West's imagined capacity to provide opportunity, it is also desired because of its privacy, nonjudgmental culture, cosmopolitanism, and supposed work-life balance.[11] Spending even a short period of time there is viewed as potentially transformative for one's career prospects in Egypt.

But for this class of young men, actually getting to the West is extremely difficult. I was often asked about diversity visa schemes, master's scholar-ships, or imaginary states. Mahmoud discovered an advertisement for work in Canada on a Facebook group for Egyptians wanting to travel and gave his number. Someone phoned and confirmed he was eligible but needed to pay a CAN$3,000 registration fee. Mahmoud asked if it was a scam, to which I said it probably was and advised him not to follow up. The desperation to migrate can sometimes lead Egyptians into exploitative relations.[12] For many the West is knowingly beyond reach and therefore not something taken seriously.[13] But for some it becomes a long-term pursuit. When I saw the paper on Saami's wall in August 2015, he confirmed that this pathway had not worked out. He failed at the first step, unable to enter a call center after being told, like many lower-middle-class youth, that his English accent was too "Egyptian." He applied for the Fulbright anyway but got rejected. As we stood before the wall, Saami said, "I haven't achieved my dream yet, but I'll keep trying, insha' Allah." He continued to spend two hours daily after work looking for opportunities to travel to an English-speaking country. Every time I saw him, there was an opportunity he was considering: becoming an Arabic teacher in the United States, signing up to a recruitment agency in the UK, or enrolling in English courses for foreigners. Working toward these opportunities, pre-paring visa applications, or changing the job title in his passport to add offici-ality provided momentum. But Saami slowly discovered he was up against a restrictive regime designed to exclude people like him. Describing a meeting at the U.S. embassy regarding a tourist visa application, he said: "The woman asked me, are you married? Do you have children? Do you have a business? How much is in your bank account? Who will fund your studies? When I answered, she said straight away, 'Sorry, we cannot give you a visa.'" Saami concluded that Western countries were suspicious that Egyptians would not return, with these questions designed to check whether they had sufficient ties. After meeting a Malaysian student at his old university, he made an alternative plan to travel to Malaysia to take an English course after discovering that Egyptians can travel as a tourist for three months.

Saami was not alone in his disappointing struggle to reach the West. Mostafa was introduced in Chapter 3, having entered the Faisal flat during my final days. Having grown up in Mahalla, a city of five hundred thousand in the Nile delta, with parents who had low-paid government jobs, he decided a dignified pathway was nonexistent. What had once been a thriving garment industry in Mahalla was decimated following 1990s economic reforms. After Mostafa obtained his business degree, his job options consisted of "boring" government administration or small-scale, poorly paid accountancy. He was rejected from a role in the army because of his father's low-status job. Mostafa described Mahalla as a place of stagnation that could not fulfill his dreams to "influence the world." He moved to Cairo initially, but soon found himself stuck in an Arabic-language call center. Mostafa lived with an aunt who resided in a compound in Cairo's outskirts after her husband's Gulf migration, and he soon developed aspirations to travel. When I met him in 2015, he told me of multiple failed attempts. In 2013 he was supposed to go to Qatar but was unable after breaking his leg, with the agent refusing to wait while it healed. Another time he heard about possible employment in central Russia, but after checking whether he would have time to study, an acquaintance told him he would "work and sleep" only on a farm. Mostafa was not keen on the Gulf, owing to its reputation for racial discrimination and pushing migrant men like his uncle into a lifetime of work. Instead, like Saami, he felt studying abroad would increase his chances of obtaining a high-skilled job in Europe or returning to open a business in Egypt. He began applying for foreign scholarships to do a master's degree. By 2015 he had applied for and been rejected from eighteen scholarships. The last was the Chevening, a UK government diplomatic effort to help "young leaders and professionals" across the world earn a UK master's degree. Successful candidates possess a different class profile than Mostafa, belonging to the upper-middle classes who enjoy international private education.

While preparing applications Mostafa experienced intense hope. It oriented his whole life outside work. Although he took time to relax, hanging out with friends and heading on occasional trips to the coast, Mostafa actively tried not to "distract" himself. He judged as "lazy" youth who were not doing everything they could to achieve social mobility. But each new rejection instigated intense sadness, in which he did not speak to anyone for days. Mostafa overcame this by scouring the internet for more scholarships before focusing his mind on each application. To keep up motivation, he called on God's power and used self-help quotes that told him not to give up, to keep straining and working on his skills. He also tried to do something different every time to improve his chances. After being fired from the call center because he spent too long off work following his injury, Mostafa searched for six months for a job with regular shifts, which enabled him to take evening courses in HR and English. By 2018 he had spent LE10,000 on courses in preparation for scholarships. To help him pass the IELTS English exam, he did language exchanges with foreigners in Cairo, initially establishing a network through me. Finally, he attended a fair for foreign master's courses at an upmarket hotel in Dokki, where he learned from university representatives how to improve his application: by focusing on one subject and making sure he had good references (although this was difficult since his university professors did not speak English). He was also told it *was* possible for public university graduates like him to get accepted. This advice provided Mostafa with renewed confidence and incited laughter about how bad previous applications had been.

By setting out the experiences of Mostafa and Saami, I want to take seriously the unsuccessful attempts of marginalized groups to migrate. Aspiring migrants are often assumed to live in a state of existential stuckedness as a result of border regimes that prevent movement. But the reality is often more complex. The lives of aspiring migrant men in Egypt constitute continuous oscillation between existential mobility and immobility, between the hope that they are moving toward a better future and the depressing sense of being stuck in life, with fear, doubt, joy, and distraction emerging in between. They experience intense hope while preparing a scholarship or visa application and taking a training course that might help, imagining the future life that might come. One man described studying and looking for scholarship opportunities in his room as his "heaven"—although his real heaven was barra (outside). However, they become depressed after a new failure. This oscillation is produced by a migratory regime that extends a meritocratic terrain of scholarships, self-help, and training into the Global South, reproducing the promise that migration is possible for anyone while exclusionary visa regulations keep actual movement restricted to a select group of highly privileged people.[14] This extension of hope provides legitimacy to migrant regimes and enables much money to be made through agents, visa fees, and training. But oscillation is also fueled by men themselves. When I pressed Saami on why he continued trying to migrate despite repeated failure, he answered:

> If I stopped dreaming and hoping, I would not be able to carry on. You need hope. You can't give up. I have faced many disappointments in my attempts to go abroad and improve my life. I get sad for a few days and then focus on the next attempt, because you need hope. I focus on the next attempt to overcome sadness. I always look to find another way because there are lots of ways to reach your goals, so if you are not successful you should not give up.

As I argued in relation to Egypt's domestic labor market, migratory regimes also produce a cruel attachment to the promise of future fulfillment and the objects in which it is embedded. Mostafa's and Saami's decisions to keep investing time and money, despite seeing scholarship and visa applications rejected time and again, represented an attempt to sustain a feeling of hope for a better future. This feeling enabled them to carry on navigating their precarious lives in Egypt. It provided status out of a sense of where they are headed in comparison to others. These activities became a crucial emotional labor that enabled them to continue participating in a domestic labor market and transnational migrant regime, while simultaneously legitimizing them.

MANAGING DOUBT

However, the shape of this labor is not permanent. Migratory structures do allow for productive openings, if not in ways initially anticipated. Attachments to migration also shift over time. For some this entails shifting tactics when it becomes clear that particular avenues will not work out. But for others this constitutes a more doubtful stance toward migration itself. After several years in Cairo, Mostafa experienced some career mobility. After completing an HR course he obtained a job in a translation company, earning LE3,000 (US$170 in 2019) per month. On the side he looked after private investment clients from a previous job as an advisor for Saudi businessmen and was trying to establish a translation company. Mostafa also got engaged to a

Dutch woman after meeting her through language exchange, thus opening the possibility of migrating on a spousal visa. But Mostafa was loath to adhere to the stereotype of "marriage for business" (gawaz al-biznis).[15] He wanted to feel like he earned it. He was also concerned by the struggles of a friend who migrated to Europe through marriage only to end up in difficulty when he fought with his wife and could not convince the authorities he was the father of their son.[16] When I met him in Egypt in 2019, Mostafa recollected previous desperation to leave:

> I used to be so restless to travel to any country; I don't have that any more.
> I have worked hard here to build up my career; I don't want to give that up
> and start again. I don't want to do just any job.

Mostafa was still enthusiastic about migration—he now managed a Facebook group that posts scholarship opportunities to thousands of members—because he knew his earning trajectory in Egypt would inhibit his ability to live the upscale life he desired, particularly in an economic context that halved the value of Egypt's pound against the dollar. But he wanted to migrate for a good opportunity, either white-collar work or study. His resistance slowly created tensions with his fiancée, who was becoming tired of waiting. Finally, in late 2019, Mostafa agreed to try living in Europe for a few months. The work involved in securing the spousal visa was far from easy. Getting married in Egypt required a certificate confirming that his fiancée was Christian. After the Dutch state refused, she managed to get one from a Christian church but was told it needed a government stamp. Initially, the embassy refused, but through her networks she managed to obtain a small stamp. This still proved insufficient for the Ministry of Justice, which asked for a bigger stamp. In the end, Mostafa's fiancée had to convert to Islam.

Mostafa's story reveals how migratory regimes allow for productive openings. But it also reveals an alternative attachment to migration among lower-middle-class Egyptians. It is not universally understood as a hopeful practice because of the precarious nature of the opportunities. For Mostafa, hearing about the struggles of migrant life, coupled with his masculine desire to avoid travel as a dependent and his own socioeconomic mobility, altered his attachment. In the end, though, the allure of Europe proved too much to resist. But this more doubtful relation becomes apparent when Egyptian men consider the more realistic avenue of the Arab Gulf. Migration to the Gulf, unlike Europe, is considered in ambivalent terms. For this class of young men it knowingly involves a lifetime of work—like a "donkey," one man said. Work-life balance in Europe is often compared favorably against the Gulf. Saudi Arabia in particular is the target of negative attention. In a conversation with Mahmoud and Ibrahim about travel, they said they would never go to Saudi. "Saudis are racist and treat anyone who works beneath them very badly," Mahmoud said, before introducing a story of an Egyptian woman who was raped by Saudi men. Ibrahim backed this up by relaying another story of a friend: "His kafil [sponsor] told him he wanted to sleep with his wife, and if he wanted to get promoted he needed to let him do it; he refused and came back." In response to the exploitation suffered by Egyptians, young men spend much time belittling Saudi, describing how it was a desert only fifty years ago compared to Egypt's three thousand-year-old civilization. Aside from exploitative relations and racial discrimination, the Gulf is perceived as a place of boredom, where there is not much to do outside work, particularly for single men. But for lower-middle-class Egyptians it remains an attractive destination for two things. It sometimes provides the potential to advance one's career in a way that is not possible in Egypt. It also provides money. Money is the key that might unlock a host of other dreams such as marriage, setting up businesses, and comfortable lifestyles.

This ambivalent relationship to the Gulf is demonstrated when men are presented with an opportunity. One evening in the Faisal flat in 2015, Mohamed instigated a conversation with me by asking, "If you got a chance to go abroad, in not such a good job, would you leave your country?" He had been offered an administrative position in a Saudi company on a salary of 2,000 riyal per month (LE4,000 at the time)—with accommodation and transport covered.[17] A discussion ensued about whether he should travel. Mohamed knew it would lead to a bigger salary than he currently enjoyed, even though his friends would say it was not good. This would open possibilities, such as saving money to marry a woman in his hometown, build a house, and put future children in a good school. Making his family comfortable was an important duty for him, as was helping younger siblings with their marriages. However, Mohamed did not want to leave Egypt. He liked being close to family. If he had a salary of LE2,500 per month and a job that had a career trajectory, he would stay. But his current job was not that. Remaining in it would ensure that his marital plans would break down—"Egyptian women are not patient," he declared. Everyone in the call center was waiting to find something better—but he was not confident of doing so in Egypt. Traveling to Saudi was a secure way of taking an upward trajectory. But he was unsure about this job opportunity, while he also feared the "boring" life and bad treatment of Egyptians. He worried about spending so much on tickets and preparation—around LE15,000, he thought—only for it not to go well: "It is not something one can go and try," he said. I suggested that migrating might open up Mohamed's future, but he shot back, "But it will close as well; if I go I will be there working the rest of my life." The big pulling factor was money: "If you go abroad it is not about anything else, life there is work only; but at least you work and get money in return, here you work and get no money."

Mohamed rejected this opportunity after consulting with his family. This gives an insight into the difficult decisions Egyptian men face when considering Gulf migration. For some, this is producing a more permanent reappraisal of migration. As described in the previous chapter, following the ruination of his prospective travel to Dubai, Ibrahim halted the pursuit of migration and proclaimed that being a respectable husband and father meant staying with his family. To justify his decision, he called on religious proverbs citing the danger of endlessly chasing money and told stories of Egyptians who had migrated and sacrificed love or returned following prolonged suffering. Another man even accused migrating Egyptians of "escaping": "They should carry on struggling and face up to the difficulties here." Increasing knowledge of the precarity of the Gulf migrant regime for lower-middle-class Egyptian men is slowly producing more doubtful attachments to migration and constructions of value by staying put.[18] However, for many the pull of monetary and career mobility proves too much to resist over time amid the state of Egypt's economy. Indeed, only a few weeks later Mohamed left for another job in Saudi Arabia. Like Mohamed, many describe travel as a forced choice because of their inability to locate employment opportunities that provide a platform for a career, marriage, and a decent lifestyle in Egypt. But as it is happening, men engage in active emotional labor—often involving family and friends—to construct migration as a hopeful act. This involves emphasizing how travel will enable them to afford marriage and decent lifestyles. But it also involves factors beyond money. Egyptian men want travel to be more than about money alone. They emphasize that it will enable them to experience different cultures as well as learn new skills and develop their career.

Many who are worried about a lifetime in the Gulf assert that they will travel for a limited time before returning. This speaks to a distinction in Arabic between migration (higra), living away from home (mughtaribiyyn), and traveling (musafiriyyn).[19] While migration is a permanent act of making a new home—often associated with European migration, ghurba (living in a strange place among strangers) and safar (travel) are more temporary states that define life in the Gulf.[20] The prospect of returning to friends and family with better financial resources produces hope. Some even position returning as a duty in order to help Egypt. But others see migration, even to the Gulf, as an opportunity to escape a place that has delivered so much pain. They emphasize their excitement to escape a stagnant labor market and economy, and Egypt's crowdedness, dirtiness, poor public services, and uneducated people. This can even be through constructing the Gulf as a step toward pastures new. After years of working in unpaid law positions in Egypt, Gamal was finally rewarded with a junior position in a commercial law firm in Saudi Arabia—after seeing a Facebook post and conducting two interviews. Acquiring the visa took weeks, during which his attachment to the position strengthened as well as anxieties about whether it was real. Although life in Saudi would be hard, he thought it was a good opportunity. The salary of 3,000 riyal (plus accommodation and courtesy car) would leave room for savings. The job could also be a step to somewhere else. His dream was London, but he would try Dubai after one year. Dubai is an exception within the Gulf in the minds of Egyptians because of its hypermodern and cosmopolitan reputation. But it is difficult to get to. Mahmoud, after deciding he needed to travel to improve his trajectory, accepted his uncle's invitation to come on a tourist visa for one month. Once there, he would look for any job to allow him to stay. Mahmoud was worried about getting into debt with his uncle and failing to find a job. But he was encouraged by friends who told him it would be easy. Mahmoud finally traveled in early 2017 after failing to find an alternative plan. He left focusing on the potential life he could reach.

So far I have revealed the emotional life of migration in the lives of young men struggling to obtain decent work in Egypt's labor market. For many, mi-

gration represents an ultimate solution to existential stuckedness. The practice of imagining and working toward it reignites hope for the future. But as a
result of the precarious social positions of lower-middle-class Egyptian men in
an international migrant regime, opportunities are few and far between, and
what opportunities there are come with risk and uncertainty. Thus, sustaining a vital sense of hope in migration in this set of circumstances takes much
emotional labor, both in overcoming the disappointment of failed attempts
and relocating new opportunities and in the doubts that plague the more realistic prospects. For most Egyptian men migration is never achieved. But for
others, migration does become a reality. Earlier I introduced four men who
migrated during my fieldwork. Saami traveled to Malaysia on a three-month
tourist visa with the intention of improving his English, Mostafa reluctantly
trialed a few months' stay in Belgium on a spousal visa, Gamal took a law job
in Saudi Arabia in the hope it might lead elsewhere, and Mahmoud traveled
on a tourist visa to Dubai to look for work that might enable him to finally
experience social mobility. These men, despite their differing destinations and
methods of travel, went full of hope for what the future might hold. What I
want to do now is examine what happens to the hopes imbued in migration
as it is lived. How is that hope threatened by the struggles of migrant life and
how is it stitched back together?

NOTHING IS PERFECT

> If you migrate with strong dreams and set goals, you will certainly get disap-
> pointed and hopeless. You need to be flexible, you know, like you are floating
> on the waves, you need to be a piece of wood going where the current takes
> you, and try not to be a nail which is struggling against the waves, because
> you will just be eternally disappointed.

I was speaking to Mostafa in October 2020 about what had by this point
been a ten-month stay in Belgium. He was describing the mindset one needs
to survive migration. Mostafa traveled three days before Christmas in 2019
to live with his wife in a studio flat in a provincial Belgian city. He left full
of expectation about growing his translation company by building up company networks. Although officially allowed to stay for five years, he originally
planned his stay as a trial and booked a return flight in March 2020. For the

first month Mostafa acted like a tourist before settling down to build his translation contacts, with the help of his wife. In March the coronavirus crisis hit and Mostafa was unable to take his flight back. He suddenly had to adapt to the idea of being in Europe longer term. Mostafa kept trying to expand his translation website but found it impossible to get business when companies were decreasing operations. As he was eating into savings, he began looking for work inside companies, calling on the several years of experience he had acquired in Egypt. However, Mostafa found nothing. The only work available—which other Egyptians were doing—was manual labor in construction. Mostafa could not bring himself to accept this work. Although emphasizing that he did not judge, it was a form of flexibility he could not accept. Instead, he began looking into further study. While his passion had always been business, he realized it would be difficult to secure an administrative job inside companies because he needed Flemish—which he had begun learning. Reluctantly Mostafa decided to retrain and do another bachelor's in information technology. He thought this a skill universally sought after. He secured acceptance in a local university and began in September 2020. Mostafa recollected how back in Egypt he had been so excited to do a degree in Europe; however, now that he had secured it he was sad at having to start his career from scratch. But he felt he had no choice.

Reflecting on his migratory experience so far, Mostafa described how he had learned to adapt his outlook on life. He no longer held on tightly to specific dreams but rather was trying to adapt based on where life took him. This was far from easy for him as a man in his late twenties who had built up work experience and expectations of what career he would follow. It would have been easier, he said, had he migrated in his early twenties, when he did not have a set idea of what he wanted to do. Mostafa experienced great disappointment when his expectations for the business did not come to fruition. He did not expect it to be so difficult to find appropriate work—and that people, even if educated, have to retrain in Europe. Mostafa left Egypt thinking Europe was a utopia. Many Egyptians come thinking that, he said—"with girls, cars, and work that you want, but it is not like that at all, it is not black and white." Mostafa did appreciate some things in Europe. He still believed in its "fairness" ('adala), whereby if you work well, you live well, unlike in Egypt—thus revealing a lingering attachment to meritocracy.

He also appreciated the system in which you can get things done easily when dealing with the state instead of the chaos of Egypt's bureaucracy. However, he did not like aspects of European culture—he had to negotiate some differences in his marriage—and was frustrated by Egyptians who wanted to completely forget Muslim or Arab culture and become European. Looking ahead, he did not want his children to grow up in Europe. But the biggest issue now was his struggles in work. As a result, Mostafa had to develop a new approach to life. He actually appreciated the destruction of the perfect image of Europe in his mind: "At least I have discovered the reality now and don't have Europe in my imagination any longer." This outlook meant being adaptive and not hanging on to particular dreams too tightly.

Other scholars have argued that a contingent mindset often emerges in response to precarity.[21] Mostafa's metaphor recalls Henrik Vigh's notion of social navigation, the act of sustaining movement in an environment that is wavering and unsettled—Vigh references the sea. But Vigh celebrates this as an agentive, skillful act.[22] Following young men like Mostafa over many years reveals how it can be an immensely painful experience that emerges from the embers of lost dreams and the images that carried them. This mindset was not unique to Mostafa. Saami went through his own lengthy process to establish a semblance of normalcy after arriving in Kuala Lumpur in November 2015. After spending a month getting to know the city, he began looking for English courses. They were extremely expensive, so he decided to look for work, only to find he needed a student visa or work permit. The work available informally was restaurant waiting, which according to Saami is not acceptable for Egyptians—it is mostly Bangladeshis and Nepalese in these jobs. Saami decided to try to change his visa by applying for a two-year master's course in linguistics (his specialism in Egypt) costing 8,000 ringgit (LE27,000). But first he needed to achieve a score of seven on an IELTS English exam. Unable to afford official courses, he self-studied. In the meantime, he left Malaysia as his tourist visa was running out. Instead of making the expensive trip back to Egypt, he went to Indonesia for five days. Upon returning, Saami was asked why he was reentering so quickly but was allowed after saying he would apply for a master's. After two months of study, Saami secured 6.5 on the IELTs but applied for university anyway before leaving again at the end of his second three months—this time to Bali with an Egyptian friend also applying for study. By this stage he had finished his savings and relied on parental support. Fortunately, Saami was accepted to a master's program and immediately began securing a student visa. Before beginning in late 2016 he had to leave Malaysia one final time.

Saami took part-time work to help fund his studies—both as a customer service agent organizing trade fairs and as an English teacher at an international school. In May 2019, just after finishing what turned out to be a two-and-a-half-year master's program after he took a term extension, Saami obtained a job offer working as a customer service agent for Arab YouTube channel operators. Before starting, he got the chance to spend forty days back in Egypt for the first time in four years. This coincided with the four-year process to obtain a stable job in Malaysia. He has now been in the job fourteen months—with a shift to homeworking since March following the COVID-19 pandemic. Saami said this was by no means his dream job—he was not using skills learned in his master's. It also represents the new work culture: "Work is like a service now rather than a family. I take a salary in exchange for work, that's it." This hinted at Saami's newfound focus away from work. He now realized he would not be a "businessman" or rich like he envisaged, but he has a job and stability. Saami was focused on another aspect of life, starting a family, which he had delayed by traveling. It would be easy for him to marry an Egyptian, he said, as they share a language and culture. But he was searching for a new home, which meant finding another family by marrying a Malaysian woman. Having family close was especially important for a future wife, he said: "I don't want to be a lonely couple." Saami asked a Malaysian friend for help. He asked his mother, who suggested her niece who worked as a doctor. They met in August 2020 and are working out if they are a suitable match—negotiating the complications of differing languages and perspectives. Saami will rent a local house as he cannot afford to buy one and is almost ready to pay the dowry and buy a ring.

Reflecting on his migration, Saami said: "there is always a bill you have to pay for any decision you take in life; nothing is perfect." For Saami, migrating meant he had sacrificed starting a family on time—he was in his midthirties now. But his younger brother had sacrificed his career by getting married so young. He now had a two-year-old son and was relying on parental support to care for him while looking for work. Saami missed his family and friends greatly, but he would never go back to Egypt: "I look at the country now like a foreigner, I don't care about it." When he returned in 2019, he saw that Egypt had become worse: "Everyone was complaining about living expenses tripling; the government has built some new infrastructure, but they still live in shit." Saami does mix with Egyptians in Kuala Lumpur, many of whom also traveled for studies. Egyptians come, he said, because Malaysia is a Muslim country and well-developed. But Saami said many want to move on to Turkey or Australia. When I asked why, he suggested it was because they do not like the Malaysian mentality: "Kuala Lumpur has three communities: local Malay, Chinese, and Indian; all three are closed, so it is difficult to establish a home here. Most Egyptians do not see it as a second home." However, Saami did not agree with trying to continually chase better: "Nothing is ideal," he said; "even in Turkey it is hard to get a job because there are many Syrians now." He had worked for so many years just to establish some stability in Malaysia and did not want to give it up. He also carried this into advising people in Egypt who asked him about it: "I don't recommend Malaysia to others, I just tell them they need to try for themselves." When I finally asked Saami whether he is happy, he fell silent initially: "It is not good to think if you are happy or not. I am thankful for my job, and I know I lack a family; I now need a family. Malaysia is not my home, but I don't have another country now; I'm okay to carry on here."

Both Mostafa and Saami, although at different stages of their migratory journey and ten thousand kilometers apart, had similar experiences. They both traveled with intense hope for the dreams they would be able to fulfill. But once they arrived, both had to work extremely hard to even achieve a semblance of stability as a result of exclusionary labor and citizenship regimes. The dreams they once had for dramatic social mobility are ebbing away. This new reality required and produced an alternative labor of hope—especially as they were entering a stage of adulthood that required settling down instead of endlessly chasing dreams. It rested on constantly adapting the image of the future they were working toward, as well as accepting its imperfections. The shift to this outlook was experienced as immensely painful. It also produced a hollowing-out of the emotional attachment to the chase of a good life. Even though both Mostafa and Saami were still working toward new hopes imbued in family, citizenship, and career progression, they were doing so not with the same urgency and conviction as before. Existing literature that has talked about this contingent way of being in the world has, following Michel de Certeau, emphasized it as a form of agentive endurance.[23] This is true—it does enable Mostafa and Saami to endure. But exploitative systems also rely on and reproduce themselves through the ways people cope within them. Indeed, it is what keeps these systems going. I now want to examine how this plays out in the Arab Gulf, where the extremes of success and failure were felt more starkly for young middle-class Egyptians.

DUBAI: THE CITY OF MIRRORS

While I had planned to go to Dubai to visit Mahmoud and Gamal, this did not work out. Originally, I intended to go for one month in October 2018, but days before my travel the story broke that a PhD student had been arrested on suspicion of being a spy. One year later I made a second plan. However, in early March of that year Mahmoud suddenly announced that he was going to quit his job and return to Egypt. Reassessing my travel, I decided to visit Mahmoud in Cairo and hear about his experience in Dubai instead, before traveling to Gamal. But after I arrived, Gamal suddenly announced that his employer had given him permission to travel to Egypt immediately to register his new baby as an Egyptian citizen. I therefore changed my tickets again and stayed in Egypt to spend time with Gamal. Although frustrating, my foiled plans to observe the lives of these young men in Dubai says much about the instabilities of migrant life for Egyptians in the Gulf. Their differing reasons for returning to Egypt also say something about the divergent paths these two men had taken. While Mahmoud's migratory hopes had been shattered, Gamal was slowly embedding himself in Dubai for the long term. But Dubai for both these men, as Gamal described during our time together in Egypt, was a city of mirrors. While it looks shiny and glamorous from the outside, it hides problems beneath the surface. Gamal was talking about the city itself but also referring to the life of an Egyptian migrant in the city. Although it offers the allure of social mobility, Dubai is experienced as precarious and limiting for many of its residents.

That I was talking to Gamal about Dubai highlights his success in en-suring that Saudi Arabia was a step. Gamal spent one year in Dammam. I never got to see him there, but on the occasions we interacted digitally he complained about having nothing to do, the restrictive culture, and his lack of control. Although he was enjoying his job and gaining good experience, Gamal started looking for work in Dubai and quickly obtained a job as an executive associate in a trade law firm. Gamal experienced dramatic social mobility through his migration, owing to his ability to obtain a high-skilled bilingual legal job. Having worked for free for many years in Egypt, in Dubai he began earning 14,000 dirhams (LE59,000) a month. Although Gamal complained that this was not much compared to the cost of living and Emirati salaries, it gave him the ability to save (his rent cost 3,000 dirhams per month). At the same time, he was getting involved in business ventures back in Egypt, helping his cousin import spare car parts and sharing ownership of his brother's gym. He also enjoyed his newfound monetary freedom. After struggling even to pay for public transport when I saw him before his migration, in 2019 he picked me up in a rental car costing LE400 per day. As we drove around, he described how he had "got carried away" with his salary through buying stuff: perfume for 500 dirhams, an Apple watch, a new phone, a new car. This spending spree had relied, Gamal told me later, on a 60,000-dirham loan from an Emirati bank. He admitted worry about his ability to repay the 10,000-dirham installments but insisted he would resolve it.

Observing migrants as they return reveals an interesting aspect of migration, namely how they experience their home countries in comparison to their previous selves. Gamal expressed repeatedly how he felt different in Egypt now, more comfortable and freer. His newfound confidence showed in his consumptive prowess, but also in the way he carried himself as he moved around Cairo. He gleefully boasted about being able to drive me, his cousin, and his sister around. He also had the boldness to exchange the rental car just because he wanted a better one, as well as refuse to pay parking charges. Gamal expressed great satisfaction about his social mobility. He had learned that "every dream is possible if you work hard and clever." He also got gratification from the fact that he had come from a poorer background:

> You know, I found out there are two kinds of Egyptians in Dubai: One [comes] from under the earth (taht al ard). They know how to hustle and deal with problems; they don't ask for help. There is another kind who come

from a high class who are quite weak. There is a guy in work who went to English-language school in Egypt; he lives in Maadi and got the job through connections. He is unaware and ignorant; he can't solve problems by himself.

Gamal found status through his mobility. It reinforced his belief in meritocracy and individual agency. But he also carried insecurity. Gamal repeatedly asked if I thought he had changed, if he had forgotten where he came from and become arrogant or judgmental. Gamal made efforts to express understanding of Egypt's poor—when he is rich, he said, he will give his friends money because many are struggling. But this conflicted with his desire to express pride. He disliked being reminded of past struggles and denied previous resentments, such as his loss of faith in God or anger with his upper-class cousins for refusing to help him in the past. Gamal's rise solidified his faith in a system that he now had to uphold to enjoy his success. Shamus Khan described how the elite legitimize privilege through developing a language of individual character traits to explain success.[24] Gamal's story demonstrates how the few who manage to experience social mobility also reinforce this language because they relied on it to maintain hope along the journey.

Alongside social mobility, Gamal had experienced dramatic transformation in his family life. After a few weeks he got into a casual relationship with a Filipino colleague, Jasmine. Suddenly Jasmine got pregnant, and Gamal knew he had to marry her, which his mother confirmed. They married in the Seychelles—halfway between Manilla and Cairo—in a private civil ceremony, as Jasmine was Christian. Gamal wanted the baby to be born in Egypt, but Jasmine desperately wanted to give birth with her family. They had a son, whom they named Joseph. Gamal described the passion and responsibility he felt. He would make sure Joseph grew up tough like him. He was also thankful the baby was a boy because he worried about raising a girl in Dubai: "She would go out and get tricked into having sex by men who claim they love her." After giving birth they discovered that obtaining a passport in the Philippines takes three months. Gamal got angry because of the expense of having to rebook flights, shouting, "You think I'm a bank!" But he told me he felt guilty: "I should have said no in the first place, but since I said yes I can't get angry." He lamented their frequent fights: "I make her cry a lot, she is one of those sensitive women who feels others' pain even if she doesn't know them; I need to adapt." As a result Gamal was being cautious to protect himself. Rather than waiting, they came to Egypt to process Joseph's citizenship. Although Gamal claimed it would be quicker, the underlying reason was making sure Joseph was Egyptian first. This would make it easier for Gamal to take him in case of divorce. Gamal also insisted Joseph would be Muslim. In order to ensure this, he was thinking about taking an Egyptian wife. Gamal admitted that he wanted to marry a younger woman, especially in case he and Jasmine got divorced. However, he insisted they had a strong relationship and trusted each other: "I love her a lot, she is very kind to me and loves Joseph a lot."

This couple faced many hurdles navigating a new transnational relationship while trying to raise a baby. The precarity of this situation was laid bare as they negotiated citizenship for Joseph. Gamal had secured ten days' leave from the company to go to Egypt. First, he had to go to the foreign ministry to get the Filipino birth and marriage certificates stamped. However, when he went the office was closed. Two agents in the next office said they could do it for LE1,000 per document, but he would need an Egyptian marriage certificate. He rejected their "help," but Gamal realized that the process was going to take longer. At that point I had to leave Egypt, and a week later Gamal did the same. He transferred power of attorney to his mother and left Jasmine and Joseph behind to complete the process. However, barely a week later his mother informed him that the immigration office had requested his presence to sign documents. Gamal asked permission to return to Egypt for three days, but this time his boss said no. Instead, Jasmine got a warning—which meant she had to return and leave Joseph. A day later Gamal was called into the office and told he must resign. He did so, waiving his right to a notice period because he did not want to make trouble with people who had connections. He was devastated. They suspected the manager who had fired him liked Jasmine, because he said he could file her divorce papers. Jasmine went to an Indian fortune-teller who confirmed as much but also said Gamal would find another job before his visa expired. Fortunately, one month later Gamal got another job offer, and his previous employer subsequently asked him to retract his resignation. Despite the return of stability, this series of events lays bare the complex precarities that can destabilize even successful migrant stories in the Gulf.

Overall, Gamal's story of migration is one of huge success. There is, however, a darker side to Dubai. Mahmoud arrived in January 2017 on a one-month tourist visa and stayed with his uncle. He quickly managed to find work in an call center taking taxi requests. Mahmoud had desperately tried to avoid call center work in Egypt, but in Dubai he found himself back there, earning 4,000 dirhams (LE17,000) per month. With his rent for a bed space in an eight-person room costing 1,000 dirhams, food another 800 dirhams, and commuting 1,000 dirhams, this left 1,200 dirhams (LE5,000) savings every month. For the first nine months Mahmoud solely focused on saving. This meant doing almost nothing outside work, apart from the odd meal out with colleagues from other Arabic-speaking countries such as Sudan, Algeria, and Jordan, and taking trips to malls to stare at products like he did back in Egypt. Mahmoud described it as a miserable life. He did flexible shifts six days a week of between eight and twelve hours each: two in the morning, two in the afternoon, and two at night. This made for an exhausting schedule. Before work Mahmoud ate Indian breakfast from the street—all that was available in his neighborhood because of the prevalence of Indian migrants—and after work he went home, cooked, and did chores. He did not have the energy to keep much contact with Amina, his girlfriend; they spoke once a week.

Mahmoud was not alone in this struggle. He said Dubai was hard for migrants at his level: "Nobody I met was happy, they were all just saving." But Mahmoud knew there were two kinds of Egyptian there: "One who goes to work only, saves money [to] send back to their families; they only go home two months every two years. They mostly work in sales, customer service, call centers. Then there is another kind who works in higher-paid, high-end jobs, who can enjoy all that Dubai has to offer; they can marry and eventually bring family over and settle." This speaks to a governmental migrant regime prevalent across the Gulf that is designed to demarcate between migrants who are pushed into a state of permanent temporariness and those—like Gamal—who are able to "settle."[25] Mahmoud experienced this distinction in his workplace and beyond. He complained about a sixteen-year-old "uneducated" colleague. He was one of the bidoun people—an Emirati ethnic minority denied citizenship but given Comoros nationality and some labor market privileges compared to migrants.[26] He earned 14,000

dirhams compared to Mahmoud's 4,000 dirhams for the same job, justified by Mahmoud's being outsourced but acting as a cover for racialized dis-
tinctions. Such discrepancies have consequences for one's ability to establish
permanency, as Mahmoud explained: "If you earn less than five thousand
dirhams, you cannot get a license to drive a car, you cannot get a credit
card, you cannot bring your wife to live with you or buy a flat, so there is no
long-term future for people on less than that." This was a constant source of
frustration. He tried and failed to find better work but was stuck in a system
that made upward mobility impossible. Mahmoud found it difficult to stay
motivated in these circumstances.

Various day-to-day tactics enabled Mahmoud to manage this grueling
schedule. At night he watched films on his laptop. At work itself, he described
how some employees—especially the Sudanese—hid rum in their lockers
and put it in their coffee, at least until one person got found out and fired
during a random locker check. Mahmoud and his colleagues also used to
get through their shifts by laughing at "stupid" (mostly foreign) customers.
He told me about one British woman who told him she could see the Burj
Khalifa (the tallest building in the world) from where she was standing in response to him asking for her location: "I said, 'Madame, you can see the Burj
Khalifa from any place in Dubai; can you be more specific?' but she replied,
'Do I have to do everything for you?'" They also laughed at the "stupidity"
of Indian taxi drivers. Mahmoud enjoyed imitating the interactions he had
with Indian drivers who got lost. This reflects an argument made by Samuli
Schielke that in the Gulf states it is common for different national migrant
groups to ridicule one another.[27] He describes this as a form of "subaltern
racism" that enables migrants to assert value in a system that strips them of
self-worth based on race. But Schielke points out that it is not only a subaltern
response to precarity but an intentional technique of power exercised by Gulf
states by fostering competition between different migrant groups by keeping
the numbers of any one group low.

Besides these day-to-day tactics, what kept Mahmoud going during this
period was his long-term goal of saving money. However, after one and a half
years this purpose disappeared. When Mahmoud returned to Egypt in October 2017, Amina told him he had to propose. However, Mahmoud asked her
to give him six more months, as he had only just cleared debts to his uncle.

Amina reluctantly agreed, but thereafter they began fighting. For Mahmoud, this stemmed from Amina's ever-increasing demands. The biggest fight took place in April 2018 when Amina asked him to sign a prenuptial agreement in case of divorce. In response he told Amina her parents were exploiting him, which offended her deeply. They subsequently broke up for several months and stopped speaking. In August 2018 Mahmoud returned. By this point he had decided to agree to the prenuptial agreement and planned to surprise Amina by going straight to her father. However, when he arrived, she announced she was to be engaged to somebody else. Mahmoud was crushed. He told me he cried for a week afterward. In 2019 we spent hours recollecting where things had gone wrong. Mahmoud expressed much anger at Amina and Egyptian women in general for marrying for money:

> Amina started out different, she wanted to just marry in any way, and said we could live any way, but when I started the process she kept bringing more demands, first it was LE10,000, then LE20,000, a rented flat first, then you have to buy one. It might have been her parents' demands rather than her. I climbed up all these steps from just two pounds in my pocket when I couldn't afford to go to anywhere. She was with me for that, then she just left me.

Mahmoud was angry that Amina had let monetary issues come between their love. By contrast, he positioned himself as too "Western." Because he had grown up not having parents as role models and watching Western movies, he prioritized falling in love over monetary negotiations. He was also upset by how fast Amina moved on and concluded that women must have shallower emotions. Mahmoud reminisced about past efforts he had made to please her. However, he also admitted mistakes. His biggest regret was not proposing before he returned to Dubai in 2017. She had talked so much about marriage and he delayed, which hurt her a lot: "I had the money to buy the shabka [gold], but I was scared of failing to meet their expectations." Mahmoud's lack of trust because of his parents and endless career disappointments led him to jeopardizing his marriage. He also regretted not communicating with Amina in Dubai: "Sometimes it would be a week without messaging, but I was just so focused," he said; "I worked fourteen hours a day and had loads to do and did not have energy, but I missed her so much."

Mahmoud had experienced the most dramatic rupture imaginable to his migratory hope. He returned to Dubai despondent. He carried on the call center job but described how he "went crazy and started spending loads of money," sacrificing his savings. Mahmoud began enjoying the shallow consumptive releases Dubai had to offer. He managed to rent a car by taking out a loan and paying 8,000 dirhams for a license. He also began going to the gym and posting Instagram pictures of lavish food, outings to the desert and the beach, and new products he bought (see Figure 5.1). These pictures, he said, were designed to make Amina jealous. He also began drinking and going to nightclubs. At one festival he attended in March 2019, he paid 1,000 dirhams for entry and free drinks. He showed me videos of belly dancers and fountains of alcoholic cocktails. Soon after this event, Mahmoud had a moment of realization: "One day I was sitting in my bed and just thought to myself, I can't carry on like this; I felt a light inside me, and it made me believe in God. I made a vow to stop drinking and doing bad stuff. That's when I decided to come back." Throughout the time I had known him, Mahmoud had been actively anti-religious. But in this moment of vulnerability he turned to God. Mahmoud's decision to leave Dubai also came after a period of illness: "I went twice to the doctor and suddenly thought if it was serious I would die alone here; at least in Egypt I have family and friends." Looking back, one can see that multiple things led Mahmoud to leaving: the loneliness, exhausting work schedule, and racism that made him feel like he could not achieve anything no matter how hard he tried. But it was his breakup that removed the reason for putting up with the exploitation he suffered: "I went for her," he said; "there was no point staying after."

Back in Egypt Mahmoud developed a detached engagement with life. In 2019 we spent hours going over what happened and lamenting how he would never find love again. This pain was brought into sharp focus when we were invited to Ibrahim and Noura's new marital home. While Mahmoud had sacrificed love for the dream of migrant mobility, Ibrahim had been unable to migrate but now enjoyed the status of marriage. I told Mahmoud he seemed less angry now; "I've just given up," he responded, "I don't care anymore, I became realistic." He explained how he felt "happy" because he did not care about being happy any longer: "I am no longer chasing anything. Amina made me work so hard for

FIGURE 5.1. An Instagram photo showing an outing to Dubai's "global village." Source: Mahmoud. Printed with permission.

everything, but I have no goals right now and that gives freedom." Like
Mostafa and Saami, in response to the pain brought about by his failed
attempts to chase love and a career, Mahmoud stepped back and detached
from the race itself. He still occupied his time and found immediate value
through a new job negotiating "savvy" deals as a purchasing manager for
a construction company at an upmarket housing development, as well as
looking after his aunt and seeing friends. He also still planned for a future
by investing in a flat with a government-owned bank loan. He engaged
in sporadic searches for a new partner and expressed flashes of a yearning
for a future that would enable him to be a loving father. However, he had
little hope: "I have five percent hope I can get married because a colleague
got married at thirty-three years old; with the next rejection it will be
three percent; eventually I will give up entirely." In 2019 Amina suggested
getting back together. Mahmoud could not do it, he told me, because he

no longer trusted her: "I asked if she loved her fiancé, and she could not answer; she loved someone else within two months, I can't forgive her." What kept Mahmoud calm now was faith in God: "I know God will make it okay whatever happens; when I pray I think about how God will never let me down. I realize now it is not about being rewarded; if you fail it is part of the journey God intended, it is destiny. I have done so well, some would die of overdose if they were in my position; the journey is only getting harder but I thank God for what he has done for me."

CONCLUSION: A DETACHED LABOR OF HOPE

During my time in Egypt in 2019, Ibrahim expressed gratitude that he had stayed and married Noura rather than traveling. He looked in comparison to Mahmoud, who had migrated and ruined his relationship. While he described how his relationship gave him power to deal with life's difficulties, Mahmoud had lost motivation and care for life itself. One could say therefore that migration had produced Mahmoud's emotionally detached approach to life, alongside Mostafa's and Saami's. For all three, migration had ruptured the utopian images of the future that made their lives livable in Egypt—with Mostafa having to begin a new bachelor's degree and Saami taking a job as a customer service agent. Only Gamal had managed to stitch together a semblance of what he had imagined by obtaining a high-status legal job, although he did not expect fatherhood to come so quick and was struggling in his relationship. However, this emotional journey is not unique to migrants. Inside Egypt, as the men I have spoken about in this book got older, they experienced a dramatic scaling down and the complete loss of countless dreams they once had in the realm of career, relationships, and lifestyles. Despite Ibrahim's pride and satisfaction in the aftermath of his marriage, he too had painfully given up grand visions of becoming an entrepreneur in the mold of Steve Jobs—and now focused on more immediate goals and pastimes. In 2019 he even took an accountancy job in 10th of Ramadan, the place he had previously described as a "tomb for youth." Eslam continued working in a low-paid, insecure customer service job in a Vodafone store while painstakingly preparing a marital flat. Adel also moved to 10th of Ramadan to work in an accountancy job on a low salary, especially considering the inflation that has gripped Egypt's economy in recent years.

All of these men over time lost the vigor they once exuded as they discussed their future trajectories. Downscaling one's dreams is in part understood as a normal aspect of making the transition from youthhood to adulthood in Egypt, but it is also the product of a capitalist system that is producing and making money out of stimulating hopes that are impossible to reach, while making even the achievement of stability—a stable job, a loving relationship, and a comfortable lifestyle—extremely difficult for so many. Each of these men went through periods of despair, where they stopped engaging in the pursuit of a good life. For Mahmoud this even led to suicidal thoughts. However, states of despair did not become permanent. All continued, even after the most painful disappointments, to engage in the pursuit of careers and marriage. Through doing so, they all managed to locate some form of private-sector work and still hold out hope for marriage, with the necessary support of parental savings. In many cases they also repositioned their hopes into faith, fatherhood, marriage, and less cosmopolitan lifestyles.

But the immensely painful transition from chasing grand dreams to accepting one's lot in life leaves its mark on the body. Retaining engagement in the aftermath requires a different way of being, or a different form of emotional labor, which relies on adaptation, renewal, sacrifice, and imperfection. It requires a more detached or disassociated stance toward the world in order to protect oneself from further pain. Since 2011, Lauren Berlant has developed her arguments on cruel optimism by examining the dissociative state of being in life that involves turning away from a world of injury, negation, and contingency that endures as a defining presence for biopolitical subjects.[28] This is a state—materially signified by the bodily "shrug"—in which people let go of the normative aspirational markers of the future that they have been chasing, in favor of life in the durative present. This does not mean that people do not engage in labors that provide hope for the future: getting married, having children and securing better futures for them, building a house, buying a car, saving for holidays. But they do so with less urgency and conviction, and with a hollowed-out emotional attachment to these aspirational pursuits. As this chapter makes clear, this labor again often maintains emphasis on the individual to cope with the disappointing world around them. Even the select few who do experience social mobility, like Gamal, also judge those who do not make it, because their success becomes seeming evidence of the meritocratic principle in which they invested so heavily. I want to end the book in the concluding chapter by discussing what a more collective response to the difficult individualized labors of hope that many must navigate might look like.

CONCLUSION

IN 2018 I CAME ACROSS a short film shared among Egyptians on Facebook. It was called "Happiness," by London-based illustrator Steve Cutts. The film starts with a crowd of rats waiting for a packed London tube to "nowhere." It then pans out to the city streets, again full of rats but also advertisements promising happiness in exchange for all kinds of commodities—coffee, films, cereal, theater shows. The film follows the attempt of one rat to find happiness. First, he goes to a Black Friday sale, where rats are fighting to secure products. The battered and bloody rat exits with an HD television but quickly drops it to jump into a new convertible car. After a few seconds of bliss driving through the city, he becomes stuck in a traffic jam. While sitting there, he gets a parking ticket, his wheels stolen, and graffiti drawn on his car before it starts raining. Looking despondent, the rat notices a billboard advertising a beer called "happiness," alongside the slogan *drink, forget, smile.* The rat climbs into the billboard and downs the beer, before doing the same to whiskey and vodka bottles. He finally gets a bottle stuck on his head and falls into the street, where thousands of rats pass without noticing. A piece of paper hits his face: a prescription for happiness. He meanders into a clinic, "sponsored by happimeds," and falls into a jar of tablets produced by "Grazon Smithe Klump." The rat is suddenly transformed into a dream world of nature, birdsong, and Disney characters. He jumps into the air and starts to fly over a palace before losing his wings and falling back into the dark, dense city. As he lies flat on his stomach in a back street, a hundred-dollar bill floats by. The rat begins to sniff and chase it, but it keeps getting away. He follows it into an elevator and into a room where it rests on a table. He finally reaches it before being snapped by a mousetrap on what turns out to be his desk. The film ends by panning out to thousands of rats trapped on their desks, typing away frantically.

Some who shared this video used it to critique atheistic Western life-styles—where people find fulfillment in hedonistic consumption instead of placing faith in God. But others recognized their own lives in it. Although the video was produced in an entirely different context, they saw a similarly protracted cruel pursuit of a feeling they had been chasing for years. Mah-moud, for example, told me upon watching it, "I have tried so long to find satisfaction [rida] and chase my dreams, but each time I think I am close it proves to be false. It is different in Egypt, though; we can't even buy the ticket to happiness!" I mentioned in Chapter 2 that young lower-middle-class Egyptian men struggle to empathize with an existential critique of the cruel pursuit of fulfillment within a capitalist system that relies on never-ending consumption and progress. Instead, their critique arises as they struggle to locate much movement at all toward the satisfaction that is materialized in a set of pillars that have come to define the good life in middle-class Egypt—internationalized private employment, durable romantic intimacy, and lavish cosmopolitan consumption lifestyles. As men chase those pillars, they en-counter "objects"—a training course, a scholarship application, an employ-ment fair, a self-help guru, a successful entrepreneur, a Hollywood movie, a new job, or a migration opportunity—that promise to provide the pathway toward them. These objects generate a feeling of hope that rests on the meri-tocratic notion that individuals are in charge of their destiny. But the pillars of prestigious employment, durable intimacy, and desirable lifestyles keep eluding the grasp of many lower-middle-class Egyptians. They meet repeated rejection from job and scholarship applications, get nowhere with finding start-up funds, become stuck in humiliating and unstable work, and face the ruination of romantic attachments. These experiences induce feelings of disappointment, despair, and anger. Life for these men becomes a constant effort to dispel these feelings and continue participating in the pursuit of a good life.

RECENTERING (EMOTIONAL) LABOR

This effort is what I have called the emotional labor necessary for people to cope within economic systems that produce a disconnect between the aspirations they encourage and the capacity they provide to realize them. I have placed direct focus on the practices—alongside social relations and moral terrains—that maintain a psychological state that enables people to keep engaging in the pursuit of normative good life fantasies. These include practices that provide temporary distraction and relief from the humiliation, frustration, boredom, and anxiety that emerges within the everyday routine of working in low-end jobs and the inability to experience movement toward better ones. For young middle-class Egyptian men, this entails engaging in satirical humor, watching lighthearted television, scrolling through social media, window shopping, and organizing outings with friends. As well as providing distraction, these activities offer momentary opportunities to occupy an aspirational subjectivity—to be youthful, modern, Muslim men—thus providing self-worth amid jobs that strip away this privilege. But the practices required to cope with low-status jobs and precarious situations take another form for those yearning to escape—those that keep alive a sense of hope for better things. This entails returning again and again to objects—self-help literature, religious discourse, Hollywood movies, stories of successful friends—that promise mobility to be in the hands of individuals, and objects such as training courses, applications, and migration routes that promise direct access to it. By opening up the realm of love, I also revealed how engaging in casual intimacy and building longer-term romantic attachments can provide both fleeting desire, excitement, and validation for young men, alongside purpose and hope that can compensate and provide motivation for difficult career pursuits.

I have argued for these practices to be seen as a form of emotional labor. This maps onto a vital endeavor to expand the practices we recognize as "labor": an endeavor inspired by feminist literature identifying the vitality of reproductive work within capitalist value creation alongside a recognition that the majority of the world has long preserved life outside stable wage relations. It involves moving beyond the narrow confines of the "productive" realm, which seems to have a direct relation to the economic and placing focus on all kinds of life-sustaining activities (and their associated kinship relations, sociality, affects, and moral narratives) that are abducted into "the expansion of money value."[1] Key also is recognition that the reproductive realm is not only the realm of women, although caring practices take place in highly gendered ways that incite a gendered politics. This project is still in its infancy, and much more work is required to reveal the hidden labors that produce value in and for capitalism. While some may hesitate to stretch the definition of labor too far, it is an effective way of connecting the realm of everyday practice with political economic effects under a hegemonic capitalist context. Expanding existing use of emotional labor, I have placed direct focus on the practices that go into maintaining emotional states that sustain the bodies of those engaged in the toil of preserving life and value creation. The practices of distraction and hope-making described—in the spheres of consumption, jobs, and love—although very often not exchanged directly for a wage, are key in enabling Egyptian men to keep offering themselves as labor. At once both individualized and collective endeavors, these practices enable them to endure as participants within low-status, low-paid jobs, and within a precarious, segmented labor market more broadly. They therefore represent a key, underexplored part of capitalist value creation through the extraction of labor.

A renewed focus on labor is important amid a trend in ethnographic scholarship to focus on postcapitalist survival and hope-making. These literatures have given the impression that dominant political and economic regimes have vacated the material and emotional worlds of marginalized peoples, and that those peoples have in turn begun to forge livelihoods and create hope for the future outside and against those regimes. But the empirical reality remains that most people continue to invest and participate in capitalist regimes that continue to churn out powerful promises of fulfillment. It is vital for us— rather than constantly seeking out resistant or even durable subjects—to come to terms with why capitalist regimes, despite producing huge inequalities, precarities, and hardship, continue to capture the attention and energy of people who appear harmed by them. Conceptually, the notion of labor helps with this project by centering the relationship between the activities, knowledges, and techniques that go into keeping hope alive, and their political economic and ideological origins and effects. Literature on both everyday practice and emotion-affect have positioned these realms as beyond the reach and entrenchment of hegemonic ideological and material formations. They are positioned as realms that represent the contingency of power relations and within which alternative forms of life emerge. A key aim within this book has been to place focus back onto the politics of everyday practice and emotion. This is not to suggest that these realms cannot birth new forms of resistance. Rather, the ways in which affects, emotions, and agencies emerge amid certain moralities, social relations, biopolitical techniques, and flows of capital, as well as how they become key mediums through which systems of inequality, governance, and exploitation are reproduced and challenged, must be subject to empirical research across a range of spheres.

In this book I have implemented this approach by following the everyday emotions, affects, and agencies that emerge in the lives of educated under-employed Egyptian men. I argued that their emotional labor of survival is a key realm in which legitimacy for Egypt's capitalist regime is won on a daily basis. Practices of distraction provide individualized avenues for reliev-ing negative emotions that build up within difficult jobs and a difficult labor market, while the practices making up the labor of hope reproduce a meri-tocratic moral economy that retains focus on individuals as determinants of success. Low-end workers replicate and forge an emotional attachment to this moral economy because of its inherently hopeful quality: it eternally offers the prospect that they remain in charge of their destiny rather than structural factors beyond their control. This moral economy is vital in enabling these men to survive, but this survival is not necessarily something to be celebrated, as it reinforces the legitimacy and secures the reproduction of a precarious, highly unequal capitalist regime. It leads to the focus of many people, from trainers and self-help gurus to struggling call center workers and those who experience a little mobility, being kept on the individual and their attitude, passion, and drive rather than on structural inequalities and a lack of oppor-tunities, which means that those attitudes can matter little.

I have focused on the political economy and governmental techniques alongside the everyday social creativities that are producing this emotional labor. It is being driven by a discursive and material formation of objects, narratives, and capital flows that have a complex geography, evolving from globalized circulations of commodities, Hollywood movies, entrepreneurship expertise, soft-skills training, and self-help, alongside Egyptian and Islamic discourses of humor, respect, destiny, and moral responsibility. It is spread by formalized private, governmental, and third-sector organizations that commodify, survive, and profit from these emotional labors. These include film and television, football, tobacco industries, fashion industries, social media, and comedians that provide opportunities for workers to distract and assert their "true" self momentarily, alongside self-help gurus, training centers, recruitment agencies, and entrepreneurial ecosystems that attract clients and "beneficiaries" by promising to unlock future success. However, throughout the book I have also argued that this emotional labor cannot be understood only as a set of practices coerced from above. Rather, dominant political economic and moral circulations interact with and get taken on, altered, and sometimes rejected within the daily lives of young middle-class Egyptian men who place great social value on being light, humorous, and hopeful, while developing creative forms of humor, sociality, and consumption alongside tactics of job-seeking, skill development, and religious piety to induce these emotional states. Going forward, research must retain a nuanced approach that combines focus on dominant knowledges and material techniques with the ethical and creative responses of those engaged in the toil of preserving life to understand fully the production of certain material and discursive landscapes.

It is important to finally consider how widespread this form of emotional labor might be. Throughout the book I have suggested that the practices and experiences I am describing are specific to a youthful male middle-class group in Egypt who are facing a stark disconnect between their aspirations for a globalized private-sector career, a cosmopolitan consumption lifestyle, durable marriage, and a precarious reality of becoming stuck in low-status, low-paid service work that leads to huge difficulties in affording marriage and desirable lifestyles. However, the condition of disconnection is far from unique to them. Middle-class Egyptian women face their own version, as record numbers graduate from university and develop aspirations for high-skilled careers but face more structural unemployment than men and have to wait ever longer to open a household—which remains a key marker of social value for them. It would be an important project to delve into the practices that Egyptian women are developing to cope with the experience of this disconnect. But far beyond middle-class Egypt, contemporary capitalist economies and cities are producing agonizing disconnections. They encourage and profit from the widespread production of aspiration through expanding access to education, making visible the careers and lifestyles of a national and global elite on social media, television, roadside billboards, and their in-built uncertainty that produces a proximity to socially mobile relatives or friends. However, they are also producing greater levels of impoverishment, competition, and precarity as capital-intensive growth, volatile economies, and neoliberal labor regimes fail to generate sufficient secure, well-paid employment and access to dignified lifestyles.

Amid a disconnect between expectations and realities, people find all sorts of ways to cope with the negative feelings that emerge during the tumultuous pursuit of their aspirations, as they face job rejections or firings, get stuck in precarious contracts, struggle to save money, or face ruined relationships. Overcoming these setbacks takes constant emotional work, both collective and individual. While scholarship must be attentive to localized practices, social relations, and forms of morality, the objects, practices, and spaces that provide brief distraction and relief described in the book—cigarettes, gyms, television, social media, football, and shopping malls—are not unique to contemporary Egypt. They represent mechanisms of transitory pleasure for huge numbers of people in diverse contexts. At the same time, the ubiquity of meritocratic logics is not unique to Egypt. The notion that achievement depends on the reach of one's dreams and willingness to work hard for them is being spread by politicians, training and education, entrepreneurs, films, self-help gurus, religious preachers, and those navigating difficult labor markets. Many critique these logics for legitimizing inequalities, but they carry hugely optimistic allure for people struggling to achieve their dreams in life. While it is vital that the power of this allure is properly recognized—as I have tried to do here—in the final section I would like to spend some time considering how we might reflect on turning attention to more collective labors of hope amid the continued production of structural impoverishments and precarities within contemporary capitalist regimes.

A COLLECTIVE LABOR OF HOPE?

To end I would like to directly address a question I have received many times while presenting this work: what about the existence or emergence of resistance among the young men I spent time with? In the book I have attempted to write against an overwhelming focus within ethnographic accounts of survival on practices that represent the emergence of alternative, postcapitalist forms of life. This is born out of an affective pull within scholarship to locate optimism by seeking out resistant subjects. I have put forward the notion of an individualized labor of hope, a set of practices key to enabling people to survive an unjust capitalist regime but reinforcing it through reproducing the cruel notion that any individual can achieve self-improvement through hard work. But this does not preclude the vitality of cultivating a labor of hope that is more collective in nature. This labor may produce a feeling of hope for the fulfillment of dreams or enhancement of livelihoods that does not rest on the notion of individual power. Rather, it rests on the formation of collectives that work together toward common goals or on the prospect of changing the structural barriers inhibiting the ability of people to achieve dignified lives.

Other scholars have demonstrated how a democratization of consumerist aspirations can act as a stimulus for collective claims-making.[2] As I have shown in this book, there are an abundance of moments where young men who are navigating a treacherous labor market demonstrate critical awareness of the structural barriers that prevent them from reaching the aspirational pillars of the good life in middle-class Egypt. In the aftermath of job rejections, amid long periods spent in low-status, low-paid, insecure jobs, and in the wake of ruined relationships, men briefly turn their individual and collective anger toward corruption, educational inequality, nepotism, and a lack of available jobs. For this they latch on to a complex geography of critique, a mixture of Egyptianized jokes and stories from prominent comedians, social media, and friendship circles alongside globalized artistic production—indeed Steve Cutts's film *Happiness* was produced in London for Western audiences. For some, over time their emotional labor of hope also became more performative, skeptical, and detached. In different periods they therefore demonstrate a critical stance that reveals the fragility of their compliance within an unjust economic system, a stance that might represent the potential for solidarity and collective action to emerge that is targeted at changing the system.

When I traveled to Egypt in autumn 2019, an interesting set of events took place. Mohamed Ali, a forty-five-year-old businessman and former actor who liquidated his assets and moved to Spain, posted a series of videos online accusing the president and military of corruption. Ali was the former owner of a private contracting business that worked on projects for the military. He claimed to be owed millions of Egyptian pounds and fled the country over fears of retaliation. Ali also accused Sisi of squandering state funds to build presidential palaces as well as allocating projects as favors to generals in his close circle. His combination of insider knowledge and machismo populist rhetoric gave him huge popularity—his videos received millions of views.[3] However, although he called repeatedly for nationwide protests, only a few scattered protests surfaced, with several hundred arrests taking place as Egypt's security forces effectively shut down the entire downtown area and began random checks on phones for content supportive of Ali's messages.

Ali's videos struck a chord with Egyptians increasingly angry at the state of the country and economy, which was making it more difficult to lead dignified lives—especially in the aftermath of the flotation of the Egyptian pound in 2016, which halved its value against the dollar. When I spoke to Eslam, Adel, and Mahmoud about the videos, they had all watched them. They agreed with almost everything Ali was saying: "Egypt is a place of massive inequality, where you have a big difference between rich and poor; we are really struggling to survive and it is only getting harder as the cost of living is getting so high," Eslam whispered cautiously while we sat in an ahwa near his home. However, none of these men had any intention of protesting. They feared a repressive security state, while also disbelieving in the potential of changing anything through protest, having invested in this belief during the 2011 uprising only to see no improvement in their life prospects. In fact, during one of the Friday protests, I was far away from Cairo with Mahmoud on a short holiday on the Red Sea. He described being thankful to be away. This holiday represented, again, the more individualized emotional labors that young men engage in in order to navigate their painful pursuits of jobs.

A collective labor of hope could therefore look like participation in protest. But for the duration of the fieldwork that contributed to this book from 2014 to 2019, I witnessed no participation in collective action challenging the structures within which these individuals were operating, either in the streets or at their workplaces. This does not mean that overt protest or union activity did not take place during this period. However, there are various material, moral, and affective barriers to the formation of protest in present-day Egypt. First and foremost, the return of an extremely repressive security regime incites great fear of harassment, imprisonment, or worse among the population. Second, my fieldwork took place in the shadow of a 2011 uprising that from the vantage point of a few years later is viewed as a failure. Finally, though, the formation of a moral economy that incessantly places responsibility for success upon individuals makes it difficult to develop a moral language to collectively criticize structural problems. People who do criticize structural problems are often judged for being negative or complaining. Upholding this moral economy is stimulated by a powerful affective pull. People navigating precarious labor markets are pulled back toward narratives focusing on individual power because of their hopeful quality, and away from those focusing on structural barriers because they induce depression in this context. Meritocratic narratives are indeed so powerful because they offer up the enticing possibility that individual persistence can overcome structural barriers.

This also demonstrates how hegemonic structures can secure legitimacy without necessarily duping their subjects. Instead, legitimacy and stability can be secured affectively. While navigating a precarious labor regime on a daily basis, even if people understand very well structural issues such as nepotism or a lack of available jobs, they cannot afford to focus on these things for long. Once dreams have been surrendered and people have adapted to the new realities they are faced with, it is often too painful to look back on the wreckage of lost dreams. People want to feel that their current and future lives will add up to something. They therefore learn to value and construct meaning within the lives they lead, finding ways to cobble together a fulfilling and meaningful life. Throughout my attempts to follow the lives of these men, it therefore always felt misplaced to place much attention on the need for collective action. As researchers we need to respect the ways in which people navigating oppressive regimes cope and survive, even if we consider those ways to be cruel. However, it is also important to recognize the imminent unpredictable potential for the emergence of sudden forms of collective action and resistance.[4] The acute awareness, humor, and critique of structural problems in Egypt's economy could provide the foundation for protest. Indeed, the sudden explosion of mass protest in 2011 is perhaps a good illustration of this.

In a context where many people remain attached to chasing good-life fantasies through individualized navigations of contemporary labor markets, what then might a collective labor of hope look like? While I have argued that the coping strategies of the men I was following should not be romanticized or celebrated, we must recognize how new social relations can emerge out of the conservative everyday pursuit of livelihoods. Indeed, feminist scholars have argued that a masculinized focus on visible collective action can elide the—often ambivalent—politics bound up within everyday practice.[5] As I outlined, some men did manage to experience social mobility. Relying on the help of family and friends in the form of money, connections, and educational resources, they took advantage of small openings within labor markets and migratory regimes. This may be tempting to analyze as what Asef Bayat calls quiet encroachment, resulting in a small redistribution of resources—remember, for example, Mostafa, who managed to acquire personal private-investment clients while keeping his job in a financial investments call center.[6] However, the fact that some are able to experience mobility within these regimes provides additional legitimacy to meritocratic logics. Furthermore, even though many rely on social relations in the form of money and connections, those who achieve relative success remain inclined to explain their success based on individual perseverance.

As men engage in the difficult pursuit of social mobility, the emotional labor of distraction and hope is forging new pastimes, forms of humor and critique, and networks of support, solidarities, and empathies between men and women. Out of the rubble of lost dreams, new standards of middle-classness in the realm of employment and lifestyles may be emerging, as well as new meanings of what it means to be a Muslim or a man. Recall how Ibrahim began to emphasize proximity to his family, the dangers of endlessly chasing money, and the benefits of village life in the aftermath of his inability to obtain his entrepreneurial dream or migration abroad. The impact of this adaptation is already being felt in the realm of gender relations. Women and men are being forced to endure longer periods before marriage. This elongation is giving middle-class Egyptian women more—albeit circumscribed—opportunities to chase their own careers, while forcing young couples to navigate forms of gendered respectability and religious piety as they manage tricky premarital relationships. However, it is also leading to the targeting of more anger and frustration toward Egyptian women among men as they hold up an idealized image of "clean," nonmonetized love. For most this attitude is not preventing engagement in the financial necessities of marriage, but in many cases marital norms are being stretched as parents have to step in to help, and women and their families have to show greater flexibility by letting go of their own aspirations in order to facilitate men's struggles in the labor market.

More work is needed to establish the novel forms of living that are emerging among middle-class youth in contemporary Egypt. But this analysis should not sideline the intense pain and hardship that continues to be produced by structural forces that reach far beyond their control. Egypt's authoritarian neoliberal regime is creating a stark disconnect between the aspirations it is encouraging and the means it provides for so many not just to be able to achieve them but to lead dignified lives at all. In lieu of the ability of many Egyptians navigating this economy to concentrate on those forces for long, I want to end the book by reminding us of the need for policy makers, development professionals, and commentators to redirect *their* collective labor of hope away from individual responsibility and toward the structural causes of disconnection and precarity in Egypt's labor market and wider economy. Since economic liberalization in the 1990s and early 2000s, the country has struggled with a severe deficit of formal, well-paid white-collar jobs. There are dramatic discrepancies between the quality and pay of private-sector jobs in the internationalized economy and those outside it. Low-paid, insecure service and sales work, especially in the BPO industry, does not provide a long-term solution to this deficit. It produces immense difficulties in working toward marriage, buying a home, and looking after families when all three are becoming ever more expensive. At the same time, upper-class Egyptians are accumulating vast wealth through property and other investments.

Meritocratic narratives encourage the logic that high-status, well-paid jobs and lifestyles can be reached by anyone. However, these narratives conceal the continued entrenchment of class inequality in the labor market. In May 2015, Egypt's justice minister Mahfouz Saber was asked in a television interview whether the son of a garbage collector could be appointed to the judiciary. Here was his reply:

> The son of a garbage collector will not become a judge, because he is not
> brought up in the right environment for this profession. Even if he becomes
> a judge, he will come across many problems and will [end up] quitting. . . .
> The rubbish collector must have done a great job raising his son and helping
> him obtain a degree, but there are other jobs that would suit him better.[7]

Saber emphasized the need for judges to come from a "respectable environment," both financially and morally. His comments caused uproar and led to
his resignation. The event recalled other cases of class discrimination. Abdul
Hamid Sheta committed suicide in 2003, at age twenty-five, after being rejected from a job as a commercial attaché in the diplomatic service. Having
scored higher than many others on the entrance exam, he was rejected because he came from a poor family, with the Foreign Ministry explaining
that Sheta was "socially unsuitable." In response to Saber's comments, former
vice president Mohamed ElBaradei tweeted his disgust, stating that "international rights charters guarantee freedom of choice of employment." The
British ambassador waded in, announcing that all are welcome to work at the
British embassy, including the garbage collector's son. The National Council
for Human Rights rapidly prepared a draft law forbidding all forms of discrimination in employment, in line with Article 53 of the 2014 constitution,
which reads: "Discrimination and incitement to hate are crimes punishable
by law."[8]

The reaction to this event was to push further for the discursive imple-
mentation of equal opportunity and meritocracy in what remains a "back-
wards," classist labor market, where recruitment is based on individual talent
and credentials rather than social background. Judging someone based on
individual merit may seem a noble pursuit, but this book has revealed the
harmful effects enacted by the hopeful extension of meritocracy and fairness
in a hierarchical capitalist system that continues to reward inherited privilege
and produce entrenched inequalities. The truth is that it is practically impossible for sons, not to mention daughters, of garbage collectors to become
judges in Egypt. High-status jobs in the public and private sector continue
to be decided by massive discrepancies in Egyptians' cultural and social capital—their educational certificates, English-language skills, connections in

high-status fields, even taste in music and ability to travel. These discrepancies are being produced within an education system that is becoming more stratified—where money can buy access to international schools, private universities, and fee-paying sections of public universities—alongside Egypt's highly segmented class structure more broadly. The language of meritocracy provides legitimacy for those decisions—but the reproduction of inequality continues to operate beneath the surface. Encouraging everyone to chase high aspirations in a system that produces entrenched hierarchies is cruel. It will continue to produce the kinds of anger and disappointment described in this book as people are unable to reach the lives they are promised. Improving this situation requires not simply telling people to work harder but tackling the structural barriers that are preventing so many from accessing a dignified life.

NOTES

INTRODUCTION

1. Over twenty-five years ago, Walter Armbrust provided a vivid description of the underwhelming swearing-in ceremony of lawyers to the Egyptian bar association, which symbolizes the plight facing Egypt's public universities. Armbrust, *Mass Culture and Modernism in Egypt*.

2. A series of large-scale quantitative studies asserted this using wage growth and consumptive capacity. Ncube and Lufampa, *The Emerging Middle Class*; Ravallion, "The Developing World's Bulging (but Vulnerable) 'Middle Class'"; Kharas, "The Emerging Middle Class."

3. This measurement was based on those spending between $10 and $100 per day. In 2011, the African Development Bank, using an alternative definition of people who spend $4 to $20 per day, stated that a rising middle class reached 31.6 percent of the population by 2010. This figure rose to an incredible 79.7 percent if the "vulnerable floating middle" (those who spend $2 to $4 per day) was included. African Development Bank, "The Middle of the Pyramid."

4. Chakrabarty, *Provincializing Europe*.

5. World Bank, "Middle-Class Frustration."

6. This report defined the middle class as those who earn more than $4.90 per day in 2005 terms. It declined from 14.3 percent to 9.8 percent between the mid-2000s and the end of the decade. Ianchovichina et al., "Inequality, Uprisings, and Conflict."

7. Credit Suisse, "Annual Global Wealth Report."

8. Wietzke and Sumner, "What Are the Political and Social Implications"; Kochhar, "A Global Middle Class."

9. This is a damning analysis, and it maps onto Thomas Piketty's analysis that demonstrates how all but 1 percent of the world's population has seen real wealth fall or stagnate since the mid-twentieth century. Piketty, *Capital in the 21st Century*. For evidence of these trends in the Middle East, see Alvaredo and Piketty, "Measuring Top Incomes."

10. This approach to middle-classness stems from Weberian and Bourdieusian understandings of class, which have been used and complicated in studies of the performance

of middle-classness in different contexts of the Global South. Although scholars must be wary about extending the purchase of the concept, research has overcome this issue by applying empirical historical analyses. Lentz, "Elites or Middle Classes?"; Liechty, *Suitably Modern.*

11. Ryzova, *The Age of the Efendiyya.*

12. Galal Amin estimated that Egypt's middle class increased from 19 percent in 1955 to 45 percent in 1986. The middle class in 1986 encompassed families who earned between LE300 (US$420) and LE10,000 (US$14,200) per month, a varied populace incorporating extreme affluence and modest living. Amin, *Whatever Happened to the Egyptians*, 31–37.

13. University enrollment tripled between 1952 and 1970, while by the early 1980s over half the nonagricultural workforce—and 20 percent of the total—was employed by the state. Richards and Waterbury, *A Political Economy.* The private sector was limited to land ownership (although a cooperative system monitored and controlled it), buildings (though rents were controlled and heavily taxed), construction, light industry, 25 percent of national exports, and 75 percent of internal trade. The government controlled infrastructure, heavy and medium industry, institutions of foreign trade, and financial operations. Zaalouk, *Class, Power and Foreign Capital.*

14. Walter Armbrust provided a useful definition of Egypt's middle class—colloquially labeled el-muwaẓafiyyn (the employees)—during this time: "Middle class does not correlate with a material standard of living. Egyptians who have at least a high school education, and therefore basic literacy and familiarity with how modern institutions work, generally consider themselves middle class. Egyptians who think of themselves as middle class expect a lifestyle free from manual labor. In the media, the ideal of middle class is often associated with modernity, bureaucracy, and office work, and it is portrayed as having a degree of familiarity with an ideology of national identity that seeks to balance local Egyptian and classical Islamic cultural referents." Armbrust, "Bourgeois Leisure," 111.

15. By 1975 the public deficit was LE1.3 billion (US$3.3 billion) and the trade deficit was LE1 billion (US$2.5 billion). Zaalouk, *Class, Power and Foreign Capital*, 55. Government technocrats and a lingering bourgeoisie called for greater space for private-sector activity to aid their business interests and desires for European goods. The state encouraged saving and entrepreneurship by introducing concessions on rent controls, higher wages for some bureaucrats, and tax exemptions on certain company profits. Jankowski, *Egypt.*

16. The shortfall was due to military expenditure to the United States, defaults on loans to entrepreneurs, and falls in oil prices in the wake of the 1990–1991 Gulf conflict, which reduced migrant remittances. Rutherford, *Egypt After Mubarak.*

17. Kienle, *A Grand Delusion.*

18. Mitchell, *Rule of Experts.*

19. Salem, *Anticolonial Afterlives.*

20. The lives of this new "upper-middle class" provided the focus for two books: de Koning's *Global Dreams* and Peterson's *Connected in Cairo.* They fit within a broader body of work revealing how affluent middle-class groups forged new lines of distinction in Latin America, South and East Asia, and sub-Saharan Africa on the back of

late-twentieth-century economic liberalization. Caldeira, *City of Walls*; Fernandes, *India's New Middle Class*; Zhang, *In Search of Paradise*; Mercer, *Middle Class Construction*. Scholarship on the hardship caused by these processes has concentrated on poor populations pushed into the "informal" city and "nonwaged" work. Singerman, *Avenues of Participation*; Ismail, *Political Life*; Davis, *Planet of Slums*. While this produces powerful imagery of divided cities, with the walled off upper-middle-class beneficiaries of capitalist development inhabiting a distinct city from the masses who are deemed "unnecessary" for neoliberal growth, it glosses over more interstitial experiences, and particularly more challenging middle-class lives. Lawson, "De-centering Poverty Studies." Placing attention on these populations is fruitful as it debunks the core myths of nations becoming more prosperous, fair, and democratic, while also encouraging solidarity between the middle classes and the poor to combat their malign effects.

21. Sims, *Understanding Cairo*.

22. From the 1970s onward, lagging production and expanding consumption steadily devalued the Egyptian pound. In the mid-1970s the Egyptian pound (LE) was equal to US$2.50. In the mid-1990s this had more than reversed: the dollar was equal to LE3.40. By 2011, the pound had dropped to US$6, before declining after the revolution to over US$8 by 2015—it has since declined even more. The minimum government salary was LE1,200 (US$150) per month in 2014, increased from LE800 before 2011. The lower-middle classes engage in additional activities to supplement salaries—for example, acting as land brokers or engaging in small-business operations outside government employment. These activities provide important funds, sometimes used to invest in land to secure against rising house prices; however, they do not provide a buffer against financial hardship.

23. A UNDP Arab Human Development Report described the education system as providing programs "dominated by didactic not interactive instruction with a drive to install loyalty, obedience, and support for the regime in power, besides being drenched in social inhibitions and religious taboos." Mehrez, *Egypt's Culture Wars*, 101. As a result, a concurrent system of private tutoring has developed, but this is highly differentiated in quality by financial power. In the report, public universities are reported to "lack adequate financial, human and material resources and provide poor-quality education that is at once mediocre, dogmatic and conservative." Mehrez, *Egypt's Culture Wars*, 95.

24. In 2000–2001, 20 percent of the college-age population (ages 17–22) were enrolled in higher education, compared to just 6.9 percent in 1970. De Koning, *Global Dreams*, 48.

25. Some 110,000 pupils attend nineteen private universities while 1.6 million attend twenty-three public universities. European Commission, *Overview*.

26. Youth unemployment (ages 15–29) stands at 29 percent (23 percent for men and 53 percent for women). Among Egypt's 2.3 million university graduates, 34 percent are unemployed, compared to 2.4 percent of those without education. Assaad and Krafft, "Youth Transitions in Egypt."

27. Amin, "Egypt Country Report."

28. Those entering the public sector upon leaving university declined from 70 percent to 20 percent between 1970 and 1996. Assaad and Krafft, "Youth Transitions in Egypt."

29. In Egypt, "informal" employment—without social or legal protections, a con-

tract, or regular wages—has long constituted a major segment of the economy. Among wage workers who have a secondary education, only 42 percent have a formal work contract. Ghafar, *Educated but Unemployed*. Colloquially, *informal* often means working in the streets rather than in an office.

30. Egypt has a global BPO market share of 16.9 percent. Brussels Research Group, "Egypt Is Considered." Some 16 percent of employed youth work in service and sales work, whereas only 6 percent of young men have professional jobs.

31. Anouk de Koning described how a dual labor market emerged in the aftermath of economic liberalization, with internationally oriented sectors that provide wages on average five times those of comparable domestic-facing firms. De Koning, *Global Dreams*.

32. A 2014 labor market transitions survey found that half of young workers earned between LE500 and LE999, with 25 percent earning between LE1,000 and LE2,999 per month. Barsoum et al., "Labour Market."

33. The word *sha'by* has been used since the 1940s by the media before it came into daily language. Ghannam, *Remaking the Modern*, 79. It comes from the word *sha'b*, which means "people" or "folk" but is distinct from the word *balady* (local or popular)— or *ibn al-balad*, which defines an authentic, traditional Egyptian identity. El-Messiri, *Ibn al-Balad*. After Egypt's infitah, *sha'by* has become a derogatory term to describe the lower classes in middle- and upper-class discourse. There are positive connotations, though, around sha'by life being "fun."

34. After the 2011 uprising, Asef Bayat announced the emergence of a young "middle-class poor." These were people "with high education, self-constructed status, wider worldviews, and global dreams who nonetheless are compelled—by unemployment and poverty—to subsist on the margins of the neoliberal economy as casual, low-paid, low-status, and low-skilled workers . . . and to reside in the overcrowded slums and squatter settlements of Arab cities. Economically poor, they still fantasize about an economic status that their expectations demand—working in IT companies, with secure jobs, middle-class consumption patterns, and perhaps migration to the West." While he does not speculate as to how large this population might be, various employment, education, and survey data outlined in the previous section gives some insight. Bayat, "A New Arab Street."

35. Ghannam, *Live and Die*; Naguib, *Nurturing Masculinities*; Inhorn, *The New Arab Man*; Norbakk, "A Man in Love."

36. See Assaad and Krafft, *The Egyptian Labor Market*, for discussions on female unemployment.

37. Disconnection is a concept coined by James Ferguson to counter a dominant narrative that globalization, economic liberalization, and new technologies were creating heightened connectivity. Drawing on work in the Zambian copperbelt, Ferguson described disconnection as a material process through which populations are "thrown aside, expelled, or discarded" from dominant circulations of capital and value creation. Ferguson also alludes to disconnection as a subjective condition as he describes how Zambian mineworkers had to come to terms with the withdrawal of the promise of an economic boom. Ferguson, *Expectations of Modernity*, 236.

38. There are similarities with Ted Gurr's concept of "relative deprivation," which describes the discrepancy between what people think they deserve and what they actually think they can get. Gurr, *Why Men Rebel*. It also echoes other concepts, such as "waithood" or "timepass," which describe how youthful populations are unable to reach independent adulthood, classed aspirations for a good life, and gendered expectations placed on men or women. Honwana, *The Time of Youth*; Jeffrey, *Timepass*; Cole, *Sex and Salvation*. But I favor the term *disconnection*, as it foregrounds the gap between aspirations and chances, while not assuming how this is experienced in daily life.

39. Heiman, *Driving After Class*. Separate literature has explored how capitalist economies are offering up a greater capacity for aspiration, without providing the means to achieving them. Appadurai, *Modernity at Large*; Weiss, *Street Dreams*.

40. Disconnection is impacting other middle-class populations. Like Egypt, many postcolonial states created a middle class out of state education and employment to build national identity, drive economic development, and extend political control. Heiman et al., *The Global Middle Classes*. However, as they underwent economic liberalization, these populations have experienced instability. While education continues to expand, economic changes associated with the spread of market relations, retraction of the state, and expansion of financial and commercial industries have reduced public employment and failed to generate sufficient secure white-collar work. Harvey, *A Brief History of Neoliberalism*; Boltanski and Chiapello, *The New Spirit of Capitalism*. Long-term employment has often been replaced by unstable sectors, with BPO industries exemplifying this trend. This has created masses of educated labor stuck in unemployment or employment that does not reflect their skills or provide security. Jeffrey et al., *Degrees Without Freedom?* A rising youth demographic often exacerbates this problem.

41. Interest in the emotional experience of capitalist relations is indebted to feminist anthropological critique of the Enlightenment's masculinist focus on individual rationality. This critique revealed that the present is not experienced through "rational" or "conscious" thought processes but rather first and foremost through emotion or bodily affect. Illouz, *Cold Intimacies*; Lutz, *Unnatural Emotions*; Ahmed, *The Cultural Politics of Emotion*.

42. Questions persist over whether hope constitutes an emotion itself, a nonrepresentational modality akin to affect, or a belief sustained by affect or emotion. Crapanzano, "Reflections on Hope."

43. Jackson, *Life Within Limits*, xi.

44. Miyazaki, *The Method of Hope*.

45. Ernst Bloch argued that hope is intrinsic to a consciousness formed in anticipation of the future. Bloch, *The Principle of Hope*. But it is also fueled by a sense of insufficiency, a sense that there is "more to life than what exists for us in the here and now." Jackson, *Life Within Limits*, xii. While psychoanalytical approaches relate this to a Lacanian sense of lack, Jacques Lacan understands desire as being fueled by a perpetual sense of lack, a lack of recognition from others. According to this notion, "desire's raison d'etre is not to realise its goal, to find full satisfaction, but to reproduce itself as desire." Žižek, *The Plague of Fantasies*, 38. It rests on separation between the desiring subject and the object that is desired. By contrast, anxiety arises if there is nothing left to be desired.

46. Schielke, *Egypt in the Future Tense*, 23.

47. Ethnographic work has explicated the intricate temporal and emotional experience out of what Bruce O'Neill in his research with homeless men in Bucharest describes being "cast aside" from the pursuit of a meaningful life based on secure jobs, affordable housing, lasting intimacy, and adhering to hegemonic gender roles. O'Neill, *The Space of Boredom*; Allison, *Precarious Japan*; Coleman, "Austerity Futures."

48. Philosophical work includes Ernst Bloch's setting up of a dialogue between Christianity and Marxism and David Harvey's mapping out of a "dialectical utopianism." Bloch, *The Principle of Hope*; Harvey, *Spaces of Hope*. Ethnographic scholarship explicates the practices invoking what Hirokazu Miyazaki terms a "temporal reorientation" of knowledge among marginalized communities. Miyazaki, *The Method of Hope*, 52; Mains, *Hope Is Cut*; Pedersen, "A Day in the Cadillac"; Zigon, "Hope Dies Last"; Janeja and Bandak, *Ethnographies of Waiting*. This has also been framed as temporal agency. Ringel and Moroşanu, "Time-Tricking." It also echoes a broader trend in ethnographic writing asserting the generative possibilities thrown up by uncertain economic arrangements, in that they engender the adaptive capacity of marginalized populations to engage in resistance or forge livelihoods seemingly beyond capitalist regimes of value and accumulation. Scholars have used terms like "navigation, "improvisation," and "hustle" to interpret survival strategies. Vigh, "Wayward Migration"; Thieme, "The Hustle Economy"; Cooper and Pratten, *Ethnographies of Uncertainty*.

49. Walker and Kavedžija, *Values of Happiness*.

50. Capitalist regimes are said to have vacated the "near future" and started governing in anticipation of endangerment rather than expectation of future progress. Guyer, "Prophecy and the Near Future"; Zeiderman, *Endangered City*.

51. Berlant, *Cruel Optimism*, 24.

52. Henrik Vigh's concept of social navigation (or dubriagem) describes how people "disentangle themselves from confining structures, plot their escape, and move towards better positions." Vigh, "Wayward Migration," 419. The words *agent, agency*, and *agentive* are used time and again to describe the propensity of people to relocate hope or "trick time" in times of precarity and uncertainty. This work stems conceptually from de Certeau's differentiation between strategies and tactics. Strategies, linked to institutions and power structures, involve the production of spatial formations, while tactics are used by individuals to navigate environments. De Certeau, *The Practice of Everyday Life*.

53. Laura Bear argued that the anthropological focus on ethics ignores the continued production of inequality and accumulation through the temporal and emotional landscapes of capitalist modernity. It needs to be combined with analysis of the knowledges associated with bureaucratic and corporate institutions, and techniques that create new material formations. Bear, "Anthropological Futures."

54. Distinguishing between emotion and affect originates in the seventeenth-century work of Benedictus de Spinoza. Affect describes a "prepersonal intensity corresponding to the passage from one experiential state of the body to another." Deleuze and Guattari, *Anti-Oedipus*, xvii. Affects inhabit a transpersonal terrain, what Ben Anderson labels an "atmosphere" within which bodies/objects encounter one another. Anderson, "Affective

Atmospheres." Personal feelings emerge through these encounters. They constitute the conscious ways people make sense of and provide a language to transpersonal intensities with repeated experience.

55. This approach to affect stems from the work of scholars such as Antonio Negri and Derek McCormack, among others. Negri, "Value and Affect"; McCormack, "An Event of Geographical Ethics." Ben Anderson argued that research must do more to consider how affective capacities become the "object-target" of biopolitical techniques and apparatuses, and how collective affects become part of the "conditions" for the birth of new forms of biopower. Anderson, "Affect and Biopower."

56. Williams, *Marxism and Literature*; Illouz, *Cold Intimacies*; Stewart, *Ordinary Affects*. Anthropological work on emotion has also helped theorize how it is shaped by dominant political, social, economic, and cultural arrangements. Abu-Lutz and Lughod, *Language and the Politics of Emotion*; Lutz, *Unnatural Emotions*; Richard and Rudnyckyj, "Economies of Affect."

57. Work has exposed how the production of certain affects/emotions is crucial in financial modeling, encouraging consumption, governing spaces and populations, and extracting value from labor. Hochschild, *The Managed Heart*; Konings, *The Emotional Logic of Capitalism*;. Schüll, *Addiction by Design*; Davies, *Nervous States*. But there remains a long way to go to understand the relationship between emotions and modes of capitalist accumulation, exploitation, and gendered, racialized, and colonial inequalities—in other words, the emotional politics of contemporary capitalism.

58. This might be funneled through the attempts of various institutions, industries, or dominant logics to encourage certain behaviors such as resilience, endurance, or entrepreneurialism, or create happy citizens. Kohl-Arenas, *The Self-Help Myth*; Cabanas and Illouz, *Manufacturing Happy Citizens*; Grove, "Agency, Affect."

59. Recent work in anthropology has examined the everyday politics of hope in different spheres, tracing how it sometimes provides the grounds for accumulation and inequality but also for the emergence of sociality, which challenges those processes. Sanchez, "Relative Precarity"; Cross, "The Economy of Anticipation"; Lorey, *State of Insecurity*; De Boeck, "Inhabiting Ocular Ground."

60. Hochschild, *The Managed Heart*; Hochschild, *The Outsourced Self*. A related term is Hardt and Negri's notion of affective labor, which posits the broad shift from material to immaterial labor in late capitalism. But this has come under heavy criticism for reifying a false gendered dichotomy between mental and manual labor. Hardt and Negri, *Empire*; Donatella, *Immaterial Labour*.

61. This builds on scholarship recognizing that all life-sustaining labor is affective, immaterial and material in its effects and practices, and literature analyzing the cultural terms through which workers consent to labor. Burawoy, *Manufacturing Consent*; Willis, *Learning to Labour*; Yanagisako, *Immaterial and Industrial Labor*.

62. These discussions began in the 1970s and 1980s with a focus on women's domestic labor but has expanded to constitute the "fleshy, messy, indeterminate stuff of everyday life" that goes into biological reproduction; the subsistence, education, training, and psychical support of the labor force; and the provisioning of care needs. Katz, "Vagabond

Capitalism," 711; Dalla Costa and James, *The Power of Women*; Federici, *Caliban and the Witch*; Picchio, *Social Reproduction*. More recent work examines the privatization of social provisioning as well as the public goods that provide the subsistence of daily life. Bhattacharya, *Social Reproduction Theory*.

63. This has produced a vigorous discussion of different types of "nonwaged" labor. Power and Hall, "Placing Care"; Elyachar, "Phatic Labor"; Ferguson and Li, "Beyond the 'Proper Job'"; Narotzky and Besnier, "Crisis, Value and Hope"; Monteith et al., *Beyond the Wage*. Despite calls to leave the concept behind, labor remains a relevant analytic while capitalism remains hegemonic because it still represents a vital measure of social value, and life-sustaining activity continues to be abducted into "the aim of the expansion of money value" in various ways. Narotzky, "Rethinking the Concept of Labour," 41.

64. Harvey and Krohn-Hansen, "Dislocating Labour."

65. Two articles discuss practices of hope-making as a form of "work" or "labor"; however, neither fleshes out the political economic relations of these practices. Pedersen, "A Day in the Cadillac." Elliot, "The Make-Up of Destiny."

66. Care and emotional labor are typically understood to be outside the boundaries of hegemonic masculinity. Connell, *Masculinities*. Recent studies have tried to masculinize care, demonstrating how men do engage in care while not losing sight of the gender politics of these practices. Jordan, "Masculinizing Care?"; Eisen and Yamashita, "Borrowing from Femininity."

67. This invites a note on questions of scale. It is difficult to say what portion of Egypt's middle class, or general population, is caught within this labor of hope. Employment figures suggest a large proportion of educated youth living with a disconnect between their aspirations and realities. Recent surveys have revealed widespread trepidation toward Egypt's future and stubbornly high aspirations for migration, especially amid educated youth. Since Egypt's 2011 uprising, studies demonstrate a decline in optimism about the future. Roushdy and Sieverding, "Panel Survey"; Giesing and Hassan, "Between Hope and Despair." While the ethnographic method cannot answer questions of scale, it provides a more accurate picture regarding undulations of hope and despair than surveys that offer a glimpse of a moment in time.

68. There is a wealth of research explicating the socioeconomic, gendered, cultural, geographic, historical, and institutional inequalities within which contemporary research is enmeshed. Spivak, *A Critique of Postcolonial Reason*; Kapoor, "Hyper-Self-Reflexive Development?"

69. They argue that paying close attention to uncomfortable emotions helps build "novel epistemological techniques for studying the politics of knowledge production and the landscapes of power in which we, as researchers, are embedded." Laliberté and Schurr, "Introduction." An extended discussion of my research ethics can be found in Pettit, "Uncomfortable Ethnography."

70. Feminist researchers have long advocated creating intimate, reciprocal relationships as a corrective to the inequalities embedded in the masculinist tradition of "objective, distant, rational" research. Oakley, "Interviewing Women"; Uddin, "Decolonizing Ethnography."

71. Examining this relation opens questions about the politics of helping interlocutors. Bhan, "Moving from Giving Back to Engagement."

CHAPTER 1

1. The names of people, organizations, and some locations and other details have been changed to ensure anonymity in the book.

2. Youth unemployment has long been a priority for developmental and state intervention. Much employment-related development assistance is focused on demand-side factors, but attention also goes toward enhancing the skills of populations. The origins of this focus lie in Gary Becker's concept of human capital, but it has intensified with increased emphasis on more vocational forms of education. Becker, *Human Capital*; Ansell, "Shaping Global Education." At the same time, recruitment industries and entrepreneurship infrastructures have experienced rapid growth in recent years. World Employment Federation, "Economic Report 2020."

3. "Self-fashioning" (takwin an-nafs) is an increasingly important lens through which Egyptians pursue the goal of "finding wealth and a place in life." Simcik-Arese, *The Commons*, 229; Asad, "Thinking About Tradition." Scholars have examined how this heightened focus on "self-fashioning" has manifested in the increased propensity of self-help literature (Kenney, "Selling Success"); entrepreneurship, empowerment, and creative programs (Elyachar, *Markets of Dispossession*; Atia, *Building a House in Heaven*); and claims to private property (Makram-Ebeid, "Precarious Revolution"; Simcik-Arese, *The Commons*).

4. There are similar training economies emerging in other neoliberalizing postcolonial contexts. Young et al., "Beyond Improvisation?"

5. A 2015 International Labour Organization survey found 30 out of 230 youth unemployment initiatives offering soft-skills training to educated youth in Egypt, which translates into 160,000 graduates. But this training extends much deeper, through self-employed "career coaches" and online material. It is also on the rise, with one organization introducing their program into all public universities.

6. Schulz, "The Importance of Soft Skills."

7. International Youth Foundation, *Getting Youth in the Door*, 1.

8. Young, "Egyptian Education System."

9. This claim is proved by figures such as "30% of unemployed youth refused a job because they felt it 'did not match their level of qualification.'" Ghafar, *Educated but Unemployed*. The onus is put on youth rather than available jobs.

10. According to the IYF, Egyptian workers are "short-sighted," only considering "short-term financial gains" rather than "longer-term benefits" such as "career development, pensions, and insurance." International Youth Foundation, *Getting Youth in the Door*, 8.

11. It valorizes work as a means for self-realization and moral value, produces the disciplined workers required by low-skilled employers, and makes the individual responsible for employment outcomes. Korteweg, "Welfare Reform"; Bergmo-Prvulovic, "Subordinating Careers to Market Forces."

12. Khan, *Privilege*; Littler, *Against Meritocracy*; Scharff, "The Psychic Life of Neoliberalism"; Sukarieh, "On Class"; Bröckling, *The Entrepreneurial Self*.

13. Akhil Gupta argues that "we have to consider how governmentality is itself a conjunctural and crisis-ridden enterprise, how it engenders its own mode of resistance and makes, meets, molds, or is contested by new subjects." Gupta, *Governing Population*, 96.

14. Ralph, *Renegade Dreams*, 79.

15. Anderson, "Affect and Biopower."

16. Tucker, "Affect and the Dialectics of Uncertainty"; Adams, *Markets of Sorrow*; Auyero, *Patients of the State*; Clotfelter and Cook, *Selling Hope*.

17. Schüll, "Addiction by Design."

18. Hurrell et al., "More Than a 'Humpty Dumpty' Term."

19. This reflects what previous scholars have identified, that "familiarity and comfortableness with 'barra,' an imagined First World abroad" is an essential marker of upper-middle-class belonging. De Koning, *Global Dreams*, 65.

20. *Ibn al-nas* was originally an Ottoman term describing military officers and notables but now connotes someone who is well-raised, who has a good background. Sons of the people are, as a result, respectful (muhtaram) and polite (mu'addab), but they are also educated and able to follow international consumption trends—thus the term is tied to wealth. Crucially, this can only come from historical privilege, not from getting rich quick. If a family becomes rich and sends their child to a "fancy private school," but they are uneducated and still live in slums ('ashwa'yat) surrounded by sha'by people, they would not develop this mentality.

21. This anecdotal evidence is backed up by quantitative analysis demonstrating how social mobility in Egypt has drastically declined in recent decades. Binzel and Carvalho, "Education, Social Mobility and Religious Movements."

22. Jeffrey, *Timepass*.

23. This reflects a short passage in *Pascalian Meditations* where Pierre Bourdieu describes how "waiting" might be "one of the privileged ways of experiencing the effect of power." It rests on "delaying without destroying hope, on adjourning without totally disappointing, which would have the effect of killing the waiting itself," and is particularly salient in cases that "depend significantly on the belief of the 'patient,' and which work on and through aspirations, on and through time, by controlling time and the rate of fulfilment of expectations." It is an "art of turning down without turning off, of keeping people motivated without driving them to despair." Bourdieu, *Pascalian Meditations*, 228.

24. According to TFJ, 76 percent of its graduates remain employed after three months.

25. The failures of entrepreneurship as a development strategy have been much critiqued in development studies. Dolan and Rajak, "Remaking Africa's Informal Economies"; Elyachar, *Markets of Dispossession*.

26. During the first part of my fieldwork I lived with other Europeans who were working in research and development NGOs in a shared flat in Mounira near downtown Cairo.

27. Seth Schindler has argued that poor people's inhabitation of shopping malls in

India represents a subversive act. In this middle-class Egyptian context, I am more skeptical of this interpretation. Schindler, "A 21st-Century Urban Landscape."

28. Atia, *Building a House in Heaven*; Elyachar, *Markets of Dispossession*.

29. Noura was referencing the book *Outliers: The Story of Success* by Malcolm Gladwell.

30. Herrera, "The Precarity of Youth."

31. Anderson, "Becoming and Being Hopeful," 736.

32. Mitchell, *Rule of Experts*.

33. Khan, *Privilege*.

CHAPTER 2

1. This reflects the changing political economies of many Egyptian cities in the late twentieth century. Many cities that used to be manufacturing hubs—for example, in textiles—faced decline as factories moved abroad in search of lower costs and simultaneously government recruitment declined.

2. Despite want, many people are put off or prevented from coming to Cairo by the cost of living or lack of connections. My interlocutors did rely on familial support initially but managed to survive longer-term on meager salaries and in cheap, dilapidated, crowded apartments. They did enjoy gendered privilege of movement. The early twenties are a life stage for men in which a certain level of roaming is expected and encouraged. Ghannam, *Live and Die Like a Man*. Female migration was rarer but not unheard of, often constrained by parental fears and having to live with family.

3. Schielke, *Egypt in the Future Tense*, 10.

4. Literature has considered how big cities as imaginaries become spaces of indeterminacy, within which new opportunities can arise at any moment. Simone, "People as Infrastructure."

5. Sims, *Understanding Cairo*.

6. I did explore working in the call center as well. However, the only accessible route for me was the English-language call centers, which attract a higher class of employee than the group I was following.

7. Woodcock, *Working the Phones*.

8. This factory did take its toll on workers' bodies. Many developed health problems, such as hearing or speech impairments, and became sapped of energy. One man was laid off because of a speech impediment he developed at work.

9. Allison, *Precarious Japan*; Mains, *Hope Is Cut*; Cvetkovich, *Depression*; Wilkinson and Ortega-Alcazar, "The Right to Be Weary?"

10. O'Neill, *The Space of Boredom*; Ralph, "Killing Time."

11. Anderson, "Time-Stilled," 751.

12. Berlant, *Cruel Optimism*; Jackson, *Life Within Limits*.

13. Political science literature has long understood the emergence of protest or resistance to be a complex, contingent process. Chalcraft, "Egypt's Uprising"; Beinin, *Workers and Thieves*. Furthermore, scholars have theorized how consent can be won despite the

"partial penetration" of dominant discourses. Willis, *Learning to Labour*; Yurchak, "Everything Was Forever."

14. Mittermaier, "Bread, Freedom, Social Justice."

15. At the time of fieldwork, although there were still protests, many people experienced protest fatigue and constant fear of state violence.

16. Anderson, "Time-Stilled."

17. Froehle, "The Evolution of an Accidental Meme."

18. Know Your Meme, "Forever Alone."

19. El-Khachab, "Living in Darkness."

20. Wedeen, *Ambiguities of Domination*; Siegman, "Playing with Antagonists"; Goldstein, *Laughter out of Place*.

21. Humor may represent a "cynical acceptance of the regime's inevitability as well as subversion of its intent and propaganda. The idea is not to take the joke's funniness or political function at face value, but to dig deeper into the concrete historical circumstances which allow the joker to be co-opted by hegemonic discourses while criticizing, satirizing, or mocking them." El-Khachab, "Compressing Scales," 337. For young Egyptians, humor went hand in hand with national pride. I was told that they could make jokes, but if I started doing it they would not be happy.

22. El-Khachab, "Compressing Scales."

23. Schielke wrote about how young men in a rural village in Egypt's delta attempt to escape boredom through a number of daily activities: watching football and other kinds of television, hanging out in cafés, going to weddings, joking, walks, flirting, internet chat, pornography, and smoking hashish. Schielke, *Egypt in the Future Tense*.

24. Taking selfies and posting them on social media is often derided as a narcissistic, self-absorbed, and attention-seeking practice, but various researchers have recognized their vital role in facilitating self-assertion, social connection, and a right to certain space. Datta, "Self(ie)-Governance."

25. The first mall in Egypt was built in 1989, and there are now around twenty-five in Cairo—with varying degrees of exclusivity and price. Malls arose out of a combination of land speculation from private investors (including wealthy Egyptian families), Gulf real estate companies wishing to reproduce the region's extravagant malls, and a "global" urban modernization project headed by the Egyptian state. Ghannam, *Remaking the Modern*. There are rumors that the army is involved in construction and evidence of mall building as an avenue for money laundering. Shopping malls map onto the consumption trends picked up by Egyptians living in the Gulf, suburbanization processes in Cairo, and preexisting class schemas. Mona Abaza estimated that 20 percent of Egyptians can afford to shop in malls (still three million people in Cairo); however, it may be far less in many malls where products replicate European pricing. Abaza, "Egyptianizing the American Dream."

26. This activity reflects a shift in markers of middle-classness in Egypt and beyond toward aspirational consumption. Schielke, "Living in the Future Tense."

27. Harvey, *The Condition of Postmodernity*. Walter Benjamin, writing on the Paris arcades—which foregrounded the modern mall—similarly posits that these consumer

dream-houses placed people in a "dream-like state." The utopian visions of material abundance therein—what Benjamin terms wish-images—veil the "material scarcity and exploitative labor that form the structural course of societies based on class domination." Buck-Morss, *The Dialectics of Seeing*, 118. They provide a "momentary, fleeting experience of fulfilment dimly anticipatory of a reality that is not yet." Buck-Morss, *The Dialectics of Seeing*, 111.

28. Schindler, "A 21st-Century Urban Landscape."

29. Abaza, "Egyptianizing the American Dream," 216.

30. Allison, *Precarious Japan*; O'Neill, *The Space of Boredom*.

31. Diab, "The World Cup."

32. Mains, *Hope Is Cut*.

33. Yurchak, "Everything Was Forever"; Davies, *The Happiness Industry*.

34. Gilbert, "Disaffected Consent," 33.

35. Berlant, *Cruel Optimism*.

CHAPTER 3

1. Schielke, *Egypt in the Future Tense*, 23.

2. This is an interesting debate regarding the morality of using wasta in Egypt. Even though many do not approve of it, they use it because conditions are difficult. But Adel's discursive stance demonstrates the moral power of meritocracy. Making it on your own secures self-respect, and using wasta secures the opposite. One consequence of this might be the hiding of its use, and thus the maintenance of a discursive terrain of meritocracy, even though it is not reflected in reality.

3. Miyazaki, *The Method of Hope*.

4. Wacquant, *Punishing the Poor*.

5. The term *moral economy* has been used in a variety of ways to examine how moral/cultural norms impinge upon economic practice. Thompson, *The Moral Economy*; Scott, *The Moral Economy*; Carrier, "Moral Economy." Here I am using the term to consider how a concentration of morality within the individual shapes the way in which economic marginality is constructed as deserved and influences people to continue investing in labor markets.

6. Miyazaki, *The Method of Hope*. See also Clifford-Collard, "'Things Should Be Better,'" for a similar argument. This is also encompassed by the Islamic concept of al-qadr, or predestination, which means that God knows everything and has already decided everything that will happen in the future.

7. Difficulties can also be explained as part of God's intention to prevent people from doing wrong or experiencing more hardship. However, in this chapter I focus on narratives that sustain hope, which was the more common practice among the men I followed.

8. Mahmood, *Politics of Piety*; Schielke, *Egypt in the Future Tense*.

9. Another participant actually tried to find a part-time call center job to take alongside an English course but was repeatedly told he needed to commit full time. This in-

duced an angry proclamation that companies just want to keep Egypt's youth as "slaves" rather than allow them to progress.

10. Berlant, *Cruel Optimism*, 24.

11. Jeffrey, *Timepass*.

12. A *sarsagi* is somebody who hangs out on the streets, not engaging in productive activities, perhaps engaging in petty crime. The irony is that the man on the book cover traveled to the Gulf, got married, built two houses, and made a career in customer service after the photo was taken. Adel denies recognition of a fellow mukafih in order to represent himself as one.

13. This has similarities with Sharad Chari's notion of "toil," which the Indian Gounder class uses to explain their mobility. Chari, *Fraternal Capital*.

14. Kenney, "Selling Success."

15. I was reminded of the character of Davies in Harold Pinter's *The Caretaker*, who keeps on talking about getting a new pair of shoes, an act that would symbolize the start of a journey to a better future.

16. Berlant, *Cruel Optimism*.

17. In *Cruel Optimism* Berlant discusses the compulsion to sustain the pretense of "normal" life in the aftermath of events that shatter it.

18. Jackson, *Life Within Limits*, xii.

19. This reflects notions of social death used before in the social sciences. Bourdieu describes social death as a life lived without being known and recognized, being insignificant. He focuses on those experiencing chronic underemployment, poverty, and neglect. Bourdieu, *In Other Words*.

20. Cvetkovich, *Depression*, 17.

21. Research on waithood or stuckedness has argued that it is a state that holds imminent potential for radical change as people engage in acts of resistance which provide renewed hope. Hage, "Waiting Out the Crisis." Unemployed young men are seen as especially susceptible to participation in revolt. Enria, "Love and Betrayal."

22. Kathleen Stewart describes practices of hope-making as the "daydream of being included in the world": "This is the daydream of a subject whose only antidote to structural disenfranchisement is a literal surge of vitality and mobility. A subject whose extreme vulnerability is rooted in the sad affect of being out of place, out of luck, or caught between a rock and a hard place, and who makes a passionate move to connect to a life when mainstream strategies like self-discipline or the gathering of resources like a fortress around the frail body are not an option. A subject who is literally touched by a force and tries to take it on, to let it puncture and possess one, to make oneself its object, if only in passing. A subject for whom an unattainable hope can become the tunnel vision one needs to believe in a world that could include one." Stewart, *Ordinary Affects*, 116.

23. Literature has demonstrated how consent can be won despite increasing disaffection among oppressed populations. Yurchak, "Everything Was Forever"; Gilbert, "Disaffected Consent."

24. In the case of Paul Willis's working-class lads, distrust of meritocracy contributes to acceptance of low-level jobs. Willis, *Learning to Labour*.

25. For D. Asher Ghertner, the democratization of consumerist aspiration in the context of "world-class" city-making in Delhi stimulates attempts by the urban poor to exercise claims on the city. They are claims that become intelligible only through the hegemonic discourses of the "world-class" city; thus, they reproduce hierarchical class and caste schemes, yet they are still able to demand participation. Ghertner, *Rule by Aesthetics.* Laurence Ralph notes a similar phenomenon of claims-making in the context of Chicago's gang members who, despite injurious pasts, work to improve both their individual and collective lives through the act of dreaming. Ralph, *Renegade Dreams.* Both lay bare how individualized, often consumerist, aspiration can be formative of collective claims for improvement.

26. I use the word *compliance* because it is a term that does not necessarily require the belief of the participant. Scott, *Weapons of the Weak.*

CHAPTER 4

1. Schielke, *Egypt in the Future Tense*, 85.

2. Abu-Lughod, *Veiled Sentiments*; Masquelier, "The Scorpion's Sting"; Wardlow and Hirsch, *Modern Loves*; Marsden, "Love and Elopement."

3. Abu-Lughod, *Veiled Sentiments.*

4. McDowell, *Redundant Masculinities?*

5. Fortier et al., "The Trouble of Love."

6. Schielke, *Egypt in the Future Tense*, 104.

7. Aal, *I Want to Get Married!*; Singerman, *The Economic Imperatives of Marriage;*. Kreil, "Territories of Desire."

8. Wynn, *Love, Sex, and Desire.*

9. This builds conceptually on the long-standing feminist recognition of the intimate labors of care that enable labor participation in the realm of relationships. These labors of care are frequently geared toward maintaining people's emotional states. Kwon, "The Work of Waiting"; Boris and Parreñas, *Intimate Labors.*

10. Cole, *Sex and Salvation*; Masquelier, "The Scorpion's Sting."

11. Honwana, *The Time of Youth.*

12. Lower-middle-class Egyptian women in general are more dependent on marriage—although many are ambitious about their career in their early twenties and enjoying the process of working toward it.

13. A narrative has developed in the media and religious circles that this period is dangerous. Kreil, "Territories of Desire."

14. Egyptian women are normally referred to before marriage as *banat* (girls).

15. Fernandez, "Remaking Selves."

16. Schielke notes that "much of life is not characterized by moral concerns, and sometimes people quite consciously avoid considering a possible moral aspect of their action." Schielke, *Egypt in the Future Tense*, 56. Aymon Kreil goes further to suggest that moral frameworks differ according to context. He states how Egyptian men "can defend the preeminence of intimacy in the realm of the family or the importance of strictly abiding

to religious injunctions and then put this principle aside for a conversation with friends in a coffee shop." Kreil, "Territories of Desire," 177.

17. The practices described in the chapter are heteronormative, which reflects the prevalence of heteronormative masculinities and sexualities among this class of young men, and indeed in Egypt generally. There have been notable recent struggles over LGBTQ rights in Egypt, culminating in the tragic suicide of Sarah Hegazi in 2020. For broader discussions on sexualities in the Middle East, see Delatolla, "Sexuality as a Standard of Civilization."

18. Egyptians use this term to describe all forms of sexual activity apart from penetration in a context where penetrative sex is impossible because women must be virgins at the time of marriage.

19. I admitted surprise that this man was so open about sex. He expressed annoyance about how judgmental Egyptian culture was regarding sexual relations; he much preferred the Western notion of privacy. He flippantly argued that he was not doing something bad: "Why would God punish me? He would punish people who kill and steal from the poor." Again, this reveals the ambivalent nature of moral frameworks in that they differ according to instrumental needs of specific contexts. As this man joyfully recollected his sexual experiences, he asserted defiance against moral codes that judged him.

20. Osella and Osella, "Friendship and Flirting."

21. In late 2016 Egypt floated its currency, which devalued it against the dollar by 50 percent.

22. A gama'iyya is attractive when people need to buy something quickly—such as part of an engagement, a deposit, or a commodity such as a car or mobile phone. According to some, it helps discipline people into saving, but many avoid them because of conflict that may arise if people stop contributing. An alternative for depositing savings is the post office.

23. For many Egyptian men, marriage becomes a desperate horizon of striving that does not necessarily need love and indeed is sometimes opposed to love. While the ideal is to have both, love is recognized as an unstable basis for longevity.

24. Egyptian men dating European women has become common. Karkabi, "Couples in the Global Margins."

25. Urfi marriages are conducted by a Muslim cleric in the presence of two witnesses. However, they are not officially registered and are not legally financially binding on the man.

26. Ghannam, *Live and Die Like a Man*.

27. Schielke, *Egypt in the Future Tense*, 87.

28. This represents a form of social reproduction in the marriage market. Bourdieu, "Marriage Strategies."

29. Many women also express this expectation in middle-class Egypt. During an interview with two young unmarried women, I asked whether they want to work: "Of course," one replied, "it is common now. I want to work to feel important, to feel I am doing something useful not just in the house. Also it helps out the family and helps us be more open-minded, to understand what is going on at work, in the street, in the world.

Home can get very boring." But after marriage, they insisted they would stop working: "I want to take care of children, we will have lots of responsibilities, and men prefer women to stay home. Only if the family needs more money would I work." Often, though, this is not possible because of economic necessity.

30. Despite Noura's flexibility, altering expectations can be difficult to take for women. One woman described how she had been engaged for one and a half years because her fiancé was struggling to find a flat on his low government salary. Initially she wanted to get a flat in the upmarket area of Maadi, but it was too expensive. They were now looking in the lower-class to lower-middle-class area of Faisal, which she was unhappy about. The delay had put a lot of stress on their relationship, but she insisted her family would give the man time.

31. I met a few young men who were trying to become freelance trainers in soft skills, having failed to get desirable work elsewhere. This represents an interesting, if cruel, consequence of the soft-skills training focus alongside structural youth unemployment.

32. Narotzky, "Rethinking the Concept of Labour," 41.

CHAPTER 5

1. Fayed, "Foreign Min. Warns Egyptians."

2. Migration was largely an "internal" phenomenon with mainly men moving to Cairo, Alexandria, and industrializing towns along the Suez Canal and the Nile delta to work and get an education. On the back of migrant labor, Nasser industrialized the country and improved access to housing, education, healthcare, and government jobs, thus turning domestic migration into a pathway toward a middle-class life. Abu-Lughod, "Migrant Adjustment to City Life"; Zohry, "Rural-to-Urban Labor Migration."

3. Egyptian women have been more restricted in their ability to chase employment dreams abroad. Instead, they have been encouraged to stay put and, predominantly, consider migration only through marriage. This is slightly less so for upper-middle-class women, who increasingly move abroad to study or work in high-end professions.

4. Although European visa regulations have become even stricter, Egyptians have been able to find their way to Europe since the mid-1980s, initially to southern Europe and from there to other countries, using short-term tourist or student visas or unauthorized entry.

5. Naceur and Rollins, "Europe's Migration Trade."

6. Ungruhe and Esson, "A Social Negotiation of Hope"; Elliot, "The Make-Up of Destiny"; Zharkevich, "'We Are in the Process'"; Kleist and Thorsen, Hope and Uncertainty.

7. Jeffrey, "Foreword," xiv.

8. A similar argument can be found in Pettit and Ruijtenberg, "Migration as Hope and Depression."

9. Hage, "A Not So Multi-Sited Ethnography," 470.

10. According to Ghada Barsoum and her colleagues, who conducted a large-scale survey on Egyptian youth and labor market dynamics, 50 percent of respondents declared a wish to migrate. Barsoum et al., "Labour Market Transitions."

11. Samuli Schielke describes how Egyptians describe how they are migrating for more than money—for experience, freedom, rights, excitement. Schielke, *Migrant Dreams*.

12. On another occasion a man told me about a chance to travel to Korea through the help of a company in Cairo. They told him he could go for three months on a tourist visa, look for work once there, and thereafter apply for a work visa. It would cost LE50,000 upfront. However, he could not contact the one person who had supposedly done it, which stimulated me and another friend to tell him to be careful.

13. The option of traveling by boat across the Mediterranean is not something people in this class of young men take seriously. They declare that they want to migrate through official channels.

14. This insight builds on work revealing how transnational mobility regimes structure the movement of different kinds of classed, racialized, and gendered subjects. While some experience transnational mobility as a routinized, seamless, and pleasant act, others are exposed to the prolonged waiting, enforced immobility or mobility, and blockages that are produced by border regimes. Kleist and Thorsen, *Hope and Uncertainty*; Glick Schiller and Salazar, "Regimes of Mobility."

15. Marriage between Egyptian men and European women has become an increasing phenomenon, particularly in Egypt's tourist resorts But men are often judged for marrying for visa purposes. Karkabi, "Couples in the Global Margins."

16. Mostafa's friend married through a non-state-sanctioned religious marriage, meaning he could not get a residency permit. His claim to fatherhood was denied when his wife refused to cooperate with the DNA test. This story shocked Mostafa, who expressed disbelief at the way a father was treated in Europe.

17. The average monthly salary in Saudi in 2017 was 6,000 riyal (US$1,700) per month. But Arabs get paid much less. In 2014, the government mandated that private-sector companies that hire Saudi nationals must pay them a minimum of SAR5,300 (US$1413) while expats must be paid at least SAR2,500 (US$665) (without accommodation and travel). Among Egyptians I met, starting salaries ranged from 2,000 to 4,000 riyal.

18. This builds on an anthropological literature that has in recent years analyzed the emergence of doubt in relation to dominant structures and belief systems. Pelkmans, *Ethnographies of Doubt*.

19. Schielke, *Migrant Dreams*.

20. Schielke notes the differences between ghurba and safar. Safar as travel is "associated with the promise and possibility of movement, while ghurba is the condition of disconnection from a full life that one may have to endure as a consequence of that movement." Schielke, *Migrant Dreams*, 7.

21. Jeffrey, *Timepass*; Thieme, "The Hustle Economy."

22. Vigh, "Wayward Migration."

23. De Certeau, *The Practice of Everyday Life*.

24. Khan, *Privilege*.

25. Kanna, "Flexible Citizenship in Dubai"; Vora, *Impossible Citizens*.

26. *Bidoun* literally means "without" in Arabic. The bidoun people have a long history of hardship and discrimination in the Gulf.

27. Schielke, *Migrant Dreams*.

28. Berlant, "On Being in Life"; Berlant, *On the Inconvenience*.

CONCLUSION

1. Narotzky, "Rethinking the Concept of Labour," 41.

2. Ghertner, *Rule by Aesthetics*; Ralph, *Renegade Dreams*.

3. Arman, "Money and Image."

4. Sarah Hughes argued for a wider view of resistance in its emergent form, in "subjects, materials, spaces and temporalities which do not always cohere to an (expected) resistant form and yet condition the possibility for future claims to be made." Hughes, "On Resistance in Human Geography," 1143.

5. Thomas, *Political Life*.

6. Bayat, *Life as Politics*.

7. Hussein, "Draft Law."

8. Even though the constitution (redrafted in 2014) calls for the equal treatment of all citizens, no specific directive or regulation addressing discrimination in recruitment existed.

BIBLIOGRAPHY

Aal, Ghada Abdel. *I Want to Get Married!: One Wannabe Bride's Misadventures with Handsome Houdinis, Technicolor Grooms, Morality Police, and Other Mr. Not Quite Rights*. Austin: University of Texas Press, 2010.

Abaza, Mona. "Egyptianizing the American Dream: Nasr City's Shopping Malls, Public Order, and the Privatized Military." In *Cairo Cosmopolitan: Politics, Culture and Urban Space in the New Globalised Middle East*, ed. Dianne Singerman and Paul Amar, 193–220. Cairo: American University in Cairo Press, 2006.

Abu-Lughod, Janet. "Migrant Adjustment to City Life: The Egyptian Case." *American Journal of Sociology* 67 (1961): 22–32.

Abu-Lughod, Lila. *Veiled Sentiments: Honor and Poetry in a Bedouin Society*. Berkeley: University of California Press, 1986.

Adams, Vincanne. *Markets of Sorrow, Labors of Faith: New Orleans in the wake of Katrina*. Durham, NC: Duke University Press, 2013.

African Development Bank. "The Middle of the Pyramid: Dynamics of the Middle Class in Africa." *Market Brief*, April 20, 2011. https://www.afdb.org/en/documents/document/market-brief-the-middle-of-the-pyramid-dynamics-of-the-middle-class-in-africa-23582.

Ahmed, Sara. *The Cultural Politics of Emotion*. Edinburgh: Edinburgh University Press, 2004.

Allison, Anne. *Precarious Japan*. Durham, NC: Duke University Press, 2013.

Alvaredo, Facundo, and Thomas Piketty. "Measuring Top Incomes and Inequality in the Middle East: Data Limitations and Illustration with the Case of Egypt." Economic Research Forum, Working Paper no. 832, May 2014.

Amin, Galal. *Whatever Happened to the Egyptians: Changes in Egyptian Society from 1950 to the Present*. Cairo: American University in Cairo Press, 2000.

Amin, Ghada. "Egypt Country Report: Policies and Mechanisms for Integration into the Workforce and Job Creation." Arab Republic of Egypt Ministry of Education and GIZ, March 2014.

Anderson, Ben. "Affect and Biopower: Towards a Politics of Life." *Transactions of the Institute of British Geographers* 37 (2012): 28–43.

———. "Becoming and being hopeful: towards a theory of affect." *Environment and Planning D: Society and Space.* 24 (2006): 733-752.

———. "Affective Atmospheres." *Emotion, Space and Society* 2 (2009): 77–81.

———. "Time-Stilled Space-Slowed: How Boredom Matters." *Geoforum* 35 (2004): 739–754.

Ansell, Nicola. "Shaping Global Education: International Agendas and Governmental Power." *International Development Planning Review* 37, no. 1 (2015): 7–16.

Appadurai, Arjun. *Modernity at Large.* Minneapolis: University of Minnesota Press, 1996.

Arman, Leila. "Money and Image: Framing Mohamed Ali's Face off Against Sisi." *Mada Masr*, September 24, 2019. https://www.madamasr.com/en/2019/09/24/feature/culture/money-and-image-framing-mohamed-alis-face-off-against-sisi/.

Armbrust, Walter. "Bourgeois Leisure and Egyptian Media Fantasies." In *New Media in the Muslim World: The Emerging Public Sphere*, ed. Dale F. Eickelman and Jon W. Anderson, 106–132. Bloomington: Indiana University Press, 1999.

———. *Mass Culture and Modernism in Egypt.* Cambridge: Cambridge University Press, 1996.

Asad, Talal. "Thinking About Tradition, Religion, and Politics in Egypt Today." *Critical Inquiry* 42, no. 1 (2015): 166–214.

Assaad, Ragui, and Caroline Krafft. "Youth Transitions in Egypt: School, Work, and Family Formation in an Era of Changing Opportunities." Economic Research Forum, Working Paper no. 14-1, October 2014.

Assaad, Ragui, and Caroline Krafft, eds. *The Egyptian Labor Market in an Era of Revolution.* Oxford, UK: Oxford University Press, 2015.

Atia, Mona. *Building a House in Heaven: Pious Neoliberalism and Islamic Charity in Egypt.* Minneapolis: University of Minnesota Press, 2013.

Auyero, Javier. *Patients of the State: The Politics of Waiting in Argentina.* Durham, NC: Duke University Press, 2012.

Barsoum, Ghada, Mohamed Ramadan, and Mona Mostafa. "Labour Market Transitions of Young Women and Men in Egypt." International Labour Office, Work4Youth Publication Series no. 16, June 2014.

Bayat, Asef. *Life as Politics: How Ordinary People Change the Middle East.* Stanford, CA: Stanford University Press, 2009.

———. "A New Arab Street in Post-Islamist Times." *Foreign Policy*, January 26, 2011. https://foreignpolicy.com/2011/01/26/a-new-arab-street-in-post-islamist-times/.

Bear, Laura. "Anthropological Futures: For a Critical Political Economy of Capitalist Time." *Social Anthropology* 25, no. 2 (2017): 142–158.

Becker, Gary. *Human Capital.* New York: Columbia University Press, 1975.

Beinin, Joel. *Workers and Thieves: Labor Movements and Popular Uprisings in Tunisia and Egypt.* Stanford, CA: Stanford University Press, 2015.

Bergmo-Prvulovic, Ingela. "Subordinating Careers to Market Forces? A Critical Analysis of European Career Guidance Policy." *European Journal for Research on the Education and Learning of Adults* 3, no. 2 (2012): 155–170.

Berlant, Lauren. *Cruel Optimism*. Durham, NC: Duke University Press, 2011.

———. "On Being in Life Without Wanting the World (Living with Ellipsis)." Lecture at the NYU Gallatin Center, November 16, 2016. https://gallatin.nyu.edu/utilities/events/2016/11/LaurenBerlant.html.

———. *On the Inconvenience of Other People*. Durham, NC: Duke University Press, 2021.

Bhan, Gautam. "Moving from Giving Back to Engagement." *Journal of Research Practice* 10, article N14 (2014).

Bhattacharya, Tithi, ed. *Social Reproduction Theory: Remapping Class, Recentering Oppression*. London: Pluto Press, 2017.

Binzel, Christine, and Jean-Paul Carvalho. "Education, Social Mobility and Religious Movements: The Islamic Revival in Egypt." *Economic Journal* 127, no. 607 (2017): 2553–2580.

Bloch, Ernst. *The Principle of Hope*. Cambridge, MA: MIT Press, 1995.

Boltanski, Luc, and Eve Chiapello. *The New Spirit of Capitalism*. Translated by Gregory Elliot. London: Verso Books, 2007.

Boris, Eileen, and Rhacel Salazar Parrenas, eds. *Intimate Labors: Cultures, Technologies, and the Politics of Care*. Palo Alto, CA: Stanford University Press, 2010.

Bourdieu, Pierre. *In Other Words: Essays Toward a Reflexive Sociology*. Translated by Matthew Adamson. Stanford, CA: Stanford University Press, 1990.

———. "Marriage Strategies as Strategies of Social Reproduction." In *Family and Society: Selections from the Annales, Économies, Sociétés, Civilisations*, ed. Robert Forster and Orest Ranum. Baltimore: Johns Hopkins University Press, 1976.

———. *Pascalian Meditations*. Stanford, CA: Stanford University Press, 2000.

Bröckling, Ulrich. *The Entrepreneurial Self*. London: Sage, 2016.

Brussels Research Group. "Egypt Is Considered One of the Fastest-Growing Offshore Destinations in the World and Its BPO and IT Industries Are Gaining Global Market Share." 2019. https://brusselsresearchgroup.org/egypt-is-considered-one-of-the-fastest-growing-offshore-destinations-in-the-world-and-its-bpo-and-it-industries-are-gaining-global-market-share/.

Buck-Morss, Susan. *The Dialectics of Seeing: Walter Benjamin and the Arcades Project*. Cambridge, MA: MIT Press, 1991.

Burawoy, Michael. *Manufacturing Consent: Changes in the Labor Process Under Monopoly Capitalism*. Chicago: University of Chicago Press, 1979.

Cabanas, Edgar, and Eva Illouz. *Manufacturing Happy Citizens: How the Science and Industry of Happiness Control our Lives*. London: Polity Press, 2019.

Caldeira, Teresa. *City of Walls: Crime, Segregation and Citizenship in São Paulo*. Oakland: University of California Press, 2001.

Carrier, James G. "Moral Economy: What's in a Name". *Anthropological Theory* 18, no. 1 (2018): 18–35.

Chakrabarty, Dipesh. *Provincializing Europe: Postcolonial Thought and Historical Difference*. Princeton, NJ: Princeton University Press, 2000.

Chalcraft, John. "Egypt's Uprising, Mohammed Bouazizi, and the Failure of Neoliberalism." *Maghreb Review* 37, no. 3–4 (2012): 195–214.

Chari, Sharad. *Fraternal Capital: Peasant-Workers, Self-Made Men, and Globalization in Provincial India*. Palo Alto, CA: Stanford University Press, 2004.

Clifford-Collard, Niamh J. "'Things Should Be Better'—Immobility, Labour and the Negotiation of Hope Amongst Young Ghanaian Craftsmen." *Environment and Planning D: Society and Space* 39, no. 5 (2021): 810–826.

Clotfelter, Charles T., and Philip J. Cook. *Selling Hope: State Lotteries in America*. Cambridge, MA: Harvard University Press, 1991.

Cole, Jennifer. *Sex and Salvation: Imagining the Future in Madagascar*. Chicago: University of Chicago Press, 2010.

Coleman, Rebecca. "Austerity Futures: Debt, Temporality and (Hopeful) Pessimism as an Austerity Mood." *New Formations* 87 (2016): 83–101.

Connell, Raewyn W. *Masculinities*. Berkeley: University of California Press, 1995.

Cooper, Elizabeth, and David Pratten, eds. *Ethnographies of Uncertainty in Africa*. Basingstoke, UK: Palgrave Macmillan, 2015.

Crapanzano, Vincent. "Reflections on Hope as a Category of Social and Psychological Analysis." *Cultural Anthropology* 18, no. 1 (2003): 3–32.

Credit Suisse. *Annual Global Wealth Report*. 2015.

Cross, John. "The Economy of Anticipation: Hope, Infrastructure, and Economic Zones in South India." *Comparative Studies of South Asia, Africa and the Middle East* 35, no. 3 (2015): 424–437.

Cvetkovich, Ann. *Depression: A Public Feeling*. Durham, NC: Duke University Press, 2012.

Dalla Costa, Mariarosa, and Selma James. *The Power of Women and the Subversion of the Community*. Bristol, UK: Falling Wall, 1972.

Datta, Ayona. "Self(ie)-Governance: Technologies of Intimate Surveillance in India Under COVID-19." *Dialogues in Human Geography* 10, no. 2 (2020): 234–237.

Davies, Will. *The Happiness Industry: How the Government and Big Business Sold Us Well-Being*. London: Verso Books, 2015.

———. *Nervous States: Democracy and the Decline of Reason*. London: Norton, 2019.

Davis, Mike. *Planet of Slums*. London: Verso Books, 2006.

De Boeck, Filip. "Inhabiting Ocular Ground: Kinshasa's Future in the Light of Congo's Spectral Urban Politics." *Cultural Anthropology* 26, no. 2 (2011): 263–286.

de Certeau, Michel. *The Practice of Everyday Life*. Berkeley: University of California Press, 1988.

de Koning, Anouk. *Global Dreams: Class, Gender, and Public Space in Cosmopolitan Cairo*. Cairo: American University of Cairo Press, 2009.

Delatolla, Andrew. "Sexuality as a Standard of Civilization: Historicizing (Homo) Colonial Intersections of Race, Gender, and Class." *International Studies Quarterly* 64, no. 1 (2020): 148–158.

Deleuze, Gilles, and Felix Guattari. *Anti-Oedipus: Capitalism and Schizophrenia*. Minneapolis: University of Minnesota Press, 2004.

Diab, Khaled. "The World Cup Was Supposed to Distract Egypt from Misery. It Made Things Worse." *Washington Post*, June 25, 2018. https://www.washingtonpost.com/news/posteverything/wp/2018/06/25/the-world-cup-was-supposed-to-distract-egypt-from-misery-it-made-things-worse/.

Dolan, Catherine, and Dinah Rajak. "Remaking Africa's Informal Economies: Youth, Entrepreneurship and the Promise of Inclusion at the Bottom of the Pyramid." *Journal of Development Studies* 52, no. 4 (2016): 514–529.

Donatella, Alessandrini. "Immaterial Labour and Alternative Valorisation Processes in Italian Feminist Debates: (Re)exploring the 'Commons' of Re-production." *Feminists@Law* 1, no. 2 (2012): 1–28.

Eisen, Daniel B., and Liann Yamashita. "Borrowing from Femininity: The Caring Man, Hybrid Masculinities, and Maintaining Male Dominance." *Men and Masculinities* 22, no. 5 (2019): 801–820.

El-Khachab, Chihab. "Compressing Scales: Characters and Situations in Egyptian Internet Humor." *Middle East Critique* 26, no. 4 (2017): 331–353.

———. "Living in Darkness: Internet Humour and the Politics of Egypt's Electricity Infrastructure." *Anthropology Today* 32, no. 4 (2016): 21–24.

Elliot, Alice. "The Make-Up of Destiny: Predestination and the Labor of Hope in a Moroccan Emigrant Town." *American Ethnologist* 43, no. 3 (2016): 489–500.

El-Messiri, Sawsan. *Ibn al-Balad: A Concept of Egyptian Identity.* Leiden, Netherlands: Brill, 1978.

Elyachar, Julia. *Markets of Dispossession: NGOs, Economic Development, and the State in Cairo.* Durham, NC: Duke University Press, 2005.

———. "Phatic Labor, Infrastructure, and the Question of Empowerment in Cairo." *American Ethnologist* 37, no. 3 (2010): 452–464.

Enria, Luisa. "Love and Betrayal: The Political Economy of Youth Violence in Post-War Sierra Leone." *Journal of Modern African Studies* 53, no. 4 (2015): 637–660.

European Commission, European Education and Culture Executive Agency, Y. Elshayeb, and D. Samy. *Overview of the Higher Education System: Egypt.* Publications Office 2017. https://data.europa.eu/doi/10.2797/247851.

Fayed, Hanan. "Foreign Min. Warns Egyptians Against Emigrating to Liberland." *Cairo Post*, April 19, 2015. https://web.archive.org/web/20150706222616/http://www.thecairopost.com/news/146887/news/foreign-min-warns-egyptians-against-emigrating-to-liberland.

Federici, Sylvia. *Caliban and the Witch: Women, the Body and Primitive Accumulation.* New York: Automedia, 2004.

Ferguson, James. *Expectations of Modernity: Myths and Meanings of Urban Life on the Zambian Copperbelt.* Berkeley: University of California Press, 1999.

Ferguson, James, and Tania M. Li. "Beyond the 'Proper Job': Political-Economic Analysis After the Century of Labouring Man." Working Paper no. 51. Cape Town, South Africa: University of the Western Cape, Institute for Poverty, Land and Agrarian Studies, 2018.

Fernandes, Leela. *India's New Middle Class: Democratic Politics in an Era of Economic Reform*. Minneapolis: University of Minnesota Press, 2006.

Fernandez, Sandra. "Remaking Selves and Remaking Public Space: Combating Sexual Harassment in Cairo Post 2011." Unpublished thesis, St. Andrews Research Repository, 2018.

Froehle, Craig. "The Evolution of an Accidental Meme." *Medium*, April 14, 2016. https://medium.com/@CRА1G/the-evolution-of-an-accidental-meme-ddc4e139e0e4.

Ghafar, Adel Abdel. *Educated but Unemployed: The Challenge Facing Egypt's Youth*. Brookings Institute Policy Briefing, July 2016.

Ghannam, Farha. *Live and Die Like a Man: Gender Dynamics in Urban Egypt*. Stanford, CA: Stanford University Press, 2013.

———. *Remaking the Modern: Space, Relocation, and the Politics of Identity in a Global Cairo*. Berkeley: University of California Press, 2002.

Ghertner, D. Asher. *Rule by Aesthetics: World-Class City Making in Delhi*. New York: Oxford University Press, 2015.

Giesing, Yvonne, and Reem Hassan. "Between Hope and Despair: Egypt's Revolution and Migration Intentions." CESifo Working Paper no. 9237, August 13, 2021. https://ssrn.com/abstract=3904539.

Gilbert, Jeremy. "Disaffected Consent: That Post-Democratic Feeling." *Soundings: A Journal of Politics and Culture* 60 (2015): 29–41.

Glick Schiller, Nina, and Noel B. Salazar. "Regimes of Mobility Across the Globe." *Journal of Ethnic and Migration Studies* 39, no. 2 (2013): 183–200.

Goldstein, Donna. *Laughter out of Place: Race, Class, Violence, and Sexuality in a Rio*. Berkeley: University of California Press, 2003.

Grove, Kevin. "Agency, Affect, and the Immunological Politics of Disaster Resilience." *Environment and Planning D: Society and Space* 32, no. 2 (2014): 240–256.

Gupta, Akhil. "Governing Population: The Integrated Child Development Services Program in India." In *States of Imagination: Ethnographic of the Post-Colonial State*, ed. Thomas B. Hansen and Finn Stepputat, 65–96. Durham, NC: Duke University Press, 2001.

Gurr, Ted. *Why Men Rebel*. Princeton, NJ: Princeton University Press, 1970.

Guyer, Jane. "Prophecy and the Near Future: Thoughts on Macroeconomic, Evangelical, and Punctuated Time." *American Ethnologist* 34, no. 3 (2007): 409–421.

Hage, Ghassan. "A Not So Multi-Sited Ethnography of a Not So Imagined Community." *Anthropological Theory* 5, no. 4 (2005): 463–475.

———. "Waiting Out the Crisis: On Stuckedness and Governmentality." In *Waiting*, ed. Ghassan Hage, 97–106. Carlton, Vic.: Melbourne University Press, 2009.

Hardt, Michael, and Antonio Negri. *Empire*. Cambridge, MA: Harvard University Press, 2006.

Harvey, David. *A Brief History of Neoliberalism*. New York: Oxford University Press, 2005.

———. *The Condition of Postmodernity*. Oxford, UK: Blackwell, 1989.

———. *Spaces of Hope*. Oakland: University of California Press, 2000.

Harvey, Penny, and Christian Krohn-Hansen. "Dislocating Labour: Anthropological

Reconfigurations." *Journal of the Royal Anthropological Institute* 24, no. 1 (2018): 1–202.

Heiman, Rachel. *Driving After Class: Anxious Times in an American Suburb.* Oakland: University of California Press, 2015.

Heiman, Rachel, Carla Freeman, and Mark Liechty, eds. *The Global Middle Classes: Theorizing Through Ethnography.* Advanced Seminar Series. Santa Fe, NM: School for Advanced Research Press, 2012.

Herrera, Linda. "The Precarity of Youth: Entrepreneurship Is Not the Solution." *Mada Masr,* February 11, 2017. https://www.madamasr.com/en/2017/02/11/opinion/society/the-precarity-of-youth-entrepreneurship-is-not-the-solution.

Hochschild, Arlie Russell. *The Managed Heart: Commercialization of Human Feeling.* Berkeley: University of California Press, 1983.

———. *The Outsourced Self: Intimate Life in Market Times.* New York: Metropolitan Books, 2012.

Honwana, Alcinda. *The Time of Youth: Work, Social Change and Politics in Africa.* Hartford, CT: Kumarian Press, 2012.

Hughes, Sarah. "On Resistance in Human Geography." *Progress in Human Geography* 44, no. 6 (2020): 1141–1160.

Hurrell, Scott, Dora Scholarios, and Paul Thompson. "More Than a 'Humpty Dumpty' Term: Strengthening the Conceptualization of Soft Skills." *Economic and Industrial Democracy* 34, no. 1 (2012): 161–182.

Hussein, Walaa. "Draft Law Pushes Equal Opportunity in Egypt." *Al-Monitor,* May 21, 2015. https://www.al-monitor.com/originals/2015/05/egypt-jobs-meritocracy-favoritism-judiciary-parliament.html.

Ianchovichina, Elena, Lili Mottaghi, and Shantayanan Devarajan. "Inequality, Uprisings, and Conflict in the Arab World. Middle East and North Africa." MENA Economic Monitor, October 2015.

Illouz, Eva. *Cold Intimacies: The Making of Emotional Capitalism.* New York: Polity Press, 2007.

Inhorn, Marcia. *The New Arab Man: Emergent Masculinities, Technologies, and Islam in the Middle East.* Princeton, NJ: Princeton University Press, 2015.

International Youth Foundation. Getting Youth in the Door: Defining Soft Skills Requirements for Entry-Level Service Sector Jobs. April 2013. https://iyfglobal.org/library/getting-youth-door-defining-soft-skills-requirements-entry-level-service-sector-jobs.

Ismail, Salwa. *Political Life in Cairo's New Quarters. Encountering the Everyday State.* Minneapolis: University of Minnesota Press, 2006.

Jackson, Michael. *Life Within Limits: Well-Being in a World of Want.* Durham, NC: Duke University Press, 2011.

Janeja, Manpreef, and Andreas Bandak, eds. *Ethnographies of Waiting: Doubt, Hope and Uncertainty.* London: Bloomsbury, 2018.

Jankowski, James. *Egypt: A Short History.* Oxford, UK: Oneworld, 2000.

Jeffrey, Craig. "Foreword." In *Ethnographies of Waiting: Doubt, Hope and Uncertainty,* ed. Manpreet K. Janeja and Andreas Bandak, xiii–xv. London: Bloomsbury, 2018.

———. *Timepass: Youth, Class, and the Politics of Waiting in India.* Stanford, CA: Stanford University Press, 2010.

Jeffrey, Craig, Patricia Jeffery, and Roger Jeffery. *Degrees Without Freedom? Education, Masculinities and Unemployment in North India.* Stanford, CA: Stanford University Press, 2008.

Jordan, Ana. "Masculinizing Care? Gender, Ethics of Care, and Fathers' Rights Groups." *Men and Masculinities* 23, no. 1 (2020): 20–41.

Kanna, Ahmed. "Flexible Citizenship in Dubai: Neoliberal Subjectivity in the Emerging 'City-Corporation.'" *Cultural Anthropology* 25, no. 1 (2010): 100–129.

Kapoor, Ilan. "Hyper-Self-Reflexive Development? Spivak on Representing the Third World 'Other.'" *Third World Quarterly* 25, no. 4 (2004): 627–647.

Karkabi, Nadeem. "Couples in the Global Margins: Sexuality and Marriage Between Egyptian Men and Western Women in South Sinai." *Anthropology of the Middle East* 6, no. 1 (2011): 79–97.

Katz, Cindi. "Vagabond Capitalism and the Necessity of Social Reproduction." *Antipode* 33, no. 4 (2001): 709–728.

Kenney, Jeffrey. "Selling Success, Nurturing the Self: Self-Help Literature, Capitalist Values, and the Sacralization of Subjective Life in Egypt." *International Journal of Middle Eastern Studies* 47, no. 4 (2015): 663–680.

Khan, Shamus. *Privilege: The Making of an Adolescent Elite at St. Paul's School.* Princeton, NJ: Princeton University Press, 2012.

Kharas, Homi. "The Emerging Middle Class in Developing Countries." OECD Development Centre, Working Paper no. 285, January 26, 2010.

Kienle, Eberhard. *A Grand Delusion: Democracy and Economic Reform in Egypt.* London: Taurus, 2001.

Kleist, Nauja, and Dorte Thorsen, eds. *Hope and Uncertainty in Contemporary African Migration.* New York: Routledge, 2016.

Know Your Meme. "Forever Alone." Accessed April 16, 2023. http://knowyourmeme.com/memes/forever-alone.

Kochhar, Rakesh. "A Global Middle Class Is More Promise Than Reality: From 2001 to 2011, Nearly 700 Million Step Out of Poverty, but Most Only Barely." Pew Research Center, July 2015.

Kohl-Arenas, Erica. *The Self-Help Myth: How Philanthropy Fails to Alleviate Poverty.* Berkeley: University of California Press, 2015.

Konings, Martijn. *The Emotional Logic of Capitalism: What Progressives Have Missed.* Palo Alto, CA: Stanford University Press, 2017.

Korteweg, Anna. "Welfare Reform and the Subject of the Working Mother: 'Get a Job, a Better Job, Then a Career.'" *Theory & Society* 32, no. 4 (2003): 445–480.

Kreil, Aymon. "Territories of Desire: A Geography of Competing Intimacies in Cairo." *Journal of Middle East Women's Studies* 12, no. 2 (2016): 166–180.

Fortier, Corinne, Aymon Kreil, and Irene Maffi. "The Trouble of Love in the Arab World : Romance, Marriage, and the Shaping of Intimate Lives: Editors' Note." *Arab Studies Journal* 24, no. 2 (2016): 96–101.

Kwon, Jhee. "The Work of Waiting: Love and Money in Chinese Korean Transnational Migration." *Cultural Anthropology* 30, no. 3 (2015): 477–500.

Laliberté, Nicole, and Carolin Schurr. "Introduction: The Stickiness of Emotions in the Field: Complicating Feminist Methodologies." *Gender, Place & Culture* 23, no. 1 (2014): 72–78.

Lawson, Victoria. "De-centering Poverty Studies: Middle Class Alliances and the Social Construction of Poverty." *Singapore Journal of Tropical Geography* 33, no. 1 (2012): 1–19.

Lentz, Carola. "Elites or Middle Classes? Lessons from Transnational Research for the Study of Social Stratification in Africa." Working Papers of the Department of Anthropology and African Studies of the Johannes Gutenberg University Mainz 161, 2015. http://www.ifeas.unimainz.de/Dateien/AP_161.pdf.

Liechty, Mark. *Suitably Modern: Making Middle Class Culture in a New Consumer Society.* Oxford, UK: Princeton University Press, 2003.

Littler, Jo. *Against Meritocracy: Culture, Power and Myths of Mobility.* London: Routledge, 2017.

Lorey, Isabell. *State of Insecurity: Government of the Precarious.* London: Verso Books, 2015.

Lutz, Catherine A. *Unnatural Emotions: Everyday Sentiments on a Micronesian Atoll and Their Challenge to Western Theory.* Chicago: University of Chicago Press, 1988.

Lutz, Catherine A., and Lila Abu-Lughod, eds. *Language and the Politics of Emotion.* Cambridge: Cambridge University Press, 1990.

Mahmood, Saba. *Politics of Piety: The Islamic Revival and the Feminist Subject.* Princeton, NJ: Princeton University Press, 2004.

Mains, Daniel. *Hope Is Cut: Youth, Unemployment and The Future in Urban Ethiopia.* Philadelphia: Temple University Press, 2012.

Makram-Ebeid, Dina. "Precarious Revolution: Labour and Neoliberal Securitisation in Egypt." *Dialectical Anthropology* 43 (2019): 139–154.

Marsden, Magnus. "Love and Elopement in Northern Pakistan." *Journal of the Royal Anthropological Institute* 13, no. 1 (2007): 91–108.

Masquelier, Adeline. "The Scorpion's Sting: Youth, Marriage and the Struggle for Social Maturity in Niger." *Journal of the Royal Anthropological Institute* 11, no. 1 (2005): 59–83.

McCormack, Derek P. "An Event of Geographical Ethics in Spaces of Affect." *Transactions of the Institute of British Geographers* 28, no. 4 (2003): 488–507.

McDowell, Linda. *Redundant Masculinities? Employment Change and White Working Class Youth.* London: Wiley, 2003.

Mehrez, Samia. *Egypt's Culture Wars: Policy and Practice.* London: Routledge, 2008.

Mercer, Claire. "Middle Class Construction: Domestic Architecture, Aesthetics and Anxieties in Tanzania." *Journal of Modern African Studies* 52, no. 2 (2014): 227–250.

Mitchell, Timothy. *Rule of Experts: Egypt, Techno-Politics, Modernity.* Berkeley: University of California Press, 2002.

Mittermaier, Amira. "Bread, Freedom, Social Justice: The Egyptian Uprising and a Sufi Khidma." *Cultural Anthropology* 29, no. 1 (2014): 54–79.

Miyazaki, Hirokazu. *The Method of Hope: Anthropology, Philosophy, and Fijian Knowledge*. Stanford, CA: Stanford University Press, 2004.

Monteith, William, Dora-Olivia Vicol, and Philippa Williams, eds. *Beyond the Wage: Ordinary Work in Diverse Economies*. Bristol, UK: Bristol University Press, 2021.

Naceur, Sofian Philip, and Tom Rollins. "Europe's Migration Trade with Egypt." *Mada Masr*, February 1, 2017. https://www.madamasr.com/en/2017/02/01/feature/politics/europes-migration-trade-with-egypt/.

Naguib, Nefissa. *Nurturing Masculinities: Men, Food, and Family in Contemporary Egypt*. Austin: University of Texas Press, 2015.

Narotzky, Susana. "Rethinking the Concept of Labour." *Journal of the Royal Anthropological Institute* 24, no. 1 (2018): 29–43.

Narotzky, Susana, and Niko Besnier. "Crisis, Value and Hope: Rethinking the Economy." *Current Anthropology* 55, no. 9 (2014): 4–16.

Ncube, Mthuli, and Charles Lufumpa, eds. *The Emerging Middle Class in Africa*. London: Routledge, 2015.

Negri, Antonio. "Value and Affect." *Boundary 2* 26, no. 2 (1999): 77–88.

Norbakk, Mari. "A Man in Love: Men, Love, and Hopes for Marriage in Cairo." In *Reconceiving Muslim Men: Love and Marriage, Family and Care in Precarious Times*, ed. Marcia C. Inhorn and Nefissa Naguib, 47–62. New York: Berghahn Books, 2018.

Oakley, Anne. "Interviewing Women: A Contradiction in Terms?" In *Doing Feminist Research*, ed. Helen Roberts, 30–61. London: Routledge & Kegan Paul, 1981.

O'Neill, Bruce. *The Space of Boredom: Homelessness in the Slowing Global Order*. Durham, NC: Duke University Press, 2017.

Osella, Caroline, and Filippo Osella. "Friendship and Flirting: Micro-Politics in Kerala, South India." *Journal of the Royal Anthropological Institute* 4, no. 2 (1998): 189–206.

Pedersen, Mortan A. "A Day in the Cadillac: The Work of Hope in Urban Mongolia." *Social Analysis: Journal of Cultural and Social Practice* 56, no. 2 (2012): 136–151.

Pelkmans, Mathijs, ed. *Ethnographies of Doubt: Faith and Uncertainty in Contemporary Societies*. London: Tauris, 2013.

Peterson, Mark Allen. *Connected in Cairo: Growing Up Cosmopolitan in the Modern Middle East*. Bloomington: Indiana University Press, 2011.

Pettit, Harry. "Uncomfortable Ethnography: Navigating Friendship and 'Cruel Hope' with Egypt's Disconnected Middle-Class," *Emotion, Space and Society* 36 (August 2020): art. 100714.

Pettit, Harry, and Wiebe Ruijtenberg. "Migration as Hope and Depression: Existential Im/Mobilities in and Beyond Egypt." *Mobilities* 14, no. 5 (2019): 730–744.

Picchio, Antonella. *Social Reproduction: The Political Economy of the Labour Market*. Cambridge: Cambridge University Press, 1992.

Piketty, Thomas. *Capital in the 21st Century*. Cambridge, MA: Harvard University Press, 2014.

Power, Andrew, and Edward Hall. "Placing Care in Times of Austerity." *Social & Cultural Geography* 19, no. 3 (2018): 303–313.

Ralph, Laurence. *Renegade Dreams: Living Through Injury in Gangland Chicago.* Chicago: University of Chicago Press, 2015.

Ralph, Michael. "Killing Time." *Social Text* 26, no. 4 (2008): 1–29.

Ravallion, Martin. "The Developing World's Bulging (but Vulnerable) 'Middle Class.'" World Bank, Policy Research Working Paper no. 4816, January 1, 2009.

Richard, Analiese, and Daromir Rudnyckyj. "Economies of Affect." *Journal of the Royal Anthropological Institute* 15, no. 1 (2009): 57–77.

Richards, Alan, and John Waterbury. *A Political Economy of the Middle East.* Boulder, CO: Westview Press, 1996.

Ringel, Felix, and Roxana Moroşanu. "Time-Tricking: A General Introduction." *Cambridge Journal of Anthropology* 34, no. 1 (2016): 22–31.

Roushdy, Rania, and Maia Sieverding. "Panel Survey of Young People in Egypt (SYPE) 2014: Generating Evidence for Policy, Programs, and Research." Cairo: Population Council, 2015.

Rutherford, Bruce K. *Egypt After Mubarak: Liberalism, Islam, and Democracy in the Arab World.* Princeton, NJ: Princeton University Press, 2008.

Ryzova, Lucie. *The Age of the Efendiyya: Passages to Modernity in Colonial-National Egypt.* Oxford, UK: Oxford University Press, 2014.

Salem, Sara. *Anticolonial Afterlives in Egypt: The Politics of Hegemony.* Cambridge: Cambridge University Press, 2020.

Sanchez, Andrew. "Relative Precarity: Decline, Hope and the Politics of Work." In *Industrial Labour on the Margins of Capitalism*, ed. Chris Hann and Jonathan Parry, 218–240. New York: Berghahn Books, 2018.

Scharff, Christina. "The Psychic Life of Neoliberalism: Mapping the Contours of Entrepreneurial Subjectivity." *Theory, Culture and Society* 33, no. 6 (2016): 107–122.

Schielke, Samuli. *Egypt in the Future Tense: Hope, Frustration, and Ambivalence Before and After 2011.* Bloomington: Indiana University Press, 2015.

———. "Living in the Future Tense: Aspiring for World and Class in Provincial Egypt." In *The Global Middle Class: Theorizing Through Ethnography*, ed. Carla Freeman, Rachel Heiman, and Mark Liechty, 31–56. Santa Fe, NM: School for Advanced Research Press, 2012.

———. *Migrant Dreams: Egyptian Workers in the Gulf States.* Cairo: American University in Cairo Press, 2020.

Schindler, Seth. "A 21st-Century Urban Landscape: The Emergence of New Socio-Spatial Formations in Gurgaon." In *Sarai Reader 2007: Frontiers*, ed. Monica Narula et al., 499–508. Delhi: Centre for the Study of Developing Societies, 2007.

Schüll, Natasha. *Addiction by Design: Machine Gambling in Las Vegas.* Princeton, NJ: Princeton University Press, 2012.

Schulz, Bernd. "The Importance of Soft Skills: Education Beyond Academic Knowledge." *Journal of Language and Communication* 2, no. 1 (2008): 146–154.

Scott, James C. *The Moral Economy of the Peasant: Rebellion and Subsistence in Southeast Asia.* New Haven, CT: Yale University Press, 1976.

————. *Weapons of the Weak: Everyday Forms of Peasant Resistance*. New Haven, CT: Yale University Press, 1985.

Siegman, Jeremy. "Playing with Antagonists: The Politics of Humor in Israeli-Palestinian Market Encounters." *Political and Legal Anthropology Review* 43, no. 1 (2020): 103–119.

Simcik-Arese, Nicholas. "The Commons in a Compound: Morality, Ownership, and Legality in Cairo's Squatted Gated Community." Unpublished thesis, University of Oxford, 2016.

Simone, AbdouMaliq. "People as Infrastructure: Intersecting Fragments in Johannesburg." *Public Culture* 16 (2004): 407–429.

Sims, David. *Understanding Cairo. The Logic of a City Out of Control*. Cairo: American University in Cairo Press, 2010.

Singerman, Dianne. *Avenues of Participation: Family, Politics, and Networks in Urban Quarters of Cairo*. Princeton, NJ: Princeton University Press, 1995.

————. "The Economic Imperatives of Marriage: Emerging Practices and Identities Among Youth in the Middle East." Middle East Youth Initiative Working Paper no. 6, September 2007.

Spivak, Gayatri. *A Critique of Postcolonial Reason: Toward a History of the Vanishing Present*. Cambridge MA: Harvard University Press, 1999.

Stewart, Kathleen. *Ordinary Affects*. Durham, NC: Duke University Press, 2007.

Sukarieh, Mayssoun. "On Class, Culture, and the Creation of the Neoliberal Subject: The Case of Jordan." *Anthropological Quarterly* 89, no. 4 (2016): 1201–1225.

Thieme, Tatiana. "The Hustle Economy: Rethinking Geographies of Informality and Getting By." *Progress in Human Geography* 42, no. 4 (2017): 529–548.

Thomas, Deborah A. *Political Life in the Wake of the Plantation: Sovereignty, Witnessing, Repair*. Durham, NC: Duke University Press, 2019.

Thompson, Edward P. "The Moral Economy of the English Crowd in the Eighteenth Century." *Past & Present* 50 (1971): 76–136.

Tucker, Jennifer L. "Affect and the Dialectics of Uncertainty: Governing a Paraguayan Frontier Town." *Environment and Planning D: Society and Space* 35, no. 4 (2017): 733–751.

Uddin, Nasir. "Decolonising Ethnography in the Field: An Anthropological Account." *International Journal of Social Research Methodology* 14, no. 6 (2011): 455–467.

Ungruhe, Christian, and James Esson. "A Social Negotiation of Hope: Male West African Youth, "Waithood" and the Pursuit of Social Becoming Through Football." *Boyhood Studies* 10, no. 1 (2017): 22–43.

Vigh, Henrik. "Wayward Migration: On the Imagined Futures and Technological Voids." *Ethnos* 74, no. 1 (2009): 419–438.

Vora, Neha. *Impossible Citizens: Dubai's Indian Diaspora*. Durham, NC: Duke University Press, 2013.

Wacquant, Loïc. *Punishing the Poor: The Neoliberal Government of Social Insecurity*. Durham, NC: Duke University Press, 2009.

Walker, Harry, and Iza Kavedžija, eds. *Values of Happiness: Towards an Anthropology of Purpose in Life*. Chicago: Hau Books, 2016.

Wardlow, Holly, and Jennifer S. Hirsch, eds. *Modern Loves: The Anthropology of Romantic Courtship and Companionate Marriage*. Minneapolis: University of Minnesota Press, 2006.

Wedeen, Liza. *Ambiguities of Domination: Politics, Rhetoric, and Symbols in Contemporary Syria*. Chicago: University of Chicago Press, 1999.

Weiss, Brad. *Street Dreams and Hip Hop Barbershops: Global Fantasy in Urban Tanzania*. Bloomington: Indiana University Press, 2009.

Wietzke, Frank-Borge, and Andy Sumner. "What Are the Political and Social Implications of the 'New Middle Classes' in Developing Countries?" International Development Institute Working Paper, November 2014.

Wilkinson, Eleanor, and Iliana Ortega Alcazar. "The Right to Be Weary? Endurance and Exhaustion in Austere Times." *Transactions of the Institute of British Geographers* 44 (2019): 155–167.

Williams, Raymond. *Marxism and Literature*. Oxford, UK: Oxford University Press, 1977.

Willis, Paul. *Learning to Labour: How Working Class Kids Get Working Class Jobs*. New York: Columbia University Press, 1981.

Woodcock, Jamie. *Working the Phones: Control and Resistance in Call Centres*. London: Pluto Press, 2016.

World Bank. "Middle-Class Frustration Fueled the Arab Spring." October 21, 2015. http://www.worldbank.org/en/news/feature/2015/10/21/middle-class-frustration-that-fueled-the-arab-spring.

World Employment Federation. "Economic Report 2020." February 26, 2020. https://wecglobal.org/publication-post/economic-report-2020/.

Wynn, Lisa L. *Love, Sex, and Desire in Modern Egypt: Navigating the Margins of Respectability*. Austin: University of Texas Press, 2018.

Yanagisako, Sylvia. "Immaterial and Industrial Labor: A Critique of False Binaries in Hardt and Negri's Trilogy." *Focaal: Journal of Historical and Global Anthropology* 2012, no. 64 (2012:) 16–23.

Young, Holy. "Egyptian Education System Doesn't Prepare the Youth for Modern Jobs." *The Guardian*, August 20, 2014. https://www.theguardian.com/global-development-professionals-network/2014/aug/20/youth-unemployment-interactive-salma-wahba.

Young, Stephen, Satendra Kumar, and Craig Jeffrey. "Beyond Improvisation? The Rise and Rise of Youth Entrepreneurs in North India." *Transactions of the Institute of British Geographers* 42, no. 1 (2016): 98–109.

Yurchak, Alexei. *Everything Was Forever, Until It Was No More: The Last Soviet Generation*. Princeton, NJ: Princeton University Press, 2006.

Zaalouk, Malak. *Class, Power and Foreign Capital in Egypt: The Rise of the New Bourgeoisie*. London: Zed Books, 1989.

Zeiderman, Austin. *Endangered City: The Politics of Security and Risk in Bogotá*. Durham, NC: Duke University Press, 2016.

Zhang, Li. *In Search of Paradise: Middle-Class Living in a Chinese Metropolis.* New York: Cornell University Press, 2010.

Zharkevich, Ina. "'We Are in the Process': The Exploitation of Hope and the Political Economy of Waiting Among the Aspiring Irregular Migrants in Nepal." *Environment and Planning D: Society and Space* 39, no. 5 (2021): 827–843.

Zigon, Jarrett. "Hope Dies Last: Two Aspects of Hope in Contemporary Moscow." *Anthropological Theory* 9, no. 3 (2009): 253–271.

Žižek, Slavoj. *The Plague of Fantasies.* London: Verso Books, 1997.

Zohry, Arafa. "Rural-to-Urban Labor Migration: A Study of Upper Egyptian Laborers in Cairo." Unpublished thesis, University of Sussex, 2002.

INDEX

activities: career advancing, 92–94
advice, 95–96
affect, 13, 29–30, 194–95n54
affective attachment, 112
agentive abilities, 13, 21
alcohol: as distraction, 82–83
Ali, Muhammad, 6, 183
Amr Khaled, 88; performing morality, 89–90
anger, 56–57
anxiety: distraction and, 80–81
application process, 106–7; TFJ, 31–32
Arab Gulf: migration to, 22, 155–56. *See also* Dubai; Saudi Arabia
Arab Spring, 5
aspirations, 10, 11, 182, 203n25; individual, 30–32
Australia, 162
autonomy: and entrepreneurship, 42–43
avoidance: marriage, 124

Bali, 160–61
barra, 148, 149, 198n19
Belgium: migration to, 158–59
bidoun people, 167, 206n26
biopolitical projects/techniques, 29–30, 54, 195n55
boasting: about sexuality, 126–27
boredom, 63, 64–65, 155, 200n23

business process outsourcing (BPO), 9

Cairo: as global city, 7, 32; labor market, 52–53; migration to, 58–59, 199n2, 205n2
Cairo University, 1
call centers, 91; career progression and, 49–50; emotional costs of, 61–67; employment at, 28, 38–39, 105–6, 201–2n9; as factories, 62–63; recruitment to, 46–47; sharing experiences, 67–68
Canada, 150
capital, 7; social and cultural, 19, 43–44
capitalism, 173, 179, 193n39, 194n50; economy, 11–12; emotional politics of, 4, 195n57
career coaches, 26
career days, 29
careers, 17, 19, 118; focus on, 121–22; middle-class women, 185–86; mobility, 144–45; private-sector, 4, 20
Carnegie, Dale, 46
Chevening, 151
class prejudice, 86
collective action, 183–85
companies/corporations: international training, 24–25, 26
confining structure, 13

consumption: middle-class, 7, 180
conversation: distraction, 71–73; job training as, 40–41
coping mechanisms: humor as, 68–70
corruption, 92, 183; and middle-class loss, 65–66
cultural capital, 32
Cutts, Steve, 175, 182

dating, 136–38
deflection, 72
depression, 17, 64, 103, 104, 108–9; distraction and, 80–81; rejection and, 86–87
disconnection, 4, 11, 12, 20, 147, 192n37, 193n40
discouragement: fear of, 111
discrimination, 187
distractions: emotional labor of, 177, 185; forms of, 81–82; group outings at, 75–80; love as, 124–31; role of, 82–83; temporary, 57–58, 71–75
"Dreaming of Liberland" (film), 146
drugs: as distraction, 82–83
Dubai, 158; migration experiences in, 156, 157, 163–72

economic power: and love, 115, 116; migration and, 117–18
economic precarity: love and, 115–16
economy, 5, 7, 11, 177; globalized, 32, 42; of hope, 13–14; marriage and, 120–21
Edison, Thomas, 100
education, 5, 8–9, 190n13, 191nn23, 24, 193n40; foreign, 151–52
ElBaradei, Mohamed, 187
elites, 92. See also upper-middle class
embarrassment, 64
emotional cultures, 13
emotions, emotional states, 4, 11, 29–30, 172, 173, 176, 193n40, 196n69; and affect, 178–79, 194–95n54; anger and frustration, 56–57; call center work and, 61–62, 63–68; labor, 14–15, 95, 97,

101, 109, 177–78, 196n66; of migration, 156–58; negative, 17–18, 85; romantic attachments, 139–40
employability, 86
employment, 9, 17, 27, 35, 86, 131–32, 172–73, 187, 191–92nn28–29, 196n67, 197n10; government, 58, 106; public and private, 28, 84; youth, 23, 192n30
employment fairs. See job fairs
empowerment, 57; social, 33–34
engagement, 117, 118, 131, 143, 153–54
English courses, 26, 90–91, 152
English skills, 17, 18, 24
entrepreneurship, 19, 25, 39–40, 41, 44, 107, 172; and autonomy, 42–43
equality, 207n8; vs. equity, 68–69
ethnographic knowledge production, 18
Europe: migration to, 22, 149–50, 205n4
everyday practice: politics of, 178–79

faculties of the people, 8–9
failure: overcoming, 100
Faisal neighborhood, 59–60
family, 115, 166, 203–4n16; career struggles and, 96–97; costs of, 119–20; and migration, 161–62
fantasies, 13, 185
fatigue, 105
fear, 111
Fight Club, 57, 74; as analogy, 64–65
Fiky, Ibrahim al-, 98, 102
films: Egyptian vs. foreign, 73–74; "Happiness," 175–76, 182; Hamam fi Amsterdam, 149; The Pursuit of Happiness, 93, 94–95
finances: for housing and marriage, 135–36; migration and, 147
firings, 102–3
flats: marriage, 132–34; rented, 59–61
foreign cultural centers, 26
frustration, 56–57, 71, 79
funding: entrepreneurship, 44

Gates, Bill: as inspiration, 91
gender relations, 185–86
Germany: job opportunities, 149–50
ghurba, 157, 206n20
Gladwell, Malcolm, 43
globalization, 4, 11, 32, 115
goals: lack of, 170–71
government-sponsored programs, 24
graduation: Training for Jobs, 38
Gulf states: migration to, 155–56; work in,
    163–72. *See also* Dubai; Saudi Arabia

Hamam fi Amsterdam, 149
"Happiness" (film), 175–76, 182
health issues, 170
Higra, 157
hope, 11–12, 30, 84, 193nn42, 45; with
    conviction, 36–37; economy of, 13–14;
    labor of, 19, 110–11, 182
Hosni, Mustafa, 88
housing, 132, 133–34
humor: as coping mechanism, 68–70,
    200n21; satirical, 70–71, 177

ikti'ab, 17, 64, 103, 104, 108–9; distraction
    and, 80–81; rejection and, 86–87
iltizam, 29
impasse, 104–5
individualism, 100–101; focus on, 173–74
Indonesia: travel to, 160–61
inequalities, 53, 183, 194n53, 196n70; legiti-
    mizing, 44, 181
Information Resource Center (U.S.
    Embassy), 40
Information Technology Industry Devel-
    opment Agency (ITIDA), 46
inspiration, 31, 91–92
inspirational stories, 20
International Youth Foundation (IYF), 27
intervention, social, 160
intifah, 7
intimacy, 114, 116, 177, 203–4n16; finding,

20, 21; pursuits of, 126–31; relation-
    ships, 138–39
intimacy building: among friends, 67
Iraq, 147
Islam, 201nn6, 7; performing morality,
    89–90; practices, 88–89
ITDA. See Information Technology
    Industry Development Agency
IYF. *See* International Youth Foundation

job fairs, 18, 25, 52; experiences at, 45–52;
    UN, 39–42
JobMaster, 46, 50
jobs, 27–28, 35, 37, 85, 177; in Dubai,
    163–72; in Europe, 149–50; in Gulf
    States, 155–56, 157; high-status, 187–88;
    precarity of, 119–20; temporary, 105–6
Jobs, Steve: as inspiration, 31, 92
Jobzella, 48, 49
jokes, joking, 68–69
judgment: fear of, 111

kharuga, 75–80
knowledge: reoriented, 87

labor, 5, 19, 195n60, 196n63, 203n9; emo-
    tional, 14–15, 74, 82, 95, 97, 101, 109,
    177–79, 196n66; of hope, 110–11; of
    migration, 156–58
labor market, 15, 19, 25, 26, 35, 85, 87, 110,
    184, 192n32; Cairo, 52–53; love and,
    116–17; meritocratic, 20, 29; migration
    and, 148–49
laughter: as coping mechanism, 69–70
laziness, 87, 90–91
Liberland, 146–47
Libya, 147
living away from home (mughtaribiyyn),
    157
living in a strange place among strangers
    (ghurba), 157, 206n20
love, 113, 140; as aspirational, 114–15; as
    distraction, 124–31; and economic

precarity, 115–16; and labor market, 116–17; and marriage, 121, 144–45; romantic, 122–23
lower-middle class, 158

Mahalla, 151
Make Your Goal initiative, 31
Malaysia: migration to, 22, 150–51, 158, 160, 161–62
marginalized peoples, 12–13, 21, 114; migration of, 152–53
marital house/flat: preparation of, 21, 132–34
marketing tools: job fairs as, 52
marriage, 17, 21, 114, 116, 124, 126, 131, 170, 204n23, 206nn15, 16; costs of, 118–19; economic expectations, 120–21; financing, 122–23; love and, 144–45; and migration, 117–18; plans for, 140–41; resources directed toward, 134–35; and social status, 141–42; transnational, 165–66; urfi, 138, 204n25; women and, 168–69, 204–5n29
marriage for business, 154
masculinity, 21, 57, 69, 74, 90, 116, 124, 185, 196n66, 204n17
master's degrees, 1–2
meritocracy, 5, 21, 53, 201n2; labor market, 20, 25, 29
meritocratic logics/narratives, 87, 91, 111, 181, 186–87; of scholarships and training, 152–53
middle class, 3–4, 5–6, 7, 8, 32, 57, 176, 182, 189–10nn3, 6, 9, 10, 190nn12, 14, 192n34, 193n40; loss of, 65–66; maintaining, 9–10; women in, 125, 180–81, 185–86
migrant industry, 22
migration, 21–22, 154, 205nn3, 4, 10, 206n11; emotional labor of, 156–58; experiences, 158–62; Gulf states, 155–56; labor market and, 148–49; and labor of hope, 147–48; marginalized groups,

152–53; and marriage, 117–18, 140, 142; opportunities for, 146–47; plans for, 148–49; rural-urban, 58–59, 199n2, 205n2; social mobility, 123–24, 164–65; and standard of living, 143–44; to West, 149–51
mindset: youth, 28–29
mobility, 2, 85, 206n14; career, 144–45, 153–54; economic, 117–18; migration, 147, 149, 162–63, 164–65; social, 19, 123–24, 185, 198n21
modernization, 115
money, 191n22; and love, 113–14, 121; and marriage, 122–23, 169
moral economy. 21, 97, 110–11, 179, 201n5
morality, 81, 92, 201n2, 203–4n16; performing, 89–90; sexuality and, 125–26, 131
Mostafa, 185; career mobility, 153–54; migration, 158–60; persistence, 109–10; scholarships, 151–52; self-help, 99–100
Mubarak, Hosni, 3, 7, 147
mughtaribiyyn, 157. *See also* traveling, travel

Nasser, Gamel Abdel, 6, 8, 147, 205n2
National Council for Human Rights, 187
neighborhoods, 8, 86
neoliberal economics, 3, 25, 81
Netherlands, 149, 154
nongovernmental organizations (NGOs), 26

Obama, Barack: Middle East entrepreneurship initiative, 39
old rent law contracts, 132, 133
Omar, 134–35, 136
opportunities, 35; economically stratified, 26
orientation day: TFJ, 32
Our Future in Our Country, 50
outings; dating, 137; group, 75–80
outsourcing companies, 47

overqualification: and firing, 102–3

parents: and marriage, 119
performance: at call centers, 61–62; Islamic religious, 89–90
persistence, 109–10
pessimism, 84, 103–4
political economies, 13, 179–80, 199n1
politics: of everyday practice, 178–79; recreational activities, 81–82
precarity, 4; economic, 115–16; job, 119–20
private sector, 20, 26, 190n15
privilege, 34, 91, 198nn20, 23; legitimizing, 44, 87
promiscuity, 125
Pursuit of Happiness, The, 93; core lesson from, 94–95

Qatar, 151

recreational activities: politics of, 81–82
recruitment, 19; job, 35–36
recruitment firms, 53–54
refusal of work, 29
rejection, 126, 129; impacts of, 86–87; and persistence, 109–10
relationships, 21, 114, 135, 196n70; casual, 129, 177; establishing, 137–38; gendered, 185–86; intimate, 19, 126–29, 131, 138–39; migration and, 143–44; romantic attachments, 139–40; transnational, 165–66; trust in, 171–72
religious piety, 85
religious practice, 20, 88, 109, 131; performing morality, 89–90
religious texts, 21
resistance, 154, 207n4; collective action and, 184–85; satirical humor as, 70–71
revivalist Islam: morality, 89–90
reward, 87
RiseUp, 43, 49
rural-urban migration, 58–59, 199n2, 205n2

Saber, Mahfouz, 186–87
Sadat, Anwar, 6–7, 147
safar, 157, 206n20
sales work, 192n30; emotions of, 55–57
sarcasm, 68
satire, 70–71, 177
Saudi Arabia, 157; migration to, 147, 155–56, 158; work in, 163–64, 206n17
scholarships: foreign, 151–52; meritocracy and, 152–53; pursuit of, 109–10, 112
schools: public, 26
self-assessment tools, 48, 49
self-blame, 88
self-care, 81
self-development, 34–35, 87, 101–2
self-help, 19, 46, 99–100
self-help books, 20, 98–99
selfhood, 20
service work, 172, 192n30; emotions of, 55–57
sexuality, sex, 125–26, 127–28, 131, 138, 204nn17, 19
shame: distraction from, 79
shopping malls, 200–201nn25, 27; outings to, 76–77, 78–80
Sisi, Abdel Fattah el-, 12, 183
skill development, 85
Smith, Will: in Pursuit of Happiness, 93, 94–95
social connections, 35–36
social creativity, 111
socialist development, 6–7
sociality, 85
social reproduction, 14
social responsibility programs, 24–25
social values: middle-class, 180
soft skills, 16, 32–33, 205n31; self-development and, 34–35; training in, 18, 25, 26, 27, 30, 45–46
solitary activities, 73
stagnation, 64–65
standard of living: migration and, 144–45
start-ups, 43, 107

status, 86, 127, 202n19; loss of, 9–10; mar-
    riage and, 141–42, 143–44
stories: sharing, 67–68
structural barriers, 87–88, 98, 100–101
structures of feeling, 13
Students in Free Enterprise, 31
student visas: travel under, 160–61
suicides, 2–3, 204n17
SWOT analysis, 34–35

technological advances, 11
10th of Ramadan, 30; work in, 172–73
threats, 35
TJF. *See* Training for Jobs program
training, 19; meritocracy and, 152–53; as
    social empowerment, 33–34
training courses/programs, 18, 24–25
training economy, 26
Training for Jobs (TFJ) program, 26–27,
    30, 34, 54, 137, 198n24; application
    process, 31–32; graduation, 37–38; hope
    with conviction, 36–37; participants,
    23–24, 59; soft skill makers, 32–33
trajectories: individual, 30–32
traveling, travel, 118, 206nn12, 13; foreign,
    156–57, 160–61; under student visas,
    160–61
Turkey, 162

underemployment, 5, 9
unemployment, 180, 191n26; youth, 16,
    24–25
United Kingdom: Chevening, 151
UN fair: participants, 39–42
United States, 150

U.S. embassy: Information Resource
    Center, 40
Universities, 50, 190n13; public, 8, 26, 27
University for Modern Science and Arts
    (MSA): employment fair, 50–52
upper-middle-class, 34, 190–91n20
uprising: 2011, 3, 4
urbanization, 11
urfi marriage, 138, 204n25

Wahba, Salma, 28
waithood, 123–24, 144, 193n38, 201n21
Wasta, 35, 47–48, 102, 201n21
wealth: middle class and, 5–6
weddings: costs of, 119
West: migration opportunities, 149–51
Wolf of Wall Street, The, 74
women, 10, 81, 114, 124, 137, 144, 195–
    96n62, 204–5nn29, 30; engagement
    and marriage, 168–69; intimate rela-
    tionships, 127–29, 131; male views of,
    126–27; middle class, 180–81, 185–86;
    sexuality of, 125–26, 127–28
work commitment (iltizam), 29
work-life balance, 74–75

Yousef, Bassem, 70
Youssef, 40
Youth, 16, 23, 114, 192n30; mindset, 28–29

Zahra, 42–43, 49
*Zero to Hero: Your Guide for Everything
    About Jobs, From,* 48
Ziglar, Zig, 98